WOMAN IN THE

YEAR 2000

WOMAN
IN THE
YEAR 2000

Edited by MAGGIE TRIPP

ARBOR HOUSE
New York

No ONE PERSON . . . could possibly have written this book, and if there is credit to be given, it must be shared equally by everyone who provided their own indispensable parts of the whole.

So my thanks to the writers of the chapters who showed their courage by undertaking to assess the unknown and unprovable for their love of the subject; to Alan Tripp, without whom I could never have been a free, married woman; to my editor at Arbor House, Angela Miller, who encouraged and directed me; to Elaine Markson, my agent—a great team player; to Ellen Weinstein who was my indefatigable follower-througher; to Virginia Kinsman Henderson, former director of Continuing Education, University of Pennsylvania, with whom the first glimmerings of this book were seen ten years ago; to Helen Lapus who worked so hard to help me get this book together; also to Lee Arthur, Aimee Lee Ball, Esther Levine, Ruth Van Doren, Barbara Tripp, Sherri Larner, Lynn Obee, Alma Graham, Angela Yanovich, Bernice Sandler, Elizabeth Cless, Dr. Dorothy Harris, Jane Newitt, Margaret Dunkle, Charlotte Montgomery, Helen Puner, Bonnie Lobel and Sandra Gorney.

If I have omitted anyone, it is for lack of recall and not appreciation.

M.T.

CONTENTS

IV: ON HER NEW WORLDS

PREFACE

THERE IS NO LONGER any doubt about it. We are in the midst of the greatest revolution in the history of women. It will affect how they live, where they live, with whom they live and what they do with their lives.

Attitudes of both men and women have altered dramatically. You see it reflected in almost daily reports in the media of new accomplishments by women, new ways of raising girl-children, new relationships between men and women. You find women rejecting second class status on every front. And every survey shows that this demand for change is no longer a minority effort but the firm attitude of the majority of women—*and men.*

What is happening today clearly foreshadows tomorrow. Because forecasting human behavior is a difficult task—and certainly not one for the timid—I have asked twenty-eight informed and sensitive women and men to join me in painting this picture of women in the year 2000. The "panel" of contributors includes journalists, novelists, social critics, politicians and teachers; a biologist, an advertising executive, a filmmaker, a college student, a spokeswoman for the women's movement, a lawyer, a business woman, a theatrical director, a film critic, a TV director and a futurist.

Some of the writers are ardent feminists; some are not. But the gap between them is far less than one might have expected, because they all share a positive viewpoint on the emergence of women as individual human beings. The entire orientation of this book is, in fact, toward an understanding of the human condition and human potential as it relates to women. Future-looking based upon statistical data and abstract sociology is not for us—history is littered with the shattered forecasts of those who discounted the resiliency and inventiveness of the human mind and the creativity and resoluteness of woman's spirit.

Each chapter of this book is an individual entity. Each writer worked separately, being aware of the complete chapter list but not seeing the work of the others. Thus you may find ideas which overlap and intersect and sometimes contradict each other. I hope and believe, however, that as with a good work of art the composition creates a total impression, while still leaving room for a reader's own interpretations.

To help make the picture cohesive, the chapters are grouped under broad subjects. The Introduction positions the critical conditions of today which are the springboard for the future. Part I, *On Her Destiny*, covers woman's conditioning and expected roles. Part II, *On Her Working Choices and Rights*, examines woman's future options beyond motherhood and the home. The psychological and physical aspects of woman's life are delineated in Part III, *On Using Her Body and Mind*. And Part IV, *On Her New Worlds*, previews lifestyles in the year 2000 for women, men and children.

Since this is a single book and not an encyclopedia, some subjects have, of necessity, been omitted. For one thing, the thinking is essentially limited to women in the United States; yet one should be aware that the winds of change in this country are even now blowing across the oceans—and the ideas expressed here are surfacing in indigenous forms around the world.

Women's orientation to the future has long been centered on the welfare of their husbands and children. If women have been "provident," it has been largely limited to a savings account for a rainy day, hoping to send their sons to college and guide their daughters into a good marriage or planning next summer's vacation. Until now they have thought little about their own fulfillment, the kind of society in which a woman can reach her full potential and the forward planning and actions required for such a life. The history of mankind records a long continuum of wars, economic disasters, crime, hunger and repression. Perhaps the fuller participation of women in the future will provide new thrusts to create a better world for all of us.

The contributing authors join me in the expectation that this book will stimulate you to think more deeply about the future and to act in response to your thoughts.

M.T.

INTRODUCTION:
WHATEVER WILL BECOME
OF ME?

It's been a long time coming.

Time and again in the course of history, women's voices were raised to demand control over their own lives. Women asked for a voice in the choice of their husbands, their work, their government.

For several thousand years, women's progress was much like the frog in the well: two leaps upward and one back down.

In ancient Egypt, women entered the banking profession, became money lenders, speculators and the heads of businesses. By the time of the Roman Empire, they were back to lobbying against laws which restricted the amount of gold they could possess; and on the walls of Ancient Pompeii archaeologists found graffiti demanding an equal say in government for women.

So it went over the centuries. A Charlotte Brontë could write in *Jane Eyre*: "Women need the same opportunity as man to use their brains and then should not be confined to making pudding or knitting stockings." And men would reply in chorus: "God created women to take care of men and children."

Indeed, it was not until the Nineteenth Century here in America that women's voices began to be heard and grew steadily stronger; and it was not until this past decade that self-determination for women in every aspect of their lives became a possible dream.

To appreciate how far we have come, read some random samplings of life in American Colonial times: A man could acquire a wife by paying 120 pounds of tobacco for her. She helped him do his work and found his family, but legally she and her husband were one. All property and wealth—whether his or hers was held in his name; and all rights before the law and in the eyes of the church were his. In one colony, a husband could lawfully beat his wife with a stick, provided the stick was no thicker than the judge's thumb. And Thomas Jefferson wrote: "Our ladies, I suspect, are too wise to wrinkle their heads about politics. They are contented to soothe and calm the minds of their husbands returning ruffled from political debate. They had the good sense to value domestic happiness above all others."

If that sounds positively pre-historic, nevertheless it was all true only two hundred years ago.

Early efforts of American women centered on specific issues and were pursued by relatively small groups of women with now-historic leaders. In 1860, Susan B. Anthony and Elizabeth Cady Stanton, after a mere twelve years of annual petitions signed by thousands of women, won in the New York legislature the right for women not only to own property but to collect and control their own wages and to sue in court.

The Grimke sisters, Lucretia Mott and other women spoke out for the abolition of slavery. They helped bring the vote to the black man, but not to the white woman. Half a century later, women led by such legendary heroines as Carrie Chapman Catt finally won the vote for themselves, but the female majority lapsed into indifference and secured neither representation nor legislation to assure equality under the law.

And so it went until the middle of this century when a remarkable combination of circumstances started women thinking that their future might not, *could not* be like their past. Resurgent feminism, plus turbulent social upheaval, plus sudden technological change created the soil and climate in which the centuries-old seeds of women's discontent could grow.

The Women's Liberation Movement started with the young women who resented being put down by their male co-workers in the Civil Rights movement and who became the radical theorists of the New Feminism. It burgeoned with the entry of the middle-class women who refused to remain restricted to children, church and kitchen and founded a focal group for their demands for independence in the National Organization for Women. And most important, the dissatisfaction with second-class status filtered into the awareness of working class women.

Whether they support the New Feminism actively, or resent it or remain on the fence, Americans for the first time have become universally aware of women's demands for change. And according to those who study public attitudes, there can be no doubt as to which way the trend is going. In 1974, pollster Daniel Yankelovich reported that for the first time, "women's liberation" was favored by more than fifty percent of the eighteen-and-over population.

The central issue which comes closest to universal approval is "equal pay for equal work." It has the ring of the American Way, doesn't it? But it is deceptively simple to think that you can be for one kind of equality and stop there. For the more you think about it, the more you realize that the right to work and get paid fairly is inextricably woven in with other human rights. Freedom, once again, is indivisible.

Equality of labor requires equal respect for the person. In turn, equal respect for the person includes the right to equal education and training, to marry or not, to have children or not, to manage your own money, to have a say in where you live and how you live.

It is the recognition that all aspects of human behavior are involved in equality for women that differentiates the New Feminism from all the past.

For all its ideological strength, the New Feminism could not have had such an explosive impact were it not for a conjunction of other forces which made change the order of the day. Some examples:

- The advent of "the pill" and the sexual revolution changed the ground rules for male/female relationships. It reduced the necessity for marrying rather than living together. It permitted women to relax and enjoy sex. It gave women assurance that they could continue their life's work and devote time to children when and if they wished.
- The economics of the times permitted and/or demanded that more women work. For many women, work outside the home proved more to their liking than housework; for others, the income was essential for life's necessities or wanted luxuries.
- The new mobility made it both possible and acceptable for women to travel widely on their own, gaining exposure to new people and new ideas.
- Instant communications, especially television, brought to those who stayed home living pictures of the different kinds of lives being carved out by women everywhere.

A sudden awareness of longevity and its implications: the realization on the one hand that young women need not rush to raise a family and, on the other, that a woman—having had her children—would face forty or more years of her life when they no longer needed her.

Social and technological forces like these plus women's new awareness of their potential have begun to close the gap between men and women. For the sake of the human race, it is probably just in time. Medical experts are predicting that the average lifespan will be extended to one hundred years through new transplant techniques and through such drugs as dimethylaminoethanol (DMAE). Scientists predict that we will soon freely choose in advance the sex of our children. And astrophysicists now assume it is only a matter of time before we will be living in the uncrowded colonies of outer space. Such new worlds will demand the best thinking, the highest cooperation of both women and men.

Whatever the effect of technological advances, however, love, peace, self-fulfillment and happiness will continue to revolve around human relationships, the way people see and deal with themselves and others. So it is from the human side that this book looks at *Woman In the Year 2000.*

Where does one find reliable foresight? In addition to the eminently qualified writers of the chapters in this book, it seemed prudent—indeed necessary—to listen to the voice of people across the country, to hear what women (and a few men) are thinking about their lives today and the possibilities for tomorrow.

David Saperstein, a brilliant young film producer and the author of a chapter in this book, traveled from coast to coast and interviewed one hundred and fifty women formally and another fifty informally to gain insights to what people today see as the mores of tomorrow. What follows is his analysis of these interviews along with their tape-recorded words:

I found a positive attitude toward the future among the young. I found it less so as I spoke to older people; but when pressured, there was always some hope.

The young women and men were between fourteen and twenty-five. Projected to 2000, we were then talking about people who would be in their forties. This was the largest category of people I spoke with, and while they were idealistic, they had a tenacity that was based in good solid thinking, and facts.

The women were students—high school, college, university—working and married people. They were aware of the Sixties and the upheaval that we went through. They were educated visually (TV-films), and knew about the world. They were aware of their parent's lives . . . and goals . . . and failures. Almost all desired a "better" life, and that was usually defined in terms of more time for things they liked . . . people they liked . . . and less time chasing material (expensive) things. They were desperate for honest relationships, and rejected their parent's hypocrisy regarding marriage. They felt compassion for other people in the world, and were willing to share, not take from others. If this meant they would have smaller cars . . . less luxury . . . less to eat . . . that was okay. Ideas such as peace, sharing, working together seemed an integral part of their future.

Some quotes:

Female student: I don't think there will be as much marriage in thirty years as there is today, because today so many people marry for the wrong reasons . . . like you "have to."

Male student: I think people will live together more and more, and make a choice about marriage after. In thirty years, actually even today, the word bastard won't be so bad anymore.

Female secretary: Truthfully, I feel I want to bear children, perhaps that was taught to me too, but I really think it's something inborn . . . like an instinct. But I don't want to trade my life away for that. I mean. I have dreams of success . . . fame . . . goals . . . recognition . . . and a desire to do something meaningful with my life. Right now that's more important than bearing and raising children. I feel a little guilty about that sometimes . . . like when my mother asks me about who I'm dating, and marriage and all that. I've got to try to be more than just a housewife and that might mean waiting ten or fifteen years to have kids . . . maybe never . . .

Male student: My father works over at Whirlpool . . . he works like a dog . . . and he's tired. I guess he had to do that in his life, but I would like to do more . . . maybe have less . . . but spend more time with people.

Female student: I'm going after the best job I can get, and I'm going to compete with men for it. I think today I can do that . . . I have that right.

Stewardess: Okay . . . you remember when I told you that I was a cheerleader in high school . . . and that I went out with the quarterback on the football team . . . and that when I got to college I met this guy, and fell in love . . . and was great for four years . . . well (she begins to cry) . . . it wasn't a guy . . . it was a girl. And it was the greatest and only love of my life . . . and there was no way to deal with it where I came from. I was always treated as some sort of "thing" . . . I mean like so special . . . and so pretty . . . and no one ever touched me . . . no one ever bothered to find out who I was . . . well, this girl did . . . and I love her for it . . .

Female nurse: We are married. My husband was in Vietnam. I'm a nurse, and he is going to be an engineer. So I work . . . and he studies, and when he's finished and working then I'm going to be a doctor, and when I'm finished and working, he is going to write. I think we can support each other throughout our lives and do the things we want that way.

Female student: The idea is to work hard for a while, and then take off for a while. We are going to be teachers, and we figure we can work together and then move around after we save some bread, and then find a place and work some more. We don't really need much, and we want to see it all.

Female computer programmer: I like this work, and I'm very good at it. I don't want to be the president of the company . . . I think that's a drag, but I know I'm in a sellers' market . . . I mean people like me are in demand, so I don't take any crap from anybody.

Female artist's representative: I am not married, and I may just want to live alone. So I want to be treated equally under the law, and with insurance and pensions and bank loans. I really think that if the institutions that supply these services draw distinctions, they are really stupid. Someone is going to get my business, and I intend that's going to be a lot of business.

Commune woman: This life here works for us. My folks don't see it and that's cool . . . but it's my life, and this is how we're living now. So many hassles other people have, we don't. We have what we need and what we want. It's really beautiful here . . . I'm glad I found it.

Female factory worker: My God yes . . . I hate this place. Who would like it? I make money here, and I work hard. See, I don't have much choice . . . it's the only job in town and I don't have too much school. I guess I'll get married but I hope it's not to one of these guys . . . I want better . . . you know?

Female advertising trainee: I have an apartment and I sleep with a lot of guys . . . well, not a lot but I go to bed with guys. I see nothing wrong except I tried to talk to my mother about it and she went through the roof, so we don't mention it anymore.

Female researcher: One of the real possibilities for the near future, and projected into the longer term view is that as a woman's economic position grows, so does her choice of life styles, and the choice of male relationships. Whereas women were forced to make decisions on marriage too soon, from too small a sampling, in a way, from lack of information on the possibilities . . . both hers and her mates, economic freedom will allow her to take her time, to have many relationships, and decide when and who is right for her . . . women won't marry as young, or for the reasons they have married before . . . sex, economic security, or fear. Instead women (and men) will see the possibility of many relationships, and with a good one she will ask . . . "Is this good for me . . . what does it have to offer me . . . will it enlarge me as a person?

The second group of women (and about ten percent men) were twenty-five to forty years old. Projected to 2000, they were in their fifties and sixties. This group was all over the lot, and it was hard to get a feeling from them in general. Some people were frightened by the future, and when pressed, were negative about their lives. Were they trapped? I think so, and they were confused about their "self" . . . their "being" . . . and the life they had led up to this point. Others were planning, had hope and were more positive about their futures.

As a group I looked at them as the "doers" of our society. They were the electricity that made America run. They were the middle managers . . . the generation to which the torch was to be passed, but they weren't always sure they wanted it. All were aware of the changes in "woman's place" . . . and no one was without an opinion.

Some quotes:

Housewife: As my kids get older I think more and more about my future . . . being a wife and mother is a responsible job, and I really enjoy it . . . most of the time. My little one is in nursery school now, and next year kindergarten. I'll have more time for myself . . . my life is going to grow, and when the kids are old enough . . . in a few years . . . I'm going back to work . . . in something really interesting . . .

Female teacher: Women today don't like themselves. Their desire to please men leaves them empty and frustrated, competing with their role models . . . *i.e.,* movie stars . . . the main part of their "self" is responding to and playing off their men. Now, with the changes happening, they find themselves lost . . . don't know who they are, or how to go about finding out.

Coal miner's wife: You went down there today . . . I never been down there, and I don't want to go. It's a lousy place, and he works like a dog. I see when he gets home. That's no life for anyone, so I think those people who burn the bras are nuts. I don't want to work like my husband. That's no life.

Female head-teller in bank: I sat here as a teller for almost ten years, and now things are really heppening at this bank. I think it has to do with equal rights . . . and maybe I'm just a token, but I'm head teller now, and I think I can be a loan officer soon . . . or more. Lot's of women are coming in for loans these days.

Female factory worker: I work so we can have enough . . . you know . . . for the house and the kids. I can't say I like it, but we do get equal pay. It's hard to save anything. I want better for my kids . . . you know . . . school and that . . . my girls too . . . you know . . . but that other stuff that you see the kids doing on TV . . . you know . . . I don't like it . . . I don't like it.

Male executive (computers): If you really want to know, I don't think all of this works. I work about seventy hours a week, and I have to travel all over the place. I have a neighbor who is in the construction business . . . he's a foreman. Well, he has a boat . . . and he's home every day on time . . . he plays golf . . . uses his boat sees his family. I know too much . . . there are only three or four other people in the world that have my experience, and in a technological world, that means nothing but work for me.

Waitress (Florida): You say future, and I think about the people who come in here every day . . . the old people I mean. Boy, if that's where it all goes, then who wants to think about the future. This is really sad to see them. What kind of life do they have. All I think about is that I have to get away from here. These people are just dying.

Female president of large industrial corporation: I'm here because of my ability and they all know it. Yes, I got here because my husband died, and I had control, but I've stayed here, and we've done well, so I have no apologies to make. I know I'm rare, as far as woman being in my position in industry, but I do see the day when it will be much more common, and hooray for that.

Advertising woman (divorced): It was tough place, after the divorce. It was a bitter thing and I don't think at the time I knew all the reasons. Now, I'm calmer, and I'm glad I did it. I was just suffocating, but I didn't know why. It's not his fault . . . my husband . . . I just had to get out and find out who I was. I wish I could have both.

Female researcher: Also in dealing with the future, I think it is impossible to deal with women's roles without dealing with men's as well. If women are being seen, and see themselves, in a new way, then that means men will have to do some reappraising of their roles and attitudes. The future is going to mean different things to different age groups. Women forty-five and over in general, won't be tremendously affected by this whole movement . . . they see their lives as pretty well lived, and any change for them would be extremely difficult . . . their attitudes and ideas are pretty solid and I don't think for the most part they will be able to see the subtleties of femaleness that have been imbedded in them.

The Hudson Institute told me that true liberation would come to the blue collar world first, because we are moving toward a three day work week, where the husband will work three days and the wife will work three days, and each will have to do the "home chores" while the other is working.

Kondratieff says we are in for a lulu of a depression in the late Seventies or early Eighties, but if the trend toward more personal reward, inward reward, joy in the giving and making of a product or service, continues, then it may well fit into a changing economic environment.

I come away hopeful . . . I am positive about it, and I want to live and thrive in the world that the young people are talking about. There is very little to give up for that joy.

Margaret Mead called it a prefigurative society, where we take our clues from the young, and build unknown worlds for unknown children . . . but to do that, we must relocate the future.

Relocate the future. That is what women are about to do.

If a full understanding of the nature and extent of the changes may not yet be crystal clear, it is certain that woman's image of herself, and man's image of her, will never be the same. She is no longer defined as just a housewife, part of a couple, a mother or a grandmother—she is, and thinks of herself as, an individual person with feelings, hopes, ambitions, needs.

As the nation reaches its Bi-Centennial, the "second American Revolution" has begun. Symbolizing the necessity of making certain that the momentum will not be lost, in Boston the Women's Coalition for the Third Century (WCBC) is already drafting the Declaration of Interdependence for the purpose of "moving women's organizations and their work into a central position in our history, instead of an auxiliary position."

In the melodrama of the 1890's, the villain Greedy Gus came in to the old homestead and thundered, "If you don't pay the mortgage by tomorrow at sundown, I shall foreclose . . . unless, of course L'il Nell choose to . . ." L'il Nell cringed and cried, "Whatever will become of me?" And unless the hero Jack Dalton came to the rescue in time, she had no choice.

Today and tomorrow, women will again be asking, "Whatever will become of me?" But they are looking to themselves for the options and the answers.

If you examine the possibilities raised by our writers, agree or disagree, and act accordingly, you will be part of the mainstream that flows toward Woman in the Year 2000.

1

On Her Destiny

1 BORN FREE: A FEMINIST FABLE

by Letty Cottin Pogrebin

AT THE STROKE OF MIDNIGHT on January 1 in the year 2000, a baby was born. But for the extraordinary timing of this child's arrival, the event would have attracted small notice, for America had long ago abandoned the practice of glorifying pregnancy and romanticizing the reproductive experience. It was simply accepted that some people would choose to have children and some would not.

However, as you might imagine, this baby *did* attract considerable notice, for it was the first new life to make an appearance in lhis country on the first moment of the first day of the new millennium.

Although it was reared in a rather typical way for the period, in a sense this particular child belonged to history. A record was kept of many details of its development, its childhood experiences and milestones, resulting a well-documented story of an otherwise average child of the Twenty-first Century.

This is that story.

The child was named Millenny, in honor of the start of the third millennium, A.D. Now this may seem a peculiar name, albeit a most appropriate one for a child whose birthdate was 1/1/2000. But that is precisely the point.

You see, back in the 1960s and '70s, when women became conscious of their own identities, they insisted on retaining their own names. The children of these women were often given hyphenated appellations

3

denoting both their fathers' and mothers' family origins. By the 1990s, the next generation of babies was carrying around heavy surnames like excess baggage. (Susan Greenberg-Ryan-Orsini-Jones comes immediately to mind.)

It became tedious to call the roll in school and tougher still to fit these names on social security cards. So, about five years before the turn of the millennium, a new law was passed by the American parliament. (The country had changed to the parliamentary system of government after the second administration of Gerald Ford, when it had become abundantly clear that the age of great leaders was gone for good.)

This new law allowed babies to be given a single name, as long as that name was unique, creatively apt, and not likely to be mistaken for another. Thus, people could establish their own and their children's very special identities without accumulating cumbersome hyphens from generation to generation. As parents began to name their kids Quellala and Talnafy and Xenobia, the new one-name names became more and more inventive and frequently quite poetic.

Now you'll have to agree that Millenny was an absolutely brilliant name for the new baby. It was also mellifluous—and besides, it sounded nice.

The Man, her father, had thought up the name at the very instant the baby was born—an instant that he joyously witnessed, since he was on the spot helping the baby to emerge from The Woman's birth canal. The Man was scrubbed down and masked, but otherwise quite comfortable in his shirt sleeves. Having recently completed his six-month course in midwifery, he was entirely relaxed and confident about his role in the birth process. Actually, it was an uncomplicated delivery. The woman had chosen a combination of acupuncture and the Lamaze natural childbirth method, so she too was feeling cheerful and in control.

As for the location of Millenny's birth, it can only be called idyllic. From the moment of conception, The Woman and The Man had considered many options: a hospital seemed too impersonal and full of sickness. A clinic would be smaller, but still rather antiseptic and hyper-medical. And an at-home birth was somewhat risky, since The Woman would be delivering her first child at the age of thirty-eight—a fairly common age for first parturition, but still an occasionally tricky business.

Eventually, several months before the due date, The Woman and The Man decided to book themselves into one of the new Natal Environment Centers that were proliferating in progressive urban areas.

Here, physicians and trained midwives were on call, but not ubiquitous. Moreover, the Center offered a total parent preparation program during which The Man and The Woman could attend rap sessions with other expectant parents; question-answer meetings with experienced mothers and fathers; films of childbirth; seminars on the costs, care, bathing and feeding of infants. Visiting social service agents presented prospective parents with information about all the available child care arrangements, health facilities and other community services that were routinely available to all children.

After immersing themselves in this comprehensive education for parenthood, The Man and The Woman went on to choose a Birth Atmosphere that they felt would suit them best and be most advantageous to their baby. The Natal Environment Center showed them a dazzling array of atmospheric options, each one designed to humanize the delivery room experience and neutralize the infant's birth trauma.

The Woman considered her emotional needs, cultural tastes and biological attitudes. She decided she wanted both a mirror (so that she could watch the birth) and a video viewer set (so that she could distract herself from the labor by watching her favorite cassette films).

For the sound environment, she chose a selection of musical tapes ranging from folk rock to Gregorian chants. Impressionist paintings hung on one wall; the other walls were bathed in soft, colored light. French windows opened to a shady glen.

When labor began, The Woman took her acupuncture treatment and commenced her rhythmic breathing. She could sense and feel the contractions, without "pain" but with keen awareness. She changed positions depending on her feelings. She kneeled, crawled, stretched out, asked The Man to massage her, stood, sat or walked around as she wished.

She had read about the primitive straps, stirrups and sterile drapes that were in use up to twenty years before, but she could not imagine how women ever tolerated the helpless confinement and unnatural supine birth position. As it happens, The Woman was squatting over the mirror when Millenny was born.

The Man helped ease the baby out of its mother's body. As I reported it was he who suggested the name, Millenny, just as the baby's head appeared. The Woman interrupted her ecstasy to agree that Millenny was indeed a splendid name.

From Millenny's point of view, the birth was a great trip. There were no glaring lights, no doctor's spanking, no tight swaddling clothes, no brisk, efficient hands examining her for flaws. Instead, she took her first breaths, without screams or spasms, and her lungs cleared as she was stroked and massaged. Then she was placed in a warm water bath that felt like the amniotic fluid she had known for nine months. When all was calm, Millenny reposed on her mother's belly, where she was lavished with admiration while The Woman and The Man savored the beautiful intimacy of the moment and the music filled the air and the room was as warm as a womb.

There was great love between The Woman and The Man. They had lived together for several years cementing strong bonds of respect and shared humor. They knew each other well enough to believe that they wanted also to share the experience of having a child; they had often discussed how they would care for it together.

It happens that The Man and The Woman were among the minority of people in the country who had chosen to formalize their relationship in something that was called a "loyalty marriage," (although it was vastly different from marriages of a quarter-century before). They had entered into an agreement between themselves, outlining their expectations of one another, an equal division of responsibilities, and their goals for their relationship. Over the years, the agreement had been renegotiated and revised a few times to accommodate their changing needs; but it always contained a cancellation clause so that each party was free to leave after giving fair notice.

In any case, it was a private contract between two consenting adults and it need not concern us here. Except as one example of the many life-arrangements that were common in the year 2000. The Woman and The Man could have chosen to live together with no written contract, or to live apart, or each of them might have lived with other women or other men, or in a mixed communal situation. Then too, The Woman could have conceived a child by the man of her choice (or by artificial insemination), and raised the child as a single parent, with her friends and her community serving as the partner-parent.

(By 2000, society had evolved a mature, humane understanding that all children are our common future—and as such, we must care about them and use our collective resources and energies to nurture and enrich the life of every child.)

Perhaps, in the light of these many possible life-arrangements, The

Woman and The Man may strike you as a bit old-fashioned for having opted for a marriage agreement. Let us just say that was *their* decision. Just as it had been their decision as to whether they would use the male or the female contraceptive method in any given month.

Once they had crossed signals on their contraceptive schedule and The Woman had become pregnant unintentionally. In that instance, the decision to have an abortion was hers alone to make. She, The Man, and the law all recognized that no woman should be forced to use her body as an unwilling host throughout an unplanned, unwanted pregnancy.

As a matter of fact, pregnancy itself *could* have been utterly passé by 2000. In the late '70s, scientists had perfected the technique of laboratory fertilization, and test-tube embryos had been successfully implanted in the wombs of three women. The next step was the development of an artificial uterus. However, this appeared to most people as a terrifying misuse of technology. So in the year 1984, amid cries of "Brave New World" and "Remember George Orwell," the international scientific community had voted to outlaw such practices on moral grounds.

Medical brainpower was rerouted and a few years later, doctors found a cure for sterility. Shortly thereafter, hormone researchers invented male and female contraceptives that were completely safe (and conveniectly dispensed by the government in banks and post offices).

With such signal medical advances, the plain truth was that *everyone* could conceive, and *anyone* could prevent conception.

Which meant that adoption was virtually impossible in the last years of the twentieth century. All births were planned; all pregnancies were monitored for genetic and other defects so that all babies were born healthy; and all living children were lovingly absorbed into a humane, caretaker society with innumerable available living arrangements.

Therefore, when The Woman and The Man decided they wanted to share their lives with a child, they knew they must have one of their own. And so they did. When they were good and ready.

Oh, one more thing. By analyzing the female's fertility cycle and then precisely timing the act of conception, parents could determine the sex of their child at the point of fertilization. Choosing sex should have been big news. Instead, it turned out to be a rather ho-hum announcement for reasons which shall be clear in a moment.

All this background information is more than idle reminiscence. It is essential in order to explain why Millenny was not only a planned and wanted child, born to sensible, thoughtful parents—but a planned and wanted *girl* child, besides.

A girl as the first born child? Some people with long memories may marvel at this. For centuries male children were considered preferable —as heirs to the family fortune or enterprise, as carriers of the father's name, and as inheritors of the then-dominant male culture. We've all read those antique social psychology texts that reported studies in which twelve times more women than men wished they were the opposite sex. In the '60s, Edward H. Pohlman even found that pregnant women dreamed twice as often about male babies; and that more mothers of girl babies had post-partum depressions. In 1974, Candida and James Peterson found that of those with strong preferences for the sex of their first born, ninety percent of the men and ninety-two percent of the women wanted a boy.

This kind of male-infant favoritism faded away in the last decades of the century as the status of female human beings rose to the point where women and men became completely equal in the eyes of the law *and* one another. By the year 2000, women were casually accepted and well-represented in politics, education, business and the professions. Household roles were a matter of human ecology and personal preference, rather than sex-typed divisions of labor. Women's earning power matched men's in all fields. And the male contribution to child rearing was institutionalized in a new kind of full social parenthood which included paternity leaves, participation in the birth experience, and a role for all men (whether fathers or not) in the lives of society's children.

Critics of the feminist revolution twenty-five years before had feared role-reversal, militant women, spineless men, unisex and depravity. Instead twenty-first century society was enjoying unparalleled cultural diversity, multiple interests and strengths in each individual, fully functionings, mentally healthy women and men.

In this enlightened culture, women and men were nurturers; men and women were achievers. Women and men enjoyed full expression of their emotional selves; men and women were self-actualized creators, intellects and decision-makers. There were no pat differences between *all* men and *all* women, except those that met the eye. What enlivened the human race were the millions of wondrous differences that have always existed between one *person* and another *person,* whatever their sex.

Since girl and boy babies were greeted with these equally open-ended hopes and expectations, couples tended to choose the sex of their child on the basis of personal taste or whim. In truth, despite the capacity to plan a baby's sex in advance, most people were actually ignoring the choice process altogether and letting the sperms fall where they may.

The reason why Millenny's parents had nonetheless decided to conceive a girl was quite a simple one: both The Man and The Woman had younger brothers and they felt like having a little girl around for a change.

Once opting for a female child, how did The Woman and The Man prepare their home for the baby?

They made a soft and sturdy, eight-foot-square, sleep-and-play mat for the floor. (Cribs and playpens went out about the time automobiles converted from gasoline to batteries. It was considered simply barbaric to put babies behind bars when they could crawl and roll about freely on the sleep-and-play mat.) Millenny's mat was blue, as was her quilt and bunting and the curtains at the windows—because blue was the parents' favorite color. (They were sick to death of pink, since both of their little brothers had always had pink rooms.)

When Millenny was born her parents registered her in their food collective, so that the cooperative could order baby food and include her in meal planning when she became old enough to eat with the other members. The Woman and The Man had no kitchen in their home —only a small refrigerator for drinks and snacks and a tiny microwave warming oven. Meals were taken in groups at the collective's communal kitchen. Marketing was done on a cooperative, alternating schedule.

It was by far the most efficient arrangement imaginable—and economical too. All the members saved money by having only one set of major appliances and by ordering all their groceries and produce in bulk. No one was overjoyed when his or her turn came to serve as shopper, cook or cleaner-upper. But reciprocity made sense. It was well worth a few days on duty to get so many other days of hassle-free mealtimes.

The children of the food collective were glad to hear of Millenny's birth. That meant one more kid to share the table-setting and dish-clearing duties that were assigned also in rotation, to tpe children.

When Millenny was brought home from the Natal Environment Center, The Woman and The Man invited some of their closest friends to a Life Celebration Ceremony. (This was an alternative ritual to the

Christian christening or baptism and the Jewish *bris* for boys.) The friends brought gifts of personal significance. One wrote a song for Millenny, another gave ten nights of babysitting, someone else brought paints and made a happy mural for her wall.

The friends then drank strawberry wine and toasted the new baby with warm wishes for a life of pleasure, usefulness and satisfaction. In a short speech, each of her parents reaffirmed their hopes for Millenny and their intention to rear her with love and freedom. Both The Man and The Woman signed a pledge that Millenny would be free to leave them if at any time in the future, she felt her life would be more rewarding away from her home and her parents.

Millenny flourished in infancy. Perhaps because she was delivered without birth trauma, or perhaps because she was breast fed by her mother and rocked regularly by her father, she was a contented child who slept well and suffered no attacks of colic.

When the United States was a matriscentric child-rearing society, infants frequently suffered father-deprivation. In 1971, psychologists recorded the average time spent by fathers interacting with their babies and found it to be 37.7 seconds per day. Millenny's father spent an average of three hours each day with his daughter. Millenny's mother also devoted about three hours a day to her child—and they were joyful hours, not hours inspired by guilt or martyrdom.

The Man and The Woman invested more imagination than money into the toys and playthings that they brought into Millenny's world as she grew. The child loved bright rubber balls, shiny pots and pans, shaggy rugs and plastic prisms to catch the light.

As soon as she could sit, Millenny was able to play as long as she liked in the wading-pool-sized bathtub that was a gift of the food collective. Often The Woman, The Man and Millenny would bathe together, splashing, scrubbing and playing with things that fill and spill and float and sink. Sometimes friends would come and join them in the tub. Everyone enjoyed washing each other's bodies and feeling their slippery, soapy skins. Adults and children were relaxad about nudity, and a good group bath was considered more fun than a backyard barbeque.

When she was in her room, Millenny could lie on her sleep-and-play mat and push buttons that turned on different sounds from the tape machine built into her wall. She seemed to favor animal sounds, music box melodies and lullabyes. But most often she pushed the button that played her parents' voices speaking soothingly to her.

By mid-century Benjamin Spock standards, I guess Millenny didn't spend *that* much time with her parents. Her mother worked in the morning from nine-to-one, and her father worked from one-to-five in the afternoon. The parents had chosen this job schedule since it accommodated work, child time and home-maintenance chores into each day. (Since they believed in the dignity of housework and the inherent worth of child rearing functions, The Woman and The Man shared all these activities with enthusiasm.)

They could have done as their neighbors did: work the three-day, eight-hour-a-day plan; or the four-day week with six-hours work each day. But The Man and The Woman preferred to put in their twenty-five-hour work week over the course of five days so that they were never too tired to enjoy each other, their daughter and their friends.

The child care center was a real boon. It was not considered a father or mother "substitute" but a vital, positive catalyst for child development. The Center accepted kids of any age, race or class. And it was open twenty-four hours a day. Millenny was taken there from the time she was a month old, whenever her parents wanted their half-day before or after work to themselves, or when they put in time on community projects that fulfilled their Social Commitment Contract.

Since the year 1995, the government's poverty, education and welfare programs had proven insolubly inadequate, every citizen was required to sign a contract in which she or he guaranteed to give society six hours of time and talent every month, for the benefit of all. This plan was an equitable alternative to the old volunteerism ethic, which had caused selective exploitation of womankind in charitable projects to which men had only lent their names and money.

Where formerly women were assumed to have nothing more important to do than to give their time for nothing, the Social Commitment Contract (SCC) provided for a base minimum of volunteer work spread among men and women alike. People signed up for a rotating series of service tasks. These assignments didn't replace paid jobs, but supplemented them wherever and whenever there was immediate need. What's more, the SCC brought people into contact with a reality that Twentieth Century Americans used to avoid with a "Let Georgina do it" attitude. Thus far in its first five years SCC had delivered on its promise to unite humanity, expand interpersonal awareness and improve the quality of life. People also discovered that the lines of class, race, age and neighborhood had begun to blur and seem meaningless.

In a typical month of SCC's, doctors might contract for six hours of pruning trees in the public parks; laborers might work in oak-panelled rooms rebinding damaged library books; childfree citizens and retired elders could bring kids into their lives by helping out in child care centers. (There were lots of older people to draw upon as those born during the post World War II baby boom reached retirement age and one-quarter of the population consisted of folks over age fifty-five.)

With the work-week reduced to twenty-five hours (a change that ensured full employment in order to sustain the national economy), people had no trouble finding the six hours to fulfill their SCC each month. Automation had relieved human beings of tedious, repetitive work and thus, most jobs were tolerably interesting, if not satisfying. After a pleasant shift of paid employment, people seemed most cooperative about taking on a less challenging job for their SCC every now and then.

When The Woman and The Man worked off their contract, or went to the beach or theatre, they simply signed up for coverage at the child care center. Millenny thrived there too, for the center was staffed by caring men and women, child development specialists, painters, singers, acrobats, athletes, philosophers, dancers, craftspersons, educators, old people with patience, and young people with energy. A full-service health station at each center assured children periodic medical and dental check-ups and immediate attention for their cuts and scrapes.

In the early months, when Millenny was fed at the breast, The Woman found it convenient to bring the baby to work, rather than travel to the child-care center to nurse her. Every office and factory was required to maintain an infant lounge for just that purpose. (Incidentally, employers found that workers were more productive on the job when they were not harassed or worried about their babies.) Many fathers also brought their babies to the infant lounges—so that they could spend coffee breaks with them or bottle feed them in a quiet place. Both the infant lounges and the child-care centers were free, first rate and supported by federal funds or subsidies.

Eventually, Millenny was spending less time at the infant lounge and more time at the child care center. She attended the Margaret Mead

Center where a plaque on the wall bore a quotation from the ninety-nine-year-old anthropologist: "Child rearing is too complex for the individual small family unit to deal with." At the center Millenny had a greater variety of playmates, caretakers, playthings, attention and affection than ever was possible in the days when children were raised solely by the mother in an isolated nuclear household, where the learning environment was only as rich as the parents' pocketbooks and educational levels allowed.

This one-to-one child-rearing syndrome tended to perpetuate in the child whatever were the individual mother's hang-ups, fears and biases. Experts had also discovered that the isolation, drudgery and the pressure to be "fulfilled" had contributed to maternal child abuse as well as to women's breakdowns, drug use and alcoholism. Not so in the year 2000.

As she approached her first birthday, Millenny had been nourished by a number of devoted people of all ages: her parents (still the primary love objects and caretakers); her counsellor at the center (the forty-year-old man who was in charge of the infant group); the ancillary staff members at the center (including the older children, women and men doing their SCC's, and specialists who regularly visited child care centers to enrich the program). One of these specialists, a gymnast who came to exercise the babies, found Millenny to have a good spine, strong legs and an impressive grip for her age.

The gymnast's report presaged much that was to come. Millenny sat up by herself at six months, was a vigorous, speedy creeper, and walked quite steadily at nine months. This early physical and muscular development was accompanied by a devilish and adventurous spirit that often led Millenny into mischief.

By eighteen months she was jumping from her play cart icto mud puddles. (Since she was always dressed in functional, washable coveralls, she could scamper wherever curiosity led her.) Well before she was two, she could throw a beanbag across the room. Occasionally, with an excess of zeal, she pushed and pulled her friend Umganawa until he cried. And the teachers at the center are still talking about the time she climbed up on the trampoline and bounced herself into the sandpile.

Millenny was far more advanced in her motor development than in her verbal progress. When she did start to speak, at about two-and-a-half, her first words were "Oh, shit"—an expletive that her mother and father had never deleted from their own vocabulary. (Needless to say, no one was shocked. There was no longer a double standard for linguistic propriety as practiced by adults or children, or boys and girls. If people permitted such words to themselves, they permitted them to their children.)

Millenny's second word was "ambivalence"—since she was often of two minds and was used to hearing herself described as such. When she became more verbal, her speech was soon peppered with rhyming words which especially pleased her ear. Noticing this, her father began to read poetry to her at bedtime.

In 2002, when The Woman had to go to Mexico on a six-month business project, it was decided that she would take Millenny along. The Man would use these months for a return to school where he wanted to take courses in home economics and physics. He was a person who sought enrichment not "success." In the 1970s when he was in his teens, he had seen men driven to death by ambition and competitiveness, beset by ulcers and heart disease, and damaged by their emotional poverty. Now that men were in touch with their feelings, The Man enjoyed the freedom to express himself in many different areas.

Like most people, he considered education a lifelong endeavor, a continuing high voltage current that one plugged into at will. Since The Woman was earning enough salary, The Man felt comfortable about dropping out of his job, going to school and living on The Woman's earnings.

By the same token, The Woman was dedicated to her work, excited about the expedition and happy to take Millenny along. It would be no trouble. In all business travel, provisions were always made for the children of those workers who could not or would not leave their kids behind.

(Of course, there wasn't a hint of gossip when The Woman and Millenny left The Man at home for six months. Why should there be? Everyone understood that women and men—even those living in "loyalty marriage" arrangements—did not jettison their individual lives and interests when they formed their bond relationship.)

By the end of those six months, The Man returned to his job all the better for having mastered basic nutritional principles and having learned the effect of gamma rays on migratory birds. The Woman had completed her project and also unearthed some magnificent Mayan artifacts. And Millenny had learned to say "Oh, shit" in Spanish.

Her parents were pleased that she was very nearly bilingual after the Mexican trip and could chat easily with her Spanish-speaking friends at the day care center.

In the year 2003, when she turned three, Millenny celebrated her birthday twice. At home, on New Year's Day, her father baked a choc-olate-walnut-orange cake from a recipe he had picked up in his home economics class. The Woman, who enjoyed decorating and designing, festooned the room with Fourth of July bunting and Christmas balls and Easter Eggs and Halloween pumpkins because she felt Millenny's birth-day was like all the holidays rolled into one.

After their meal, The Man and The Woman gave Millenny a very special gift. They replaced her sleep-and-play mat with a grown-up bed; and where the mat had been, they set up a small trampoline that they had made themselves. Millenny jumped and bounced and twisted and rolled on the trampoline until she exhausted herself. Then her parents sang her to sleep in her big, new bed.

The next day, she had *another* birthday party with her friends and teachers at the Margaret Mead center. Thus began a tradition that was to last throughout her childhood: the tradition of Millenny's birthday parties with themes. Because of the extant record of many of these parties it is possible to trace the development of her wide interests through the subjects that she chose for each party theme.

To celebrate her third birthday, Millenny had asked for a Firehouse Party. The Woman, who loved to decorate, covered the little tables with red crepe paper and gave each child a tiny firefighter hat and a cupcake frosted to look like flames, with a real candle on top. Outside in the play yard, a "firepole" was set up so the children could slide down in their rush to the firetruck. Some children climbed ladders and rescued one another from the top of the jungle gym. Other children piled snow on the playhouse roof, pretended the snow was fire, and then washed the fire out with water from the garden hose. Several girls monopolized the big toy fire engine until a couple of the boys insisted on giving their dolls a ride in the vehicle. The party was a super success. When it was over, two girls and a boy announced they wanted to be firefighters when they grew up.

Millenny had no idea what she wanted to be. Anything was possible. And everything was fascinating.

When she was four, Millenny saw "The Nutcracker" ballet. That year she decided her party theme would be the Tschaikovsky ballet and all the kids would come dressed as toys or wooden soldiers. (Believe it or not none of the guests wanted to be sugarplum fairies. Fairies had lost their glamor and most kids thought they were the least interesting of all make-believe characters.)

At five, Millenny came to her own birthday party dressed as a bride (though she refused to choose a boy to dress as the groom). All her party guests were attendants and wedding guests.

She never knew anyone who got married the old, fancy way but she *had* seen a movie from a half-century ago and it had made weddings look like a carnival ball. She preened when she walked down "the aisle" in the white satin gown she'd made out of her grandmother's wedding dress. But otherwise, there wasn't much she could do with that theme, so Millenny was depressed when the party was over.

"All that fuss for one day," she complained to her parents. "And then what do you have after the ceremony but real life, which is not at all like a carnival ball." The Man and The Woman smiled and said nothing.

Finally The following year, Millenny went to school. Again, there were many alternatives. Some kids were taught at home, others in their commune study centers, still others had individualized tutoring in their child care centers until they were old enough for independent study. Millenny and her parents decided she would attend the Open Free School because it was exactly what its name implied. It was open and free and it tried to let people be the same.

Each day, many teachers and resource people came into the large, airy learning spaces to work with individual students or small groups of children. The schedule was something like college used to be twenty years ago or so.

There were small seminars for problem-solving and large classes for survey courses, guest speakers and films. Children learned to read in tutorial programs or with the help of pictures, recordings or self-made storybooks. They learned math through a combination of block building, new math exercises, computers and brain games. In history seminars, famous or powerful people weren't presented as a remote aristocracy. The children discovered and appropriated the women and men who would be their heroes. Students didn't have to know a lot of facts, but they had to understand how to *find out* facts, and what facts were, or whether there was always such a thing as a fact at all.

There were elective courses for every subject; each area was taught with different methods and materials. If one style of teaching didn't ring the bell, another style would be irresistable. By choosing what was right for them, children found their own way to knowledge.

There were no "you can'ts" or "you have to's" in the Open Free School. An orthodox educator might be surprised to see a seven-year-old girl in a metalworking class, or a twelve-year-old boy doing a project on "weaving through the ages." But most of the country's educators had discontinued the practice of categorizing youngsters by age and sex.

Gone were the spelling bees that pit the boys against the girls. Gone were the separate girl-boy lines for marching here and there—in fact there were no line-ups at all. Teachers weren't flustered when girls got into fights—for anger was seen as a gender-free human emotion—and boys were comforted, not ridiculed, when tears filled their eyes.

The textbooks used in school were full of exciting stories of women and men who had contributed to society. Battles and territorial disputes were reported as the gruesome, ruthless realities that they were. Pictures, drawings, lists and bibliographies reflected women's existence as well as men's. Textbooks also focused on children's rights and responsibilities at present and in various periods of history. And there were books that described how single people live or how ethnic groups preserve their special cultures or how past leaders made mistakes and current leaders were not infallible.

When occupational choices were described to children, both male and female counterparts were shown performing the jobs. The school had a constant stream of visiting speakers—women and men from every field who told children what workers do, what to expect from a job and how to prepare for a specialty. When students signed up for labor-and-learning apprenticeship programs, there was a remarkable positive effect on their self-esteem. Mentors from the work force served as guides for apprentices and represented strong, admirable role-models for girls and boys.

Human ecology was another course open to all children. Here kids could learn the multi-faceted art of self-sufficiency and perfect skills to help them cope with daily life. Girls and boys were taught to cook, do basic plumbing and wiring jobs, drive and repair a car or change a flat tire, sew and mend, sail a boat, build a fire, use power tools, keep a budget, read an annual report, change a baby's diaper.

In other courses, community organizers shared information about coalition politics and lobbying. Parents and child-care experts taught parenthood skills to students who thought they might want to have children someday. Revolutionaries were given a forum in which to present their radical solutions to contemporary problems.

City and country, forest and seashore, parks and streets were explored when small groups took environmental field trips.

Tired children could sleep in school; hungry children could eat there; sick children could find succor and medical care. At the Open Free School, there were no misfits because there was a place for every child.

Into this responsive learning community came Millenny with her love of poetry and her explosive physical energy. She elected four "thinking" courses, a field trip to a recycling plant and three sports courses. And that is how she discovered baseball in the first autumn of her first year at the Open Free School.

Baseball became her passion. She played with girls and boys her own age and she wheedled her way into pick-up games with older kids.

After finishing a morning at work, The Woman had often gone to professional baseball games to unwind and enjoy herself. (The Man wasn't fond of baseball; he preferred soccer.) Now The Woman began taking Millenny along. Game tickets were inexpensive because the major league teams had been nationalized several years back after a couple of pitchers got caught in a bribery scandal and one team went bankrupt.

Millenny saw her favorite player, Joanna Cobb, in action in an exciting world series game that filled the girl's dreams for weeks. Joanna had made a lightning double play, putting out the man on first and the woman on second. (Baseball's sex barrier had fallen in 1983, when the young girls who cut their teeth in Little League in the 1970s became good enough to break into the majors.)

For her sixth, seventh and eighth birthdays, Millenny chose baseball as the theme of her parties. There was always a seven-inning game to play before the birthday cake could be cut. And the party gifts included baseball caps, shirts, balls, bats and an autographed picture of Joanna Cobb. With all this gear, Millenny was a total devotée. Her red baseball mitt had been oiled and softened until it fit her hand like a second skin. She played every day and showed considerable talent for the sport. She didn't have to con her way into older kids' games anymore. All the boys and girls wanted her on their teams.

One weekend Millenny's father persuaded her to forsake baseball and go with him to a horse ranch. He enjoyed riding horseback through the woods and he wanted to share his enthusiasm with his daughter. Millenny loved the horses and the stables. In the saddle she felt like a Nineteenth-Century explorer trotting under the trees in an undiscovered land. She was quickly hooked on riding and was eager to learn how to canter.

The Man took Millenny riding at the public city stables every Saturday morning. Though some politicians had said that the horse had outlived modern city life, there were people who fought to keep such country amenities in the metropolis. Through activist efforts the stables were maintained by an ever-changing crew of horse-loving city folks who worked off their Social Commitment Contract amid the hay and saddlesoap. Now horseback riding was free to city people on a first come, first served basis.

Week after week Millenny and her father got on line at daybreak in order to reserve a horse for the first half hour. On crisp, transparent mornings they could gallop through the park without seeing another human being. Just the two of them, their horses and the wind. Neither of them minded awakening at dawn. It was a lovely way to be together doing something they both loved.

For months after her introduction to horses Millenny wore only ranch clothes, boots and chaps and Western hats. It was no surprise, therefore, when she asked for a Cowgirl-Cowboy party as her ninth birthday celebration.

The surprising thing was that this request led to one of the very few recorded disputes to have arisen between Millenny and her parents.

There had been little to argue about through the years. The Open Free School was such a positive place that Millenny did her schoolwork with gusto. She was happy in school and happy in the Margaret Mead center's after-school activity program.

No one had ever forced Millenny to go to sleep at a specific time because her parents found that when left alone, she went to bed when her body was tired.

She had never rebelled against her assignments in the food collective. It seemed fair to pitch in when everyone else was carrying a similar load. Since Millenny was interested in good health and physical stamina, she never begged for sweets once her father explained about vitamins and proteins.

Although television programs had been purged of their former violence, and sexist portrayals of macho men and vacuous women were banned from public airwaves, Millenny's parents still didn't approve of long hours in front of the TV set. To a child who loved books and sports, this limitation was painless.

No problems with friendships either: she had always been encouraged to choose her own companions.

With few reasons to lock horns, harmony had been habit-forming.

Until the Cowgirl-Cowboy party. In this altercation, The Woman and The Man exercised their authority much in the way that parents did in the last century and for centuries before that. The conflict was sparked when Millenny wanted a true-to-life Western party, and her parents drew the line at toy guns.

Even though guns had always been forbidden in her home, and all war toys were prohibited from her school and child care center, Millenny insisted that gun play was an essential part of any self-respecting Cowgirl-Cowboy party.

"Other parents allow war toys in *their* houses," said Millenny, with all the sass that children have spewed since time began. (Some things just *never* change.)

The Woman and The Man sat down with their child and talked about the futility of violence and the tragedy of war. They described how gun control laws had cut street crime in half and how world peace had been miraculously maintained for over a decade.

"Toy guns stand for real guns, Millenny. And real guns kill living things," said The Woman.

"There's no sense playing at a game that nobody can win," said The Man.

Millenny listened to her parents position. Then she thought for a long time about how objects can become symbols of one's values. She thought about having cited what "other people" do, and she realized that she couldn't live an authentic life as Millenny, if she began imitating others or adopting their standards as her own. She agreed that there would be no toy guns at her party and it was a great party—with a lassoing contest and "hayrides" on Millenny's wagon, brim full of straw, and nine prancing ponies, one for each year, painted on the birthday cake with yellow frosting.

Nine was a watershed age for Millenny. It was the year she elected to take an ethics course at school. Suddenly, right or wrong seemed to be demanding questions. Her conscience kept insisting on definitive answers. At the same time, peer pressure often promoted choices that contradicted her own instincts. When challenged to do her own thinking Millenny saw that having her parents' support made it easier to act on her opinions, no matter how unpopular.

Sometimes, her grandmothers would talk about their own childhoods, when girls were supposed to be popular above all. Both grandmas had been taught to smile sweetly and keep their opinions to themselves. It was hard to believe that, even in the '60s and '70s when Millenny's own mother was growing up, girls were raised to please and snare boys, be desirable marriage partners and worry about their looks. What a drag, thought Millenny. No wonder women had fought to change their lives.

Now don't get the idea that Millenny led a sterile, dreary existence, bereft of friends, unconcerned about her appearance, or immune to aesthetic pleasures. Of course there were times when she liked to feel clean, neat and attractive. And while it was more her style to be an outspoken dynamo, she was no stranger to contented solitude.

Every so often she would speak melodiously. Now and then, she wore diaphanous skirts, bathed in scented colognes, wrapped herself in silken garments.

Dressing up was fun. It was a form of magic; a transformation, an experiment in the laboratory of image-making. It was just that these things weren't that important. She was the same Millenny whether in baseball knickers, blue jeans or bijous. She took her *self* with her into her clothes, her games, her friendships. She was not an invention of other people's expectations. She was authentic.

As she moved into the second decade of her life, the girls and boys who became her real friends were those who understood. They were children of similar straightforwardness, children who were honest and genuine and free.

The boys had never learned to disdain girls—so communication between the sexes was zesty, loose and relaxed. Playing sports with girls was no different than playing with boys. There was no shame in losing to a girl because boys no longer had to protect the obsolete male superiority myth.

Without pretense between them, girls and boys could forge intimate friendships; without role-playing, there could be shared strengths and open confessions of weakness. Rather than waste the childhood years on teasing and enmity, girls and boys were unconsciously laying the groundwork for adult male-female relationships that would be based on respect and affection.

Just as cross-sex friendships prospered, so did same-sex friendships provide warm companionship. Boys talked to one another about their terrors as well as their triumphs. It was not uncommon for boys to hug and kiss each other in greeting, just as girls and women had always done.

Girls met on common grounds to exchange experiences, plans and dreams. In the first part of her adolescence, Millenny found girl friends who enjoyed many of the same activities. She found confidantes she could trust with her deepest feelings, and girls who seemed to understand her thoughts without a word being spoken.

One of her closest girl friends was more sexually sophisticated than the rest. This girl helped Millenny examine her own genitals and become comfortable with her awakening sexuality. While Millenny's mother had always encouraged her to masturbate and discover the erotic responses of her body, Millenny somehow preferred to discuss the subject with her friend. Female sexuality was taught at the Open Free School and all the youngsters understood that sexual pleasure and procreation were not necessarily related. But it was invaluable to have a knowledgeable friend who could make these lessons tangible.

Millenny's friend helped her to reaffirm her clitoral pride. She showed Millenny how to use a menstrual extraction kit whenever it was inconvenient to let her menstrual period run its course. She demonstrated how to insert a tampon, how to use the various female contraceptive devices, how to masturbate to orgasm.

Such intimate discussions were quite unremarkable in the year 2013. Girls and women routinely assisted one another with personal or sexual problems. Moreover, adolescent sexuality was no longer a taboo subject. America, like other cultures through the ages, came to accept the fact that when the body is ready, the spirit is usually more than willing. Nature had been trying to tell us this for a long, long time. Social mores began to change when Americans realized that the greatest immorality was, not sex, but war, hunger and assault on human dignity.

Some reactionary, narrowminded readers may assume that the girl who was Millenny's sexual tutor was a lesbian. Or that the boys who hugged and kissed each other hello, were homosexuals. The truth is that we don't know if they were or they weren't. After the year 1981, historical documents don't mention people's sexual preferences.

Apparently there was a spectacular brouhaha throughout the 1970s on the whole issue of gay rights. Some localities passed anti-discrimination legislation, and some places persisted in considering homophile men and women to be dangerous deviants. (Millenny read about this persecution in her history books and it all seemed to her as repugnant as burning witches at the stake.) Well, eventually what happened was all the gay people in the American parliament came out and all the homophiles in the church came out and all the Lesbians and homosexuals working for companies listed on the New York Stock Exchange came out, and suddenly the issue seemed academic.

So, since 1981, gay people enjoyed all their civil rights and in the twenty-first century nobody cared much about anyone else's sexual persuasion unless they were in bed together.

The Woman and The Man had always been heterosexual people. They may well have wished Millenny to choose the same avenue for her erotic pleasures. In any case, they knew from observation and from sheaves of studies and statistics that neither they nor anyone else could program their daughter's sexuality.

Years ago, parents had nearly expired trying to coerce their children into heterosexuality. Fathers had sent their sons to military schools to "make men" of them. Mothers had trundled their daughters to charm classes in the hope of making a "tomboy" ladylike and feminine. In the end, children became the women and men they were meant to be all along.

Those who judge others by an arbitrary "moral" code, must make do without information on Millenny's sexual preferences. There are no entries in this category. (I suspect recording *that* seemed as silly to twenty-first century scribes as reporting what Jezebel ate for breakfast would have been for the authors of the Bible.) The information was simply deemed irrelevant.

Unfortunately, a lot more is missing from this twenty-first century biography. For, sad to say, the story ends here. Did Millenny live on a Women's Farm or enter a "loyalty marriage?" Did she bear any children or was she unwilling to add another life to America's population of three hundred million? What work engaged her energies? We'll never know. And perhaps this information, too, is irrelevant, except as documentary minutia of the third millennium.

What *is* relevant about Millenny's story is its perspective on the making of a woman out of a child—a complex, exultant, intoxicating and beautiful process that many of us are trying hard to understand. Millenny's life provides some of the clues we need.

It took love and liberty to make the woman. It took a network of caring people. It took a responsive and resourceful social support system and an attitude that our children are our natural treasure. It took nurturant men and women and gender-free options and art and good health and friendship and physical exuberance and poetry. In a sense, Millenny was a product of the best that a humane culture had to offer. Its children were its gifts to the future.

The record stops here because along about the year 2016, Millenny tired of having her life observed so minutely. One day she decided to slip away to live in another place where the historians would never find her. Though she might someday return, leaving her home, friends and community was sad and very difficult.

She told The Woman and The Man that she wanted to lead a natural, uninspected life and take her place in the society that nourished her. Her parents loved their daughter dearly, but they cherished the brave independence that inspired her decision.

Fulfilling the promise they had made years before at the Life Celebration Ceremony, they let her go.

THE END

AUTHOR'S NOTE: If this Fable reads at times as science fiction, the fault lies in our closed minds and limited vision. For nothing in Millenny's story has been invented out of whole cloth. The patterns exist, the resources are there, the consciousness is rising. Only the commitment is lacking. Right now we have the potential to enact the life scenario imagined here. Will it take us twenty-five years to emancipate children and parents from the prison of stifling roles and outdated conventions? If I could answer that question, I would have written not a fable, but a prophesy.

2 THE FEMALE FAÇADE: FIERCE, FRAGILE AND FADING

by Jane Trahey

WHATCHA GONNA LOOK LIKE in the year 2000, baby? Whatchur image gonna be? Take a long, long look into the crystal ball. Does 2000 seem like light years away? It's not. Think back to 1950 and the picture of women then. Just take Betty Friedan's estimate of it. You don't need to research the matter. The nadir in female images was 1950. Women by and large had fled to the suburbs, abandoned careers, given up on higher education. They had bought the feminine mystique right down the line. Now take a look at 1975's female image. This is the one we live with. I don't have to spell that out either. I just want to remind you that this tiny change took twenty-five years. I look at the current façade of the average American female on television, in films, in print, on broadcast . . . and I think, "Baby, you've got a long, long way to go." If the past twenty years are a measure of how fast we're moving, I project a rather dismal picture for 2000.

But you say, "There's been so much written, so much said, so much done to raise consciousness. We have women's rights, we have legislation in the works, we have equal opportunities, we have equal pay." And I hate to pinch the soap bubble, but I wouldn't stake my reputation on this dream. We do not have equal pay. Statistics show that it's White male, Black male, White female, and Black female (in that order) who earn proportionately less by each category. Women are not paid the same salaries for the same work. Sure, we have legislation and sure, you can take your company to court, but equal pay is not here. Equal opportunities? Not true. The Equal Rights Amendment is on the docket for vote, but it has not come to fruition yet. I came into the advertising agency business in the late 1950s. At that time, there were two females who were presidents of their own agencies. I made it three. Now there are two again. In the year 2000, if we double our energies, we'll have four. But I'll have to see it to believe it.

The montage of the female I tune in on my nineteen-inch screen comes off as a pretty damaging indictment of the woman's cause. I see a vapid, waspish blonde, clutching a huge box of Tide or Cold Power and babbling away about the quality of her wash. I see her cracking up because Clorox takes her bleach away. I see her smelling Mervin's T-shirts and becoming quite orgiastic in front of her Westinghouse, while she plays submoron to the commands of a male voice-over, which chides her for not getting rid of the ring 'round husband's collar!

When, occasionally, she moves out of the laundry room, I see her as a frenetic lunatic on game shows. Here she giggles, writhes, begs for guidance from all-knowing husband hiding in the audience. If she wins, she jumps up and down with amazement. If she loses the trip for two to Hawaii, she cries. And whether she wins or loses, the current crop of game shows demeans her as a thinking being. No one even asks her to pick a "category" or to name the twenty-sixth president of the United States. All she has to do is scream in sexual ecstasy when she picks an empty box which turns out to hold the lucky number. The "game" is as challenging as pinning the tail on the donkey with your eyes wide open. Yet an endless series of palpitating young things chirp and tear-up and coo, while a patronizing master-of-ceremonies smiles indulgently at their childlike guilelessness.

In between these images, there's the woman who talks about the coffee her husband likes to drink, what denture cream keeps her uppers in, and (believe it or not) the laxative a friend told her to buy. She can't remember the brand-name, though it's the one "doctors recommend" (and judging by the pained expression on her face, she's in real trouble). But she lives for others: she loves her family, takes Geritol to keep herself strong for them, wipes up their floors with Johnson's wax, almost dies when she drops her grease can on the kitchen tile, keeps toilet bowls tidy, and chats with little men in the bathroom tank.

In the soap operas, she portrays the Good Mother, the Bad Mistress, the Home-breaker, the Conniver, the Innocent and Impregnated Teenager. In the situation comedies, she plays Lucy, or Jeannie, or Samantha with interchangeable ease.

I see her rerun as the teacher, nurse, man's best friend, lover, siren in her roles from the movies of the Forties and Fifties, when her career went "fffffft" the day Spencer Tracy ogled her. And for the day's final image, I get to look at Zsa Zsa, or Todie Williams, or the Weight-Watcher lady on the talk shows. *Woman* is daily spelled out for us as a second-banana mind. And what is even more frightening is the fact that the average house watches this travesty every day of every week for an average six and a half hours a day. In the first four years and first two children of her marriage, the typical woman is bombarded by millions of such TV impressions. And whether she averts to it or not, she absorbs this image subliminally. Worse—the message is picked up, stored and handed on down to her children.

Today there are fourteen soap operas on the networks. Of these fourteen, only two are produced by women. Men have the scene to themselves. And women writers occur in about the same proportion. Doris Quinlan, producer of *One Life to Live,* thinks that things are beginning to change a little in this regard. But she emphasizes the "little." She thinks it's important to have women in at the producer level so that they can make the "brass" more aware of women's needs today. *One Life to Live,* for example, twice highlighted women's lib this season: a woman actually played the role of a brain surgeon instead of a nurse; a pregnant girl actually turned down the culprit who finally agreed to marry her. Such episodes, says Ms. Quinlan, represent a real step forward. Having watched the average soaps, I believe her. Change comes to "soaps" with the most deliberate speed.

Thus does TV position women. Pert, well clad serfs, mesnes, slaves —not bright ones either. And why in the world not? Television is almost totally a man's turf. Out of fifty producers of prime-time network shows, I know of only two women. In the very top-level, decision-making jobs, there may be one out of fifty. And at the executive level, in any of the top five positions in any of the three major networks, it's zero to fifteen in favor of the boys' clubs. TV programming endorses and reinforces *their* image of women. And we've seen what that is. Take a look at their planning for an average day in television from August 19, 1974:

Mama Time

Farmer's Daughter—Kay is jealous. An old friend of Glen's is visiting. (Rerun)

Not For Women Only—Barbara interviews Jessica Tandy, Hume Cronyn, and Henry Fonda re the prime time of life for men and women.

Jaye P. Morgan talks about being a vegetarian.

Dennis the Menace

A sampling of cheeses and clocks from Switzerland.

Hazel—Hazel confronts the company stockholders with one of their defective vacuums.

Password

I Love Lucy—Lucy copes with sticky assignment in a candy firm.

Gomer Pyle—Carter tries to glamorize his spinster sister.

Hollywood Squares

Love of Life

Young and Restless

Jackpot

Password

I Love Lucy—Lucy finds herself out in the cold when she waits for Chris.

Zoo Review

Search for Tomorrow

Galloping Gourmet stuffs artichokes.

As the World Turns

Newlywed Game

Doctors

Mama–Kids Dinner Time

Father Knows Best

One Life to Live

Mike Douglas with Groucho, Donald Sutherland, Elliot Gould.

Room 222—Swimming champ itching to taste more of life.

Munsters—Housewife Lily tries a modeling career.

I Dream of Jeannie—Jeannie makes Tony a prince.

I Love Lucy—Ricky neatens up budget and Lucy is cleaned out.

Avengers

Bewitched—Pregnant Samantha's food cravings get out of hand.
I Love Lucy—Lucy buys a sheep to cut lawn.

Macho Crotcho Time

Cronkite
Chancellor
Mission Impossible
Mod Squad
Dusty's Trail
Police Surgeon
Dick Van Dyke
Gunsmoke
Baseball World
Rookies
Pro Tennis
Merv Griffin
Here's Lucy—Goggle-eyed Lucy and star struck friends spoil movie-making in Desi's house.
Bonanza
Dick Van Dyke
Medical Center—A young woman is stricken with hysterical paralysis after she sees her mother with a lover.
Bill Jorgensen
Perry Mason
Johnny Carson

Please note that daytime TV offered the housewife one foray into the intellectual world: Barbara Walters' interview. Cowboys, detectives, doctors, lawyers, baseball, tennis, male anchormen for news, male entertainers for talk, and a male minister to say our "nighty-nights" with.

Mama in prime-time, however, gets another blast of Lucy (even though she's had her three times earlier) and *Medical Center* is kind enough to show her a hysterical female.

In the year 2000, today's eighteen-year-old will be forty-three—with twenty-five years of TV watching stored in the grey matter of her brain. And what about the rub off on little Merwin, who also sits and watches? Don't for a moment think he's not being indoctrinated (and Mervinette is getting her lessons, too). From their perch on the supermarket cart, eighteen-month-old babies can recognize name brand products. Daily innoculations of TV really take. By 2000, when Merwin is twenty-five, his convictions and his attitudes will most certainly show the effects of the TV guide of 1974.

Tomorrow's programming won't change appreciably. It may get more or less violent. It may develop other messages than those we see now. But with twenty-four hours of TV to grind out daily, you can be sure you are going to see reruns of the movies that are being made today. These are the movies which influence the TV Movies of the Week in the Eighties and Nineties. Just as four *I Love Lucys* pop up each day now to remind us of the darling of the Fifties and Sixties, "Straw Dogs" and "Clockwork Orange" may dominate the menu twenty-five years from now. I read that "The Godfather" was sold for millions for a one night TV stand. You can be sure that this will play often in the next twenty-five years. To what degree the movies will show up and programming change, only NBC, CBS, and ABC Presidents, Mr. Schlosser, Mr. Taylor, and Mr. Rule know.

Think about the future. Can you really visualize Barbara Walters at last having a national news program without a co-anchor man? And if you can, how many Barbaras will there be in 2000? Against how many Cronkites, Chancellors, Reasoners and Smiths.

Will there be an abundance of female writers on TV shows? Will fifty percent of the directors be female? Producers? Management on networks? It's going to take numbers like this to create this change. Where will they come from?

Film schools and various learning grounds for this kind of work do not spawn many females or encourage them, at least not as of this moment. Jackie Park of NYU Film School fame says the attendance of women in writing courses is practically nil. "The ambiance for women in film is not so hot, they don't feel welcome, and it doesn't attract them. There is a scattering of women in the television workshops, but there are no writers." She hungers for females to teach courses, but the few women who have the qualifications are busy . . . If there are no teachers to be role-models and no students to watch them, then it stands to reason that in the year 2000 there will be too few female TV writers, directors, and producers to make an appreciable difference in programming.

Networks now forced to hire women do it grudgingly. The old chant is sung throughout TV land. "Send me a qualified dame and I'll hire her." Many of the current occupants of network jobs are qualified only by being male.

Women who do make it through the hazing line invariably are chucked into their traditional auxiliary roles: editing, associate producing, personnel, assistant budget makers, costuming; at a lower echelon: secretaries, go-fors, girl Fridays, readers, timers, etc. Women are not selling time to big agencies, creating their own productions, writing for prime-time, producing, directing, or programming.

A female TV producer, one of the few who has prime-time credits, taught a course in writing a year ago. Three out of sixteen students were women. A screen writing class at Columbia showed two out of fourteen. Even if statistics double, it's still a big minority for 2000.

And in 2000, when you get home from the plutonium dump, dead tired, and snap on your computer wall TV, you're going to be treated to a dish of the most anti-female cinema reruns we've ever had. "The Sting," "California Split," "Straw Dogs," "The Getaway," "The Godfather," "Clockwork Orange," "The Conversation," "For Pete's Sake," "Butch Cassidy and the Sundance Kid." These films, the hits of the Seventies, have carefully carved out a whole new image for women. It's not only exasperating, it's frightening. It's as if the male world is implicitly rebuking women for the strides they've made toward becoming free souls. *What made us think we could get away with destroying the cultural image projected for us as mother, girl next door, dumb dora, sweetness and light, virgin, sacharine sally, self-sacrificer, movie queen, it girl, most girl, and cheerleader?* How dare we! During the "fierce" years of Friedan and Steinem and Millett and Firestone and Bird and Greer, we began to change. As if in direct reaction, the cinema began to punish us. In the movies we came across almost exclusively as super whores, ball-breakers, hustler bait, grostesques, hussies, tarts, tramps, lay-arounds, inert sex objects, icebergs, dippy dames, and Lolitas. Nice, huh?

I can just hear all of us trying to convince our grandchildren that we never were these terrible harridans the movies made us out to be. Will they believe it? We'll know in 2000.

Yet we ourselves stand in line to see "Chinatown," "The Sting," and "Son of the Godfather." We happily support the industry that hates us most. And we don't even strike back in a tidal wave of protest letters.

Molly Haskell, in her book *Reverence to Rape,* gives a rundown on the movies from the Twenties to the Seventies. She says, "The Yins and Yangs of heterosexual romance, the power differential between the 'stronger' and the 'weaker' sex are not just tricks of movie propaganda, they have been the articles of faith among writers through the ages, and among these are the most independent-minded women novelists and screenwriters."

Talk about recycling a bad product. When women produce female put downs, that's really bad news. That's really believing the message and putting it into the media. Again, in discussing what she calls the "big lie," Ms. Haskell says, "The big lie perpetrated on Western Society is the idea of women's inferiority, a lie so deeply ingrained in our social behavior that merely to recognize it is to risk unraveling the entire fabric of civilization."

Will Susan Sontag, Elaine May, Joan Didion, Lois Gould, Renee Taylor, Ann Roiphe, Marguerite Duras be able to unravel the strands?

And what about publishing and women's image in 2000? Well, let's be practical. Except in very special presentations, hardcover books will probably be gone forever. Perhaps paper will be so rare, so expensive, the publishers will have to find a new way to publish, or they will perish. If nothing else, editing will be tougher. Certainly, fewer books will come out. And what about female influence in publishing in 2000? Twenty-five years ago, we had a tiny but powerful rash of women who made news. Fleur Cowles published *Flair*. A magazine that folded, but is a collector's item today. Claire Booth Luce had a decisive hand in government, and publishing, and writing. Beatrice Gould ran the *Journal* for women with IQs over a hundred, and the female half of the *Digest* team did what she could to keep the caliber at least above cooking school. Today, I can think of only one woman publisher, Helen Meyer of Dell Publishing Co. At this rate of decline, we should be fresh out of females in publishing at the turn of the century.

What about women in the magazine world? There are only a handful today and, for the most part, only in women's interests magazines.

Good Housekeeping, Red Book, House Beautiful, Better Homes and Gardens, Town and Country, Oui, Fortune, Money, Playboy, Penthouse, Time, Newsweek, U.S. Business, Forbes, Business Week, Reader's Digest, Viva, New York, New Yorker, Esquire, People, TV Guide, Sunset, American Home, McCalls, and the Ladies' Home Journal are edited by men. They all have male publishers as well.

Only Cosmopolitan and Ms. are edited by women. Only Ms. has a woman publisher. Starting from left to right, Helen Gurley Brown takes a definite posture on the role of women in the Seventies. About the subject matter of Cosmo she says, "We have had major articles on careers, on nursing, and library work. But they don't have nearly as much clout as an article on 'Find Your Second Husband Before You Divorce Your First One.' " The damage in this observation is not so much that the Cosmo girl prefers a sex piece or a divorce piece to a career piece. What is sad about it is Helen Gurley Brown's narrow estimate of women's careers. Nursing and library work . . . Talk about the water dripping on the stone. And this from a woman who herself has done extremely well in the communications world. She doesn't even think about another woman editing a magazine for a living.

Lenore Hershey of Ladies' Home Journal sticks to the familiar patterns of the past. Today, with a kind of fine madness, the magazine concerns itself with sweet and sour shrimp, framing and hanging pictures, five beautiful faces, the phantom lover, Elizabeth Taylor's fifth marriage, and Dr. Nolan on faith healing. Oh yes, we mustn't forget our visit with Cornelia Wallace. I can almost predict the menu one, five, or twenty years from now: sweet and sour frogs legs, wall coverings, the beautiful face, Jackie Onassis says farewell to Ari, Dr. Nolan on hair cancer, and—oh yes, don't forget our visit with President Percy's wife.

As for Ms., this ideological foray into the angst of today's woman at least cuts a track for women to walk in search of personal freedom and wholeness.

It's the one female freedom book. Editor: female. Publisher: female.

At a recent "Think Tank" meeting run by Betty Friedan on the future of women in the economic climate of today's world, I kept hearing, "But look where we are. Look where we've come." Okay, I thought, I must be missing something. I don't see it in the ad business at all. So I dug out a directory called *Foremost Women in Communications*. Published in 1960, it's an alphabetical listing of the big time jobs in our field. Yet I found, as my finger did the shopping, that on newspapers, women had the following titles: Women's Editor, Society Editor, Home Equipment Editor, Better Household Ideas Editor, Food and Home Editor. The volume shows that in advertising, women hang out in account work, media buying, copy, promotion, production and they don't show up as art directors, copy supervisors, presidents, treasurers. *In short, women are not decision makers.* They are not positioned where the action is. They are *not* powerful in the communication arts, where their image is created and spewed out to the world. And I sigh for what it will be like in 2000 unless women can get ownership, unless they can find funds to subsidize their ideas, their designs, sell stock in themselves, get their words heard by way of theater, tell their stories to mass media and share in running the mass media. They must publish. They must bring out their own papers, run their own stores, sell their own commercials, produce their own commercials. Otherwise, men will outbeam any image women project. Like the networks, they have the power to simply beep us out of business.

By and large, society has an image of the female as powerless and it insists on keeping it this way. The more competitive we become, the sharper our threat to male superiority. They won't take this lying down.

The "fierce" image of women on the march, so exciting in the Sixties, has quieted down. The guerilla warfare that had to be waged in lobbying, in fighting, in marching for bills on equal rights and prods for legislation for equal pay has paid off to *some* degree. But it seems to many women they've won. Today's young feminists are not so noisy, not so outraged, not so hell-bent on being heard. So they are heard less. The moan, "Oh, not that old saw again," from a male employer does have its effect. To woman's deeply implanted need for love, this is the fastest way to say, "Baby, you ain't going to get no love till you quit harping." When this happens, some women draw back from the fight, ashamed that they are boring men.

The kids I see fresh out of college who come by my door looking for jobs, help, counseling, sympathy are "fragile" not "fierce." They haven't copped out, they just think the war is over. They are doves with clipped wings who think that peace has been achieved. Freud long ago pointed out the irreconciliable antagonism between human drive and the demands of civilization. So the "fierce" woman must be tamed. In today's job market, unemployed Ph.D's find it tough to get an office "temp" job. Where can they set their sights? You got it. A husband. And thus the backslide begins.

But jobs may well get scarcer and scarcer in the next twenty-five years. If this is so, will women be the first to bite the dust? As Friedan suggests, women might be the first victims of the economic disaster. Will "a man-with-a-family" yukity-yukity-talk destroy female careers right and left once again as it did after the Second World War? Will all the things the National Organization for Women fought so hard for fall by the wayside?

What about women in newspapers and in newspaper advertising? What about women publishers of newspapers? I can think of two—Kathryn Graham of the Washington Post—who inherited the job from her husband and then turned into one of America's most exciting publishers, and Dorothy Schiff, Editor-in-Chief and Publisher of the New York Post. No women own or run any TV-affiliates either; most of them are controlled by the local newspapers.

How are women faring in retail stores? Places where they should be standouts. Well, they're not advertising or sales promotion directors. They're not presidents. Out of five thousand top retailers in the country, only two females are presidents. One owns the shop, the other has it on merit.

Even though store advertising is directed almost exclusively to women, men tell them the story.

Magazine advertising is bad enough, TV commercials are idiotic, but store advertising is positively spooky. And I hate to say it, but women write a lot of it.

Here are some choice examples from the Sunday *New York Times*. From Bendel's.

> sonia rykiel's got the message/
> big muffled sweaters/ the long swirling
> skirts/ the smoke hushed colors/ and
> the scarves that tie and toss and trail.
> but come see how wonderful all that
> fullness is on you/ right now/

From Saks Fifth Avenue: "beautiful feet should be seen and not heard."
From Bonwit Teller: "the long dress will get you applause at night. Flattering is flowering. Come meet Bob the designer."
From Bergdorf Goodman: "Midnight to moonglow. The hush that falls o'er a room as you enter."
From Bonwit Teller: "When he calls at six, asks about dinner at seven wear this elegant . . ."
From "slink it up" to "knowing tweeds" to "fluid and feminine" to

"skirts marrying blouses," on and on it goes. Only B. Altman writes of women who might be bank presidents, college professors, contenders for public office. . . . I know. I write the ads.

But let an ad be directed toward a man . . . and it is filled with information. Abercrombie and Fitch, in introducing foul weather gear the same day, would no more think of saying . . . "the hush falls o'er the deck when you come aboard . . ." than they would fight for gun prohibition. Their ad is chock full of information. A Macy ad on calculators is directed not to women who may do the checking account monthly, but to a man. It's got a whole different bead. And to further disappoint the optimist: most store copy writers are female.

Why do store managements continually sell the female one way and the male another? Will it change this idiocy of approach as we near 2000? It may. Print may go because of paper shortages. It will certainly take a different form. Be curtailed in its approach. But what will stores do then to attract and entice their fashionable customers? How will they ever tempt her to "slink in?"

I wish that women coming out of high school and college today (the fifty crowd in 2000) were "tigers." They're not. They are not struggling for equality in agencies, or in broadcasting, or in print.

Is it because there are no super bonuses for successful women? A man who succeeds gets a more intelligent, more interesting wife. Not so the other way around. A man who succeeds and is aggressive is considered sharp, a go-getter, someone to watch. A woman who is called aggressive is someone to watch . . . but *carefully*. True, in law and medicine and academia, the mating of matching degrees is not uncommon and the spinster school teacher of yesterday seems to be fading away. Is it because teaching was, and still is, acceptable to society as a proper woman's career? But what about the image of the single woman in business—with a lonely life in a two bedroom apartment in Upper East Side New York; where a fern that survived is an event, and where Maxwell's Plum is the action spot, while Southampton beaches are where you pick up your law for Saturday night?

That's not exactly a carrot to dangle in front of the successful woman's nose.

Psychologically, a woman hears nothing but a man's voice telling her what to do. Her father, her husband, her principal, professor, boss. Listen to one hundred commercials (as I did recently). In ninety-nine of them, you'll hear a male voice-over giving the "go-get-it" command. This is true for soap, soup, cosmetics, fashion, chicken—you name it. Is it that women don't listen to women? Women's schools are headed by men. The boards of directors of feminine products are men. The people who run the country and set the standards for women's needs are men. And most women's doctors (body and soul) are, too. So the "most girl" of the forties and the "it girl" of the Thirties become the "fall girl" of the Seventies for an incredible myth that men *are* hands down superior to women.

If I sound discouraging, it's because I am a total realist. I am in a business that a lot of the time is pure fantasy and I've learned to recognize fantasy—and quick. Much of the women's movement for most American women is a kind of fantasy. Much needed and much hoped for. We've come "a short way," which a male copywriter for Virginia Slims subconsciously wants us to think is a "long way." We haven't come a long way at all and we're going to go snail-slow from now on unless women stop working exclusively for men, and start working for themselves. Docile and intelligent editors must become publishers. Copy writers must become agency owners, TV producers for networks must become TV producers for themselves. Women scenario writers must begin to raise the money for their own productions. Women professors must aim to be presidents of the women's colleges. Secretaries in museums should look toward curator jobs—and settle for nothing else. Sketchers and designers in big Seventh Avenue manufacturing setups have to take a loft on their own. It's going to take time. We must expect to have as many setbacks as Blacks have had. Every time the legislature meets, we have got to be there insisting on our rights, not sitting on our silky soft hands, which reminds me, instead of being the sharp mind doing PR for a male candidate, how about running for the office yourself?

Women can't have an image in 1975, or in the year 2000, that's strong, free and vital unless they see themselves this way.

Without a healthy self-respect and a sound plan for achievement in society, financially and mentally, we'll be right back where women were in 1910, when the vote was denied to idiots, lunatics, criminals, and women. That's how the world at large saw us then and that's how they'll see us in the future unless we start functioning on a very different and supportive female platform.

3 NO MORE SAPPHIRES OR BLACK PEARLS: SELF-DEFINITION IS WHERE IT STARTS

*by Inez Turner,
Dorothy Robinson,
Deborah Singletary
and Margo Jefferson*

IF WHITE WOMEN HAVE HAD difficulty in breaking free of the present and thinking about their future, the problem has been doubly difficult for Black women. Only in the Seventies have young black women, exploring new ideas together, begun to see options for individual, independent paths and fulfillment for themselves as women. Using the technique of consciousness raising—getting together in small groups to discuss common problems openly and to gain better self understanding—the four authors of this chapter have tried to express what they hope to see in a world they will very likely live to see. It is like a book within a book: four individual ways of thinking about women's future. But, as Margo Jefferson who brought the group together has written in a covering note: "Black women are as diverse in philosophies and tactics as any independent-thinking people are and must be. To speak for all Black women would be pretentious. What follows are the thoughts (and hopes) of four of us."

Black Women—a Futuristic Definition

by Inez Turner

We sat around the room in an assortment of chairs brought in from various parts of the apartment, some of us sat cross-legged on the floor. There were ten of us saying things which in many cases we had never said to anyone before; sharing thoughts with relative strangers—things we had sometimes fought to keep from our own consciousness. We were consciousness-raising; talking about ourselves, our lives, our inner and outer conflicts. We were ten Black women, brought together by an organization of Black feminists, who were dismayed by the past and determined about the future. Our very presence in that room, talking and sharing the way we were, signaled a dawning—a dawning that would be a rude awakening for many who did not desire to see Black woman get herself together. Often we talked about the past, about the days when we did not know ourselves and did not know our sisters, but we were ever mindful of the future and determined to set ourselves right for it.

We wanted first to understand who we were. Were we grinning mammies with ample bosoms to cradle black children, white children and men children? Were we bitter sharp-tongued Sapphires who did not understand that our men should be jobless, but carefree, spineless, but king? Were we bewitching bitches who peddled sex on street corners because we were hot, not hungry?

We could hardly pick up one of the very few books which dealt with Black women without seeing at least one of these stereotypes in and between the neatly printed lines. We could seldom turn on the television set and see a Black woman whom we could identify as mother, sister, co-worker or neighbor—there was no one any of us had ever seen in the flesh. The only familiarity we had with Black women on the TV screen was that we had seen the same tired stereotypes depicted on larger screens in movie-houses and walking across the stage in theaters. It was our task to define ourselves and have our definitions free of White determinants or Black male determinants. Our definition had to encompass what our unique life experiences as Black women have been and what we saw as our present and future priorities as Black women.

One popular myth that we were anxious to dispel was that Black women were matriarchs. Sociologists determined that crime, unemployment and other ills, that were disproportionately high in Black communities, were due to a breakdown in family structure. A larger portion of Black families than white families were headed by females, so Black women stand accused of emasculating Black men! Absurd. Racism is and has been the number one problem of *all* Blacks. Many of the Black women who do head fatherless families have been forced onto welfare rolls or to support their children as domestics, clericals and hospital workers—the lowest paying jobs in the country. If Black men are deserting their families, resorting to crime and yielding to drugs, it is because racism has beat them down—not Black women. Black women and Black men were brought to this country as slaves on the same ships. The women have been brutalized, beaten and lynched too. And, in addition, when it became too dark in the fields to pick the crops, we toiled long hours in master's kitchen and cooked in some dusty corner of our own living quarters. We have suffered the indignities of indiscriminate breeding and indiscriminate rape. *No* doors have been open to Black women that have been closed to Black men. When racism doesn't get us, sexism does.

No, we are not mammies or Sapphires, or prostitutes or, as Black men have lately defined us, queens. That assumes Black men to be kings and that leaves us in the same old place, doesn't it? We reject the old stereotypes and the new. We are educated and uneducated. We are witty and dull. We are outgoing and shy, rich and poor, industrious and lazy. We are all the things humankind has ever been; and we are alive and aware and ready; ready to write our own books and command our own ships. We are ready to grow without the restraints of racism and sexism. We are ready to fight, so that the year 2000 can bring changes, so that our daughters and granddaughters will be set free from our continuing struggle.

Black Women ... Expectations and Demands

by Dorothy Robinson

The year 2000 is not so far off that it allows for distant fantasies of the better life for black women. We will still be doubly oppressed (by virtue of being Black and female). The degree of that oppression is perhaps subject to debate but neither racism nor sexism will disappear in a scant twenty-five years.

Hopefully, the major difference for black women then as opposed to now will be the dissipation of the illusions—not necessarily the dreams, but certainly the illusions—of the nuclear family, substantial wealth and a comfortable, secure, influential position within the mainstream (read: white) of contemporary society. While these specified illusions will be a reality for some Black women, they will be illusive to many others who will be forced to seek and adopt viable alternatives.

The demands and expectations of Black women involve giving to other people. We are expected to be wife, mother, teacher, servant, self-denying, obedient, ready at the drop of a hat, and prepared to adeptly cope with all situations. These demands are looked upon as woman's duties and have not even been subject to question or objection, at least not verbally for the most part. But our actions tell us something else . . .

Black women pay a heavy price for the demands made upon us. Statistics show that proportionally the highest incidence of suicide occurs among Black women. More than white men, white women and black men, we are killing ourselves out of frustration, anger and the inability to find solutions to our problems. It is unrealistic to expect this situation to change without Black women redefining who and what we are, and consciously determining what will be acceptable to us as obligations. More and more black women will begin to develop an inward orientation—that is to relate demands and expectations to our lives with all else coming after, including children and men. Our success at survival lies in the qualitative growth of ourselves.

Sexual Politix: The Women's movement and feminism threaten Black men (indeed all men). As Black women step out of the restraints of sex-stereotyped roles, relationships become more competitive both inside and outside the home. By 2000 much of the reconciliation will have occurred around the issue of roles. It will be increasingly difficult to regard or treat a woman as a plaything and get away with it. The essence of our being will not be defined in terms of sex, sexuality or femininity. We will value ourselves, and be valued, for our competence and ability to develop techniques which serve to educate and protect us. Stepping out of pres-ent day so-called feminine roles will not be a depreciation of a black woman's value but rather the reapplication of energies to productive modes of expression.

The notion of sacrifice as applied to family responsibility has been a damaging guilt factor laid upon Black women. We were taught to place our needs last in deference to man and child. Our joy was to be found in their success, in their achievement—never our own. The male outlet was always sports, or the "boys" or hangin' out among friends, reinforcing wounded self-images. Women had no such outlet. Friendships among women were never seriously encouraged. Women's relationships with each other were somehow superficial and suspect. Trust and respect among women for each other was rare. The rude awakening was to find no guarantees in sacrifice, that the man might not always love you and that your children may not even understand or appreciate your efforts. The result is a totally empty woman with nothing left of herself and for herself.

Children: At long last motherhood is being reexamined. Black women realize that having a child is a matter of choice, not obligation, and that not having a child is no indication of failure as a woman. The factors influencing this decision are: whether or not the mother is a single parent; the amount of mother's time available for the child; financial resources; child care resources; feelings toward children—like, dislike, ambivalence.

Children need not, indeed should not, be the sole responsibility of the mother. In situations where both parents are living together, the responsibility will automatically be shared. But particularly for the single parent (male or female) and working parents, public or private day care is mandatory. A community effort is needed to share child-rearing responsibilities including day care, education, recreation, transportation, etc.

Of course by 2000 day care will be government financed to a large degree and private companies, especially those housed in huge skyscrapers, will have been pressured by women to provide a day-care facility in the building so that logistically it is convenient, but also so that the parent may at any point in the day have access to her or his child. Quality day care will allow women to maintain productive *and enjoyable* lives, provide time for involvement in community activities and allow for personal growth through recreation or education. The important factor is that the responsibility of motherhood will have become less of a restrictive burden. Mother and child will enjoy each other as well as new, mutual freedoms.

What it all means: Acting as agents for our own self-interests in the year 2000, the expectations and demands of Black women will be our own. Our choices will be made on the basis of selected priorities. Obligations will be accepted on the basis of capability, need and a clear understanding of responsibility—responsibility for the sake of progress or accomplishment, not blind externally imposed regulation.

Present day insecurities will evolve into new practices of self-expression and leadership. Perhaps even new dreams will be fashioned, but from firm intent, with solid access to fulfillment.

Black Women—Building a New Self-image

by Deborah Singletary

All of the things that *some* Black women are have been exaggerated so that every line, hair and pore looms before us in monstrosity. Like a nightmare, those images have attacked all of us and we have run horrified. We became afraid to put our hands on our hips and say, "uh huh, honey, let *me* tell *you,*" because we were afraid of being Sapphires and we could not see the beauty in Aunt Jemima because familiarity breeds contempt. In its distortion our strength has seemed ugly and undesirable, and we apologize for taking care of the business that was dumped in our laps—the business that nobody else wanted. In normal perspective, all Black women can appreciate Sapphire and welcome her in our future self-definition. But there is more than Sapphire in our history, and in perspective all those women will enhance what we will become.

But what will we become? There is much that distracts and deters our growth. What is supposed to represent great strides for the Black race has often been detrimental to Black women. The increase of Black films has served as a vehicle for perpetuating old, and creating new, stereotypes of Black women; the emerging Black female disc jockeys are taught they must be sexy to be effective while sex appeal is offered to Black male disc jockeys as an option; and although there has been an increase in the number of Black female singers, the messages in the songs they sing encourage us to grasp at illusive male love while representing relationships among females as unrewarding, invalid or non-existent. The definitions of us by white sociologists and white psychologists has fed the media tainted interpretations.

As what we will become is dependent on speaking honestly and openly with each other about who we are and how we feel about ourselves, clearly we must build on the concept of consciousness raising. However, our purpose will be defeated if we run from CR back to the kitchen to prepare the meal before *he* comes home. Finding real acceptance among ourselves, we will no longer feel the need to prove ourselves by being good for men only. This means we will no longer be the buffer between oppressive whites and the Black men, who forget that racism is stifling to Black people and not just Black males. We will begin to recognize ourselves as a resource in the building of a Black nation not limiting our contribution to producing male children for leaders. We will reject being patronized as Black queens. We want the respect accorded kings.

Once the Black woman has redefined herself so that she is no longer torn between contradicting demands that she be strong, independent and everyone's mother, and on the other hand sweet, demure and retiring, she will want to be in the forefront of activity in her Black community. However, the present white and male powers are so ambivalent to Black female leadership, that to be effective she will have to waste her energies writing letters, demonstrating, explaining, protecting, arguing and pleading. She will be accused, ignored, ridiculed and hated. She will retaliate, doubt, retreat, and bounce back. And such struggles will take her away from herself. The time she might invest in improving her community will be spent proving herself, and she will suffer. And I don't foresee much change in this situation over the next twenty-five years.

It will not be enough to be more assertive and competitive with male powers, thereby compelling recognition of ourselves and our rights. The historic tradition of "get thee behind your man" is stronger in its capacity to destroy than to create. Convincing "them" that Black women will not be confined to the roles defined for us by society would take precedence over fighting for the issues important to us as members of the total Black community. Away from conflicting demands by white structures and Black men we will decide what is important to us.

Black women will consciously seek each other out in situations conducive to the growth and development of a community in our own image. The prospects are exciting. Our plans will start small. Impatient for the school system to become sensitive to the need for non-sexist, non-racist education we will develop programs such as tutorial sessions, which teach children to be conscious of the subtleties of sexist and racist oppression, while at the same time sharpening their academic skills. Such a plan might begin in someone's apartment but could conceivably result in a school run and taught by Black feminists. We can coordinate among ourselves sixteen-hour day-care services which will reflect our commitment to our Black sisters. By rotating such responsibility, no woman will be deprived of attending a consciousness raising session or other feminist meeting, of working, or of any other project that would require some time away from the responsibility of children. We will write books—novels and textbooks, poetry, short stories—creating a library of and for Black women. We will be our own publishers even if it means typing our creations on mimeograph and circulating them among ourselves. We will live, work and play in the context of our Black womanhood.

What we think, feel or wear will not be influenced by male identification. Our daughters will be raised to live, not simply to get married. Relationships with men or the desire to relate to men will not cease, however our expectations will be that these relations are only a part of our lives. Therefore, the duplicity that dating breeds will exist less and less because we will no longer feel as though we are products on display—less and less will we use sales strategy to "prospective buyers." This will provide greater capacity to develop ourselves. With the historical precedence of dating no longer valid, the traditional marriage will become less and less inevitable.

As individuals, our priorities will be our selves; and as other women are a reflection of our selves, our major commitment will be to Black women. We will not as automatically choose to spend "special occasions" with men. By the year 2000, although we will not have finished the task of reorganizing our lives, we will have gained enough momentum so that our direction and focus will be clear. No longer on the defensive, Black women will be able to work toward the control that the word matriarch implies in terms of our families when there is no male support, when we are running our own businesses and free from financial and emotional dependence on man or men. When "they" point an accusing finger at us and spew out, "Matriarch!" as an insult, we will thank them for the compliment.

Make Miracles From Leftovers: Black Women in the Arts

by Margo Jefferson

Black women have always had to do with art what they have had to do with food: make miracles from leftovers. Take music, where we have been major innovators. Artists like Ma Rainey, Bessie Smith and Ethel Waters extended the blues tradition, making the first transitions to jazz singing, and opening the way for blues recordings. Adelaide Hall, Billie Holiday, Sarah Vaughan and others created an entirely new style of instrumental singing and improvisation, leaving their marks so deeply on jazz that the best instrumentalists are still trying to equal the subtleties of the human voice. Then look at the other side. Almost no women have been instrumentalists like Charlie Parker or composers like Duke Ellington; the words and music they work with are usually men's and very often banal; much of their history is a struggle against the limits of song. Imagine the art of a Billie Holiday unfettered by a ridiculous tune like "What A Little Moonlight Can Do"; think of Sarah Vaughan freely improvising rather than stretching out the syllables of "The evening breeze/Caressed the trees/Tenderly." Consider what the irony and humor of a Carmen McRae, the political intelligence of a Nina Simone could do if they were not so often rescuing and reinterpreting unmemorable pop material.

Now, extend this situation to the other performing arts: to acting where, on stage and screen, the talents of Black women are usually routed into symbols of kitchen sass and strength, or back porch sexuality; where Cicely Tyson is one of the first actresses to be given roles that she can fulfill rather than sabotage or circumvent; where black women playwrights and directors—those given work, that is—can be counted on the fingers of one hand. Take dance. Black women were not permitted in ballet until the Dance Theatre of Harlem emerged—their bodies were considered too full and round, their temperaments insufficiently fey and austere. In modern dance a small number have performed beautifully, but almost none have choreographed. Significantly, the only two Black women to establish their own companies for any period of time are Katharine Dunham and Pearl Primus, and they acted as dance anthropologists, returning to African and Caribbean forms which no one else, in the 1940s and 1950s, cared about.

To move beyond the performing arts to writing, music composition, painting and sculpture—where culture's deepest and most lasting myths and images are created—is to come smack up against a heavily guarded and fenced territory governed by white men. Economic and cultural prejudice have combined to keep Black women excluded or ignored —oddly enough, even by black men and white women in their growing struggles for recognition. How many people know of writers like Nella Larsen, Zora Neale Hurston and Margaret Walker; of painter Margaret Burroughs and sculptor Elizabeth Catlett? Classical music composer Julia Perry is nearly unknown and unrecorded; jazz arranger and composer Mary Lou Williams retired to the church in the late 1950s and only recently reemerged. The many blues songs of Sippi Wallace, Victoria Spivey, Lovie Austin and Alberta Hunter have gone unsung and unacknowledged, while blues men everywhere are given credit for creating and sustaining the form. What will the next quarter-century bring?

Leftovers can only be used so often; new foods must be acquired, and as many women know, if you want good vegetables, you'd better grow them yourself. Black women are starting to change the forms and the demands of the arts, and thus change the grounds for judgment. And more and more, we will begin to work with and for each other—Black women directors seeking scripts from Black women writers; Black women composers seeking out and helping train Black women conductors and performers; Black women artists banding together to put on their own exhibitions. Novelists and poets like Paule Marshall, Toni Morrison, Alice Walker, June Jordan and Audre Lorde are very different, but they share a determination to bring a new subject—the lives of Black women—and new sensibilities to light. They are not bothering to prove that they can write in the style of *Ulysses* or *The Waste Land*—the old "I'm as good as you" tactic, doomed forever to failure—they are exploring their own vision, that of doubly oppressed, hence doubly perceptive people, and adopting whatever forms are necessary to express that. They are aware of their folk tradition—storytelling, crafts, blues and gospel singing. And they are involved in one of Western art's thorniest problems, that is the fusion of aesthetics with politics and morality. Why have so many major American artists been reactionary like T.S. Eliot, or fascist like Ezra Pound? Why do so many artists see themselves as guardians of a halcyon past rather than creators of a challenging future? Why are they so disdainful of history? Why do they make such rigid distinctions between "high" art and "folk" art, clinging to the former, condescending to the latter? These attitudes have worked against blacks and women—none of whom can afford the luxurious ignorance involved in avoiding history, all of whom have been wounded by the past; who, having come out of folk art and travelled through high art, can envision the two as allies, not enemies.

Black women will be in the vanguard of a growing movement over the next quarter-century to fuse forms, and assimilate and use those contradictions. Take music again. There will be more participation; it will not be unusual to see black women playing in jazz ensembles and symphony orchestras. Our predominance as jazz singers and as pop singers will be sustained; opera now boasts so many gifted black women that there will be an excess in twenty-five years. But more exciting, these diverse groups may start to come together. What they all share is a desire for new material: women like Leontyne Price and Shirley Verrett are caught in a traditional opera repertoire; women like Aretha Franklin and Mavis Staples are caught in an uninventive pop repertoire. Now, consider the unknown black women who are studying in conservatories and jazz schools; listening to Bach and Count Basie; Marian Anderson and Odetta and Martha Reeves. Why couldn't they write a piece of music that defied classification as opera, or musical comedy or jazz— something that could take in the styles and rhythms and voices of a Grace Bumbry and a Betty Carter? (There are intimations of this already: in the recent work of Mary Lou Williams, which demonstrates a love for bebop and oratorio, and in the music of the little-known Jeanne Lee, officially known as a jazz singer, but whose voice can be heard performing jazz, Latin, African and Oriental styles.) If it seems difficult to imagine, and synthesis that isn't dilettantism often seems so, think again of the Dance Theatre of Harlem: who, twenty-five years ago, could have imagined a kind of ballet that linked European classicism with American jazz movements?

Besides, so much of this is using resources already present or being developed. If a black woman really sat down to write something perfectly suited to the unique style of an Aretha Franklin, she would have to create something new; Franklin herself is a new synthesis of traditions and styles. If Toni Morrison's *Sula* or Alice Walker's *The Third Life of Grange Copeland* were made into a film with the scriptwriter and director both being black women, a new sort of truth would emerge on the screen.

Predictions are at least as much hope as analysis. The year 2000 is not as far off as we might wish, given the time it takes to make deep and lasting changes. Appropriately, two lines of the poet Gwendolyn Brooks capture the mixture of stoicism and excitement with which we observe the future.

> And I ride ride I ride on to the end— . . .
> To fail, to flourish, to wither or to win.
> We lurch, distribute, we extend, begin.

4 CHILD REARING: 2000 A. D.

By Gloria Steinem

THE YEAR 2000. It has a hopeful, science-fiction ring, so perhaps we can predict that by then there will be an understanding of how caste functions in our child-rearing operations, that there will be a concerted effort to eliminate all the giant and subtle ways in which we determine human futures according to the isolated physical differences of race or sex.

That statement may sound simple or unnatural to many of us reading it now. Simple—to those of us who accept the fact that individual differences far outstrip the group differences based on race or sex. Unnatural—to those of us who assume that physical differences pervade and shape all human capabilities. But it seems to me that the problem of caste is the most profound and revolutionary of the crises we must face. Only by attacking the patriarchal and racist base of social systems of the past—tribal or industrial, capitalist or socialist—can we begin to undo the tension and violence and human waste that this small globe can no longer afford, and that the powerless, castemarked majority of this world will no longer tolerate.

By the year 2000 we will, I hope, raise our children to believe in human potential, not God. Hopefully, the raising of children will become both an art and a science: a chosen and a loving way of life in both cases. Whether children are born into extended families or nuclear ones, into communal groups or to single parents, they will be wanted—a major difference from a past in which, whatever the sugar coating, we have been made to feel odd or unnatural if we did not choose to be biological parents. Children will be raised by and with men as much as woman; with old people, as well as with biological or chosen parents; and with other children. For those children of single parents or nuclear families, the community must provide centers where their peers and a variety of adults complete the human spectrum. For those children born into communal groups or extended families, the community must provide space to be alone in and individual, one-to-one teaching. The point is to enlarge personal choice, to produce for each child the fullest possible range of human experience without negating or limiting the choices already made by the adults closest to her or to him.

It used to be said that this country was a child-centered one. Nothing could be further from the truth. Children have been our lowest priority, both in economic and emotional spending. They also have been looked upon as a caste, although a temporary one. And that caste has been exploited as labor by relatives as well as by business people. It has been used as a captive audience or a way of seeking social status. It has finally been reduced to the status of object—a possession of that caste known as adults.

By the year 2000 there should be no one way of raising children; there should be many ways—all of them recognizing that children have legal and social rights that may be quite separate and different from the rights or desires of the adults closest to them. At last we should be nurturing more individual talents than we suppress.

5 THE FREE MARRIED WOMAN

by Maggie Tripp

THERE IS HOPE FOR MARRIAGE.

A short twenty-five years ago, such a statement would have seemed obvious. Today the problems inherent in conventional marriage are discussed at dinners and in magazines, documented in statistical reports and flashed across the television screen; and they are not significant merely in the abstract; they're happening to *your* friends, or to *your* parents, or to *your* children, or perhaps to *you.*

A number of solutions are being suggested. Group marriage. "Term marriage. Ménage à trois. Permanent singleness.

Amidst all the uproar, almost no one has noticed that one party to the marriage contract is changing many provisions of the agreement. With the reawakening of women's consciousness about themselves as individual human beings rather than as vestigial appendages of males, millions of American women will, during the next twenty-five years, be creating an entirely new kind of marriage.

The marriage ritual will remain. But the relationships within marriage will be sharply altered. The new marriage may look similar to the old marriage from the outside; but new attitudes and a mature sense of self on the part of the female partner will create a very different kind of give-and-take between married men and women.

It is this change in the woman, the understanding that she can live *with* a man and not just *through* a man—and man's inevitable recognition that such a woman makes a more desirable wife—that will be the dominant pattern of marriage in the year 2000.

In your generation or your mother's (depending on your age), belonging to a man and raising a family was the beginning and the end for a woman. She was programmed for this—or for nothing. The American ideal was to catch a man before you were too old, say twenty-two, and to take a deep breath, disappear into a suburban ranch house and not come up for air until your children ("a boy for you, a girl for me") were safely married.

Growing up female started when they covered you with a pink blanket instead of a blue one. It continued when they gave your brother a chemistry set and a doctor's kit while you got one more doll and a nurse's uniform. And when you cried, they went, "aaah, baby!" while they told your brother that crying was unnatural and unmanly. By the time you got to high school, you began to notice that boys were turned off by girls who got high marks. There developed sort of a negative correlation between intelligence and sexuality. Or, as I once heard a teen-age football star put it, "Who wants to date a girl who knows all your signals?" At college the problem intensified. These were the years in which most young women found their men. And when pushed to the choice, most young women preferred a ring on their finger to a Phi Beta Kappa key on their keyring. Matina Horner, now dean of Radcliffe, studied the achievement motivation of college men and women and found that bright women were in a double bind: in competing with men academically, the women worried not only about failure but about success. Failure was feared, but success was feared equally because it might make them appear too aggressive to be "feminine."

In sum, then, you grew up with a whole bagful of tattered shibboleths: for instance, "men are active, overt, interested in tangible things and able to conceptualize ideas," or "women are passive, feeling rather than thinking, keyed to human value but not to accomplishment."

The goal of the "real" world was marriage. And indeed women married for a variety of reasons which seemed real enough to them at the time. Most felt that they married for love—for who would want a loveless marriage? Some married to escape their parents or to avoid becoming an "old maid." Some saw marriage as a public declaration of their success for the benefit of their families or friends. Others saw their goal as a home of their own and children. Still others sought to avoid loneliness, to be protected and to find emotional support. And some few even married to avoid the burden placed on the single taxpayer.

If personal development stood in the way, if self-fulfillment was a liability, only the exceptional woman hesitated to make a quick choice. What kind of person she might be in the future and what might satisfy her needs as time went by hardly figured in the equation.

Strangely enough, while women were often the casualties of this cultural conditioning, men too may well have been its victims. As Philip Roth has written with great insight in *My Life as a Man:*

> For those young men who reached their maturity in the fifties . . . there was considerable moral prestige in taking a wife, and hardly because a wife was going to be one's maid-servant or "sexual object." Decency and Maturity, a young man's "seriousness," were at issue precisely because it was thought to be the other way around: in that the great world was so obviously a man's, it was only *within* marriage that a woman could hope to find equality and dignity. Indeed, we were led to believe by the defenders of womankind of our era that we were exploiting and degrading the women we *didn't* marry rather than the ones we did. Unattached and on her own, a woman was supposedly not even able to go to the movies or out to a restaurant by herself, let alone perform an appendectomy or drive a truck. It was up to us then to give them the value and purpose that society at large withheld—by marrying them.
>
> An awful lot of worrying was done in the fifties about whether people were able to Love or not—I venture to say, much of it by young women in behalf of young men who didn't particularly want them to wash their socks and cook their meals and bear their children, and tend them for the rest of their natural days. "But aren't you capable of Loving anyone? Can't you think of anyone but yourself?" when translated from desperate fifties-feminese into plain English, generally meant "I want to get married and I want you to get married too."

Now, suddenly, in 1975, the values and ideals of marriage have changed for men and women alike.

Few young men of today have the feelings Philip Roth has described. Young women, both within the Women's Movement and without, are demanding new arrangements between men and women. What has happened to change so radically the traditional roles and expectations?

To think clearly about the crisis in conventional marriage and to visualize a workable marriage for the year 2000, it is helpful to look back at an era when monogamous marriage appeared to work well.

A hundred years ago, woman's role in the marriage was very functional. In addition to bearing the children, she performed many specific jobs that were essential to survival. If the husband planted the corn and wheat, she made the meal and baked the bread. If the husband was ill, she was perfectly able to run the store. She often made the family's clothes, taught the children their lessons and, when need be, even took up a gun to defend the home. Women's skills and men's were complementary. A marriage was held together by mutual needs and respect—indeed by an essential interdependence.

As woman's contribution to survival diminished, the emphasis switched to her beauty and sensuality. If she could be replaced by a laundress for his shirts, a cook or a restaurant for his food or cheap labor for his store, her one uncopyable virtue was her individual femininity. If she was denied the opportunity to move into the world outside the home to test her skills, she could only hope that the mystical chemistry which brought them together would hold him to her all her life.

Against this background then, consider the conjunction of forces which have radically altered the male/female relationship.

First, and hardly the least important, is the availability of sexual intercourse without the dual risks of pregnancy and social scorn. For the man it means that marriage is no longer essential to satisfy his sex drives; for the woman it means that virginity is no longer either a prerequisite or a lure for marriage. So people need a better reason to get married than just to share the same bed.

The second change came with the removal of the social pressure to "populate the earth." With the earth already overpopulated, the addition of another infant requires due deliberation. As a result, the pressure for early marriage has greatly lessened; some unmarried young men and women are raising children as "single parents;" some young people marry with the express understanding that they do not want to have children at all; and some men and women live together, feeling no compulsion to marry at all.

A third swift change is the opening up of opportunities outside of marriage for women who want a full and fulfilling life. Slowly, but inevitably, the male-controlled outside-the-home world is yielding to the entry of women. The options are there for the woman who does not wish to answer the question "Who am I?" by simply changing her name. At a time when a motivated woman can become a computer programmer, a lawyer, a telephone repairer, a pilot, a government official, a coal miner or a superintendent of schools, marriage becomes only one of many roads to follow. A woman no longer needs to grab the first man who comes along. A woman no longer needs to give up the psychological satisfaction of self-reliance in return for the promise of bread and security.

If the opportunity for varied sexual experience, the diminished urge to bear children and the expanding alternatives for self-development and life-style were not enough to undermine the case for conventional marriage, the results of the last two decades have revealed malfunctions to shake the strongest believer. The divorce rate has shot up like an Apollo rocket—and among the "best" people—leading one to suspect that many who stay married do so out of economic necessity. Psychiatrists' offices are filled with women from outwardly "happy homes." And afternoon solo drinking bouts are the refuge of those who can't face the trauma of verbalizing their problem.

Although speaking from a man's point of view, Joseph Epstein wrote an extraordinary summation of the woman's feelings in a marriage on the rocks in *Divorced in America:*

> Your ambition and her boredom—these were two of the main spears in the side of your marriage. Twist one and the other turned with it. Because you earned a lot of money, she didn't have to work. Because she didn't have to work, she nearly choked on her freedom. Your money made possible her boredom. Bored, she disdained your ambition; ambitious, you grew tired of her boredom. She began to resent the time you spent at your desk; you, knowing her resentment, began to resent the time you spent away from it. Twist one spear and the other turned with it.

And Epstein again, summing up the core of the matter as he sees it: "The now nearly universal search for fulfillment on the part of the American women outside of their marriages is beyond question the most radical development to confront the institution of marriage in this century."

But how can a woman find self-fulfillment within marriage if she is born, raised and bred to be a dependent, and if she is thrust into the world at a point in time when her traditional roles and gratifications have been diminished? When society says, "Oh, yes, you may now go out in the world and get educated and compete but when you marry, your husband's needs come first and you must play the supportive role"?

It reminds me of the nursery rhyme:

> Mother, may I go out to swim?
> Yes, my darling daughter;
> Hang your clothes on a hickory limb,
> But don't go near the water!

This, then, is woman's dilemma: at a time when the old conventions of marriage no longer work for her and the new patterns are not yet set, where does she look for answers?

As William H. Chafe observed in *The American Woman,* the behavior of people does not change from social edict; it changes from the successful examples of people doing something which breaks the old cycle and begins a new one.

Now, in 1975, there are literally thousands of people testing a new kind of marriage. It is a marriage changed primarily by a new breed of woman—and by men who accept, desire, prefer her. She is the *un*-dependent woman. She knows what she wants and what she wants includes her own development as a self-contained entity. By the year 2000, all women of intelligence will emulate her. I call her *the free married woman.*

How do you move from captive to free? You don't do it by waking up one morning and screaming at your husband, "I'm free, I'm free. We're going to have a whole new kind of marriage." Rather, you do it through new understanding and specific actions, actions that are the mark of a free person, which communicate your needs and command his respect.

What is the free married woman like? She is a woman who has married for a different set of reasons from her mother's . . . because she has a different set of needs. She needs a man who can share her interests as she can share his, a mutually supportive arrangement. She understands love beyond sex, love of a total person, a mutual bond, a complementarianism . . . all without ownership.

Although she is a wife and mother, she is also "somebody else." Or, to be more precise, because she is already "somebody else," she can successfully be a wife and mother without being obsessed or possessed by these roles. She is, then, a whole person in her own right. She uses her talents, education, instincts, hopes, determination to fulfill the natural human instinct to "be somebody." Not John Smith's wife or Mary and Jimmy Smith's mother, but Sally Smith—in person.

She is a woman who learned a great deal about herself before she was married—her strong points, her weaknesses. What she was willing to give up and what she couldn't. And she talked to her husband about these things so that they each understood what kind of concessions or sacrifices they might be called upon to make for the other.

And she is not "waiting for the next stage of life." Waiting until the last baby is born. Waiting until the children are all in college or off to work. Waiting to complete her education or begin her life's work. Her life is a one-piece fabric, exploring, thinking, questioning, developing and feeling rewarded from cradle to grave.

The core of the proposition, then, is this: to be a free, married woman, one must have a life of one's own. And life—living, being alive, not merely eating and breathing—involves knowing what you are and what you want to become and fighting with a consuming passion to do it. Not shadow-living as a reflection of a husband's accomplishments or the vicarious thrills of one's children's progress.

A life of one's own. With a husband. With a family, if you please. Is it possible? I think it is not merely possible, I think a lasting marriage will become more and more impossible without it.

A life of one's own. To avoid the plight of an older woman who said to me, "I have given myself away to my husband and my children. And now they don't want me."

A life of one's own. To create a three-dimensional woman instead of a paper doll. A woman who can evolve and change, explore and grow even as a man can.

A life of one's own. A woman who can find a sense of self and purpose without the icy shock of divorce. A woman whose marriage brings constant discovery of new dimensions between the partners . . . because she is a changing, challenging person, a person who in the most intimate reaches of her body and mind has a capacity for yet one more unexpected dimension.

In the classes I teach, we have had many long consciousness-raising sessions about the free married woman and how to build a life of one's own. In such sessions, there is no formal teacher–student relationship but simply an open exchange of ideas among thinking human beings. Some of the recurrent questions in these sessions and the responses may help your thinking about this subject.

It's easy to say, "Be a free married woman, build a life of your own," but isn't it hard to do? How do I get started?
Consensus: You start by stopping—stopping to get to know yourself. Your feelings, your desires, your dreams, your wants. There is in all of us a "me nobody knows." But we women have to push ourselves to explore our talents and interests. You have to set aside the time. Society rushes you to grow up and then to grow old. Take time to think about what turns you on. Get yourself tested. Or just try something. What's the difference if the first thing doesn't work out? At least you'll have something to reject.

Are we saying that all married women should go out and get jobs?
Consensus: No, but I think we're saying that all women need a consuming interest beyond their families, something you can take with you all through your life. Today, 43 percent of married women are working anyway and the percentage is going up every year. You might as well try to do something that makes you happy while you're making money.
Jean: On the other hand, there's nothing wrong with doing something for the love of it. (How about the two young women who led the fight to save San Francisco Bay from being closed in by a land-fill?) And there's nothing wrong with a woman who is really into macramé or watercolors or anything creative that stretches her skills . . . something she really works at and maybe enters in local shows.

If it's o.k. to work for love or money, how does a person measure whether or not she's a success at what she's doing?
Consensus: There's a lot to be said for money because it makes it easier to do the things you want to do, or at least to survive a rainy day. But there are other guideposts for measuring the kind of work that gives you a sense of self. Here are four: 1) Your work must earn your own respect plus the respect of others. 2) Your work must be subject to progressive improvement. 3) You must love what you are doing (even though you may hate it from time to time, an expected emotion in any love affair). 4) Your work must make you stretch yourself beyond what you imagined your capacity

to be. None of these values will prevent you from making money—they may even help—but they are indispensable to the intensity needed for a life of one's own.

Margo: I think you're talking about a pretty ideal situation. In real life, you don't always have that kind of choice.

Mary: That's true but you've got to think about those things and try to work it out. And it applies to the man's life work too. The only thing to do is to sit down and decide how much money you really need and how you can make the best arrangement for both of you.

What about male attitudes? What makes you feel that men want to be married to a woman who wants "a life of one's own?" And what will it do to one's sex relationship with one's husband?

Consensus: What would make any thinking person today believe that men still want a woman who is a dependent, "clinging vine?" Everyone agrees that more and more women will be working in the future. Why shouldn't a woman work for something of value in the long pull? Living together before marriage is so commonplace that men need a reason to marry beyond sexual gratification. What better reason than that the woman whose accomplishments and growth potential make her a good partner for the long run? Or a woman whose financial contribution to the marriage makes possible a life-style they can both enjoy—without the confining burden on the husband of lifelong responsibility as the sole producer of the bread?

Marion: Some couples marry today with the advance understanding that they want no children. Surely those men want an independent wife. Couples who have children—one, two or three—clearly realize that the woman of the year 2000 will have thirty or forty more years of her life after those children are long gone. What kind of wife will the man want then? An independent one, a non-burdensome one, a person who is part of the changing world of tomorrow rather than a fading version of the little girl he married.

Maggie: You asked about sex relationships. Is this free married woman molded in an image that is compatible with sensuality? Or will her sense of self drive the man to seek sexual satisfaction elsewhere? If this question really bothers you, you are shackled to stereotypes of sexuality and social behavior that are taking their last gasps and will be dead and gone before the year 2000. Drs. Masters and Johnson, Alexander Comfort, Robert Francoeur and others have confirmed beyond doubt that the idea of woman as the passive recipient of the sex act is preposterous. Indeed, it is only the woman with a strong self-identity and desire for personal satisfaction who can bring the sex act to its highest plane of exploration and excitement. She does what she does freely, as a gift of love. The woman who performs the same acts as a submissive slave can never satisfy a man (or herself) so well—for how can you compare the duty extracted from an underling with the openly given adulation of an equal?

Diane: I'm looking for a husband but I'm very, very fussy and I refuse to compromise and if I don't find him, I don't marry. If I don't find the kind of man I seek—it's got to be more than just his saying "I'll allow you to work"—he's got to have the kind of head on his shoulders that says "I like you as a human being." I find that too few men like women. How could you really be intimate with someone whose hostility comes out in many subtle ways? I'm looking for a potential . . . somebody I can see enough "like" in so maybe I can encourage a little more. But if I don't find him, I have enough strength in me to go on. I intend to live to be 106, by the way.

Are we all implying that monogamous marriage with sexual fidelity is the wave of the future?

Consensus: No, we've been saying only that monogamous marriage is a viable way of life for a free married woman. And that a free married woman can exist only with a free married man. In that kind of relationship, the first issue is that you have a better chance of good healthy sex within the marriage. Whether or not you have sexual intercourse outside of the marriage is a separate question—and, like other questions in the marriage, it has to be settled by mutual consent.

Susan: Let's face it. Almost everyone who gets married today has had premarital intercourse. If you want to continue to have relationships with others, you and your husband have to decide that you can handle it without sacrificing the special emotional involvement that exists between you.

If you want "a life of your own," there can be conflict between your needs and his. For instance, what happens if one of you is offered a better job in another city?

Consensus: In any marriage, "free" or not, sooner or later some of your needs will conflict with some of his. Women have been taught that they come second. Remember the biblical Rachael saying, "Whither thou goest, I will go." If you start out with the premise that one partner's (read "his") needs are always more important than the other's (read "hers"), you are simply brewing the chemistry of resentment which will one day explode. Most women who feel that they must cater completely to their husband's needs simply do not have well-developed *needs* of their own. It is very difficult to balance out the needs of a man who, say, wants to change to a new line of work with the uncertainties of a woman whose head is buried in a pillow shedding tears about it.

Lynn: Let's take the specific question of the two-career family where the man or the woman has the chance to take a new job in another city. What is happening right now is no longer theory. Especially with younger couples. They take a long look at what the proposed change would do to both of their careers and interests. And they make a mutual decision. Even when the man has to give up his job to move to where the wife's great opportunity lies.

Maggie: Many big corporations are now keenly aware of this change in attitude. Some will use their personnel departments to seek a comparable opening in the new locale for the wife of the man they want to move. Many no longer insist that a man must move or lose the momentum of his career. And as more women enter the executive ranks, the question is evoking more novel answers. An editor of a New York newspaper is married to a Cleveland dentist. The head of an advertising agency in New York is married to the president of an airline in Texas. A professor of Brooklyn College is the spouse of one at Radcliffe. Each couple meets weekends, holidays and whenever possible, and they immerse themselves in each other during those days. As one of them told me, "I once figured it out. Jim and I actually spend as many hours a week together as does the average couple. And we certainly spend as much time talking, sharing our experiences, planning our lives together. We're not much for sinking into silence watching the TV set. We make every hour count. We don't expect to do this forever, but it certainly isn't hurting our marriage while we do."

How do you convince a man to accept the requirements of an independent woman? Why should a man marry a woman whose demands may conflict with his?

Consensus: It's doubtful that you can or should try to convince a man that he should marry a woman who wants "a life of her own." Any more than you should try to tell him he should want a woman who is tall or short, skinny or *szoftig,* smart or dumb. Instead you should look for a man who wants what you are; who, through instinct or education, can sense that the pleasures of a whole female person outweigh the problems; who can afford to be supportive of your need to grow because he himself is not small and fearful.

Maggie: Happily, the trend in masculine thinking favors the free married woman. Listen to what Joel Roach wrote in *Ms.* magazine: "It is enough to say that when someone has concrete power over your life, you are going to keep part of yourself hidden and therefore undeveloped, or developed only in fantasy. Your identity becomes bound up in other peoples' expectations of you—and that is the definition of alienation. It did not take long for me to make connections between the alienating ways in which Jan had to deal with me in the early days of our marriage and the way that I was dealing with my 'senior colleagues,' the men and women who had the power to fire me and did."

What will be the effect on children of this kind of marriage? What about the sheer amount of time needed to be a good mother? Isn't raising a family a full-time career . . . or at least a first priority?

Consensus: Those questions seem to assume that the children come first in every situation. Obviously, young children require time and care. As they get older, they require less and less. Starting at perhaps the age of five, most children require less care and attention than their parents insist on giving them. The child, in fact, becomes a plaything, a time occupier, a *raison d'être,* for the mother.

Mimi: Since it is inevitable that the child will someday grow up and require little or none of the mother's time, why should not the mother herself outgrow the child even as a well-raised child should outgrow her?

Lanie: And what of the father's responsibility for sharing the burden of raising the child? If the wife has the need to be out Thursday nights at her sculpture class and to work Sunday mornings in her studio, what could the husband do at those times that would be more valuable for both of them than to perform his role as caretaker for the child? In the next quarter-century, the work week will continue to shorten—and men will find, to their advantage, that caring for the children is a task to be enjoyed and shared by both parents. It won't do the kids any harm, either. The world they will grow into will be populated by both sexes; they should early on be acclimated to relating to both male and female attitudes.

Maggie: I have a very pointed quote for you on this question. Here's what Alice Rossi, an eminent sociologist, wrote in *Psychology Today* about her personal experience in spending time with children:

> Yes, women who are with or near their pre-school children throughout the day are certainly not interacting with the children all during that time. In fact, they spend about two and one-half hours a day interacting.
>
> And the point is that working mothers can plan their schedules just as well. In fact, there are advantages to this approach. One is the development of the child's sense of independence . . . but there is also another, which is the sense of family solidarity which develops from the custom of inviolate family hours. When our children were young, Pete and I tried hard to be home and genuinely available between five and eight in the evenings. These were hours of togetherness with the children. The experiences we had then—for all of us—meant a great deal.

Women's traditional tasks can't be made to disappear on demand. How about running of a household? The meals have to come from somewhere, don't they? When the dishes get piled high enough in the sink, someone has to wash them. Or do you throw them out and start over again? Maybe with a new husband?

Carol: It seems to me that those are all questions which imply that women and Brillo have a natural, God-given affinity. Gourmet cooking is a talent to be cherished and admired, but day-in, day-out food preparation and clean-up is more a necessity than a triumph.

Kathy: Men should be able to understand this. In the army, K.P. doesn't carry the same prestige nor pay as G-2. Men are able to share household chores quite nicely. Doing the dishes after dinner is much better for his digestion and waistline than plopping in front of the TV. He's tired? So are you if you're a free person who has been seriously doing your own work during that day.

Maggie: Those are all fairly obvious arguments against hanging the apron strings around the wife's neck. By the year 2000, it may be largely academic. Good food will be available, factory-prepared in ready-to-serve portions—not like frozen dinners, but ready to cook in seconds in ultra-sonic ovens. And dishes will be cleaned and dried by sonic waves in minutes. Beds will make themselves at the touch of a button. Oh, I don't know if this is exactly how it will be . . . but you can see already in our markets how much is prepared and ready to heat and eat. So can't you see that the important thing is not who will be fixing the dinner or dusting the house or any of the repetitive tasks of "homemaking"? The real question is, what will the woman of the home be making of herself?

Is this kind of marriage going to be accepted by society as a whole? I mean, can or should every woman be a free married woman? And if not, what problems will she meet in the world around her? Where will she find her friends and social acceptance?

Consensus: If you're thinking about the present, of course there are problems for the free married woman. Those women who want dependent, conventional marriage probably consider this new life-style a threat to them by its very existence. At the other extreme, some women who are fighting for women's rights feel that no form of formal marriage can be satisfactory until laws and the structure of society are changed to provide pure equality.

Sandy: Who said, "I never promised you a rose garden"? It's a question of what's important to you. You can't be friends with the whole world anyway. If you're the kind of person who is into anything from butterfly collecting to heading your own business, you won't feel too hurt if you're not included in the local sewing circle anyway.

One subject which has recurred frequently in my discussions of the free married woman—at schools, at women's groups, at cocktail parties —is money. Not surprisingly, most women feel that being genuinely independent requires some degree of financial independence. Since women have seldom enjoyed this blessing except by virtue of the largesse of men or by inheritance, the idea of being both free and married requires some different ground-rules governing money. And the rules depend upon the particular situation.

In some families, the husband and wife earn equally. They should contribute equally to the family's operating expenses and should each have the opportunity to save, invest or acquire.

In other families, the husband is the principal earner. But the wife should be given a regular share of the incremental income—the income above living expenses—which she is free to do with as she sees fit. And she should equip herself to make her own decisions as to the employment of this money to build a substantial backlog. One important reason for this is so that she will not have to stay married as an alternative to starving. The fact is, she is much more likely to stay married if differences between the spouses are not to be settled by the husband's control over the daily bread.

This is not, as some have suggested, a matter of the man paying the wife for replacing a maid. To be sure, she may be doing tasks which might otherwise require hired help. But that is a mere fragment of the picture. If a man is happy to have his wife share in building his life through making a home, having and raising children, enriching his life with her skills, broadening his world through her perspective—and if he is satisfied that this, rather than working for money, is her half of the compact—then he is getting full measure and he should recognize her need for the security that only money of one's own can provide.

Of course, a gainfully employed husband is not the total answer, either. The young married woman told me, "Money is not *our* problem, because we have more than enough to live on. But it is *my* problem because I want to lead my life as an independent woman."

From the free married woman's standpoint, money isn't everything. It won't automatically give you a sense of self. It can't define who you are. But having money, and the process of making money, will go a long way toward helping you to find out.

Finding out who you are is one of the common concerns of the captive married woman, the woman who has discarded or submerged her own person in marriage. These are the words of a bright woman in her fifties:

> I'm looking for identity, to find out who I am and how I got into this mess. I think it's coming. I feel vibrations at home. They're very mixed, but as I feel stronger about it, as I push firmly enough, it begins to change. I don't think that men are going to change radically. You have to decide who you are and go from there. But I see what is happening with the young and I want some of it to happen to me.

What is happening to the young now is what plainly forecasts the mode for the year 2000. You can get a glimpse of it from this tape-recorded conversation. It took place at a film studio where a group of young women were talking to producer David Saperstein about what kind of lives they look forward to.

David: You've really changed your thinking about how to live, haven't you?

Heather: Yes, I've started a business of my own . . . really just to make money. It came from something Lee said about how to understand and use your skills. In some ways, this is going to make my husband freer because he's so intense in what he's doing that he doesn't have time to do other things he wants to do.

David: What does he do?

Heather: He's an attorney now.

David: Does he like it?

Heather: Sometimes. But he doesn't want to do that all the time. He wants to work with children—and that doesn't pay very well. If I succeed in making some money, it could help him do things he wants to do—and I'll be doing a thing I enjoy.

David: I understand you moved to New York from Princeton.

Heather: Oh yes, and I would say the future looks much brighter to me because of how things used to be there. My relationship with my husband is much better now. I don't want to be "protected" any more. I don't want to be confined. I want to stand on my own, and I think that this has helped our relationship together. I lived in a house in Princeton with him, and we didn't do very well. I felt very isolated. I was protected physically, monetarily, in every way by him as my father had protected me before that. Actually, it was very lonely, isolating and mind-deadening. We came back to the city. I would say a lot of it was because, at the end, I was at the breaking point. It was either that or no marriage. No, we've done pretty well, the two of us. I hold more hope for the future, in the children—they're eight and four. My learning to stand by myself has taught me that they must learn to stand by themselves. I don't want them to reach thirty and still have me protecting them. I want them to handle things, reach decisions, have values, decide what paths are open to them and I think they're handling that. And my husband . . . with each bit of self-worth I get for myself, in reality his esteem for me goes up too. We've had a better relationship since he does not have total responsibility for me. He can treat me more as a person.

David: What about your new business venture—will it separate you from your husband when you're required to travel?

Heather: It's a good business because I make my own schedule and my children and husband will, I expect, be able to join me from time to time. But if they have different things to do, I won't demand that they accompany me. It's certainly different from being cooped up in a house in Princeton with two cars, a dog and a cat and everything that went with it. It's part of creating a life-style that all of us can live with.

Not every woman will want to make the same moves as Heather, but every woman who wants to be free and married should re-read and think about Heather's last sentence.

America tends to be an all-or-nothing country. In the Fifties, we felt that woman's place was in the home, that working women were marking time awaiting a suitable man, or just *any* man, and that married working women had chosen husbands who failed them.

Now in the Seventies we have shattered that stereotype. The chemistry of discontent was there and the catalyst that exploded into the new force in American society was the Women's Liberation Movement. The Women's Movement has done more to change society than can be measured by its concrete achievements alone—equal pay laws, abortion reform, affirmative action programs, etc. It is changing the way women think about themselves. It is changing the way our schools, government, motion pictures, literature, business and financial institutions look at women and portray them.

There is a radical change in women's self-image. Thanks to the emergence of successful role models in sports, business and politics, American women have a better image of themselves and their potential.

There is a radical change in opportunity for self-development. In both high schools and colleges, courses are given on the nature and accomplishments and possibilities for women. Continuing education courses are offered at almost every college for women and at some men's schools. Banks, insurance companies and industry have launched a parade of self-improvement and training courses—partly as public service and partly to fill their own ranks with qualified people to comply with the law of the land.

Finally, there is a change in women's attitudes toward men. In some ways this change is more subtle than the rest and there are only the early signs of change in men's attitudes toward women. A fundamental factor is the lessened pressure on young women to get married. With liaisons outside of marriage widely accepted, with unfolding opportunities for career development and with the acceptance of varied life-styles, young women can and do postpone the decision to marry. And with increased knowledge of their own bodily functions and nature, young women find that good sexual relations with men no longer require them to be passive partners—a behavioral fact which is making its mark upon all aspects of social intercourse between men and women.

Thus the Women's Movement is altering the temper and the vision of the American people, especially its women. Yet it has not diminished the appetite for marriage, nor is that an objective of the mainstream of the Women's Movement. In fact, if you see the effect of the Women's Movement as creating more capable, more emotionally mature, more informed women, then the rebirth of feminism may well lead to a rebirth of marriage. And it will be a marriage of minds as well as bodies, based upon dynamic growth as much as romantic love.

Speaking of romantic love, I suppose some people would say that the Free Married Woman thesis doesn't add up if I leave love out of the equation. So let me say outright that I am for love. But with qualifications.

I am against love that equates with surrender, especially unconditional surrender. After all, marriage is not a peace treaty with the victor and the vanquished. An arrangement under which the winner gives a howl of joy and the defeated a cry of defeat. In which one party becomes the master and the other the slave. How much and how long can you love a slave?

The woman who is both free and married loves in a special way which permeates but does not smother. Because she herself is constantly growing, reaching new levels of understanding and expanding her capabilities, she is able to give freely without fear of exhausting her emotional resources. Because of her ability to grow and change, she is the toughest competition against the attractions of other women. And because of her self-containment, she can give all the love a man can take—and still have reserves and depths that need be plumbed.

In looking at men and women as they behave in America today, it may not be easy for you to see the vision of marriage that I see. Divorce rates are rising. Many women are uncertain of their roles; they vacillate between the alleged security of living in a man's world and the possibilities of entering the new world of equality in fact.

While individual women may go either way in 1975, the trend of the future is already resolved. Marriage as a style of life will survive, but only in new forms which take into account the changed relationship between men and women. Men will have changed because our value-systems are changing . . . because marriage is no longer needed for sex and because women can no longer be regarded as trophies. Women will have changed because the cultural directions for women will be different. One small example: Macmillan's new First Reader says on page one, "Girls don't climb trees." Turn to page two and, sure enough, there is a girl perched happily high in a tree. Those who have seen the far horizons are seldom satisfied to remain within their own backyard.

This means that, for both men and women, there will be a renewed commitment to personal growth. Since nothing grows well in a vacuum, this means an intensified need for sharing. Psychologist Herbert Otto put it this way: "As a result of this commitment to the growth ethic, couples will experience a greatly heightened sensitivity to each other's needs."

No one has ever discovered a better medium for shared sensitivity than the one-to-one commitment of marriage.

The American male has always thought of himself as free . . . until he was married. The new American woman is about to show him that freedom is indivisible, that a marriage in which both partners are free and *un*-dependent is the only kind you can live with over time.

6 THE FRACTURED FAMILY

by Alvin Toffler

THE FLOOD of novelty about to crash down upon us will spread from universities and research centers to factories and offices, from the marketplace and mass media into our social relationships, from the community into the home. Penetrating deep into our private lives, it will place absolutely unprecedented strains on the family itself.

The family has been called the "giant shock absorber" of society—the place to which the bruised and battered individual returns after doing battle with the world, the one stable point in an increasingly fluxfilled environment. As the super-industrial revolution unfolds, this "shock absorber" will come in for some shocks of its own.

Social critics have a field day speculating about the family. The family is "near the point of complete extinction," says Ferdinand Lundberg, author of *The Coming World Transformation.* "The family is dead except for the first year or two of child raising," according to psychoanalyst William Wolf. "This will be its only function." Pessimists tell us the family is racing toward oblivion—but seldom tell us what will take its place.

Family optimists, in contrast, contend that the family, having existed all this time, will continue to exist. Some go so far as to argue that the family is in for a Golden Age. As leisure spreads, they theorize, families will spend more time together and will derive great satisfaction from joint activity. "The family that plays together, stays together," etc.

A more sophisticated view holds that the very turbulence of tomorrow will drive people deeper into their families. "People will marry for stable structure," says Dr. Irwin M. Greenberg, Professor of Psychiatry at the Albert Einstein College of Medicine. According to this view, the family serves as one's "portable roots," anchoring one against the storm of change. In short, the more transient and novel the environment, the more important the family will become.

It may be that both sides in this debate are wrong. For the future is more open than it might appear. The family may neither vanish *nor* enter upon a new Golden Age. It may—and this is far more likely—break up, shatter, only to come together again in weird and novel ways.

The Mystique of Motherhood

The most obviously upsetting force likely to strike the family in the decades immediately ahead will be the impact of the new birth technology. The ability to pre-set the sex of one's baby, or even to "program" its IQ, looks and personality traits, must now be regarded as a real possibility. Embryo implants, babies grown *in vitro*, the ability to swallow a pill and guarantee oneself twins or triplets or, even more, the ability to walk into a "babytorium" and actually purchase embryos—all this reaches so far beyond any previous human experience that one needs to look at the future through the eyes of the poet or painter, rather than those of the sociologist or conventional philosopher.

It is regarded as somehow unscholarly, even frivolous, to discuss these matters. Yet advances in science and technology, or in reproductive biology alone, could, within a short time, smash all orthodox ideas about the family and its responsibilities. When babies can be grown in a laboratory jar what happens to the very notion of maternity? And what happens to the self-image of the female in societies which, since the very beginnings of man, have taught her that her primary mission is the propagation of and nurture of the race?

Few social scientists have begun as yet to concern themselves with such questions. One who has is psychiatrist Hyman G. Weitzen, director of Neuropsychiatric Service at Polyclinic Hospital in New York. The cycle of birth, Dr. Weitzen suggests, "fufills for most women a major creative need . . . Most women are proud of their ability to bear children . . . The special aura that glorifies the pregnant woman has figured largely in the art and literature of both East and West."

What happens to the cult of motherhood, Weitzen asks, if "her offspring might literally not be hers, but that of a genetically 'superior' ovum, implanted in her womb from another woman, or even grown in a Petri dish?" If women are to be important at all, he suggests, it will no longer be because they alone can bear children. If nothing else, we are about to kill off the mystique of motherhood.

Not merely motherhood, but the concept of parenthood itself may be in for radical revision. Indeed, the day may soon dawn when it is possible for a child to have more than two biological parents. Dr. Beatrice Mintz, a developmental biologist at the Institute for Cancer Research in Philadelphia, has grown what are coming to be known as "multi-mice"—baby mice each of which has more than the usual number of parents. Embryos are taken from each of two pregnant mice. These embryos are placed in a laboratory dish and nurtured until they form a single growing mass. This is then implanted in the womb of a third female mouse. A baby is born that clearly shares the genetic characteristics of both sets of donors. Thus a typical multi-mouse, born of two pairs of parents, has white fur and whiskers on one side of its face, dark fur and whiskers on the other, with alternating bands of white and dark hair covering the rest of the body. Some 700 multi-mice bred in this fashion have already produced more than 35,000 offspring themselves. If multi-mouse is here, can "multi-man" be far behind?

Under such circumstances, what or who is a parent? When a woman bears in her uterus an embryo conceived in another woman's womb, who is the mother? And just exactly who is the father?

If a couple can actually purchase an embryo, then parenthood becomes a legal, not biological matter. Unless such transactions are tightly controlled, one can imagine such grotesqueries as a couple buying an embryo, raising it *in vitro*, then buying another in the name of the first, as though for a trust fund. In that case, they might be regarded as legal "grandparents" before their first child is out of its infancy. We shall need a whole new vocabulary to describe kinship ties.

Furthermore, if embryos are for sale, can a corporation buy one? Can it buy ten thousand? Can it resell them? And if not a corporation, how about a noncommercial research laboratory? If we buy and sell living embryos, are we back to a new form of slavery? Such are the nightmarish questions soon to be debated by us. To continue to think of the family, therefore, in purely conventional terms is to defy all reason.

Faced by rapid social change and the staggering implications of the scientific revolution, super-industrial man may be forced to experiment with novel family forms. Innovative minorities can be expected to try out a colorful variety of family arrangements. They will begin by tinkering with existing forms.

The Streamlined Family

One simple thing they will do is streamline the family. The typical pre-industrial family not only had a good many children, but numerous other dependents as well—grandparents, uncles, aunts, and cousins. Such "extended" families were well suited for survival in slow-paced agricultural societies. But such families are hard to transport or transplant. They are immobile.

Industrialism demanded masses of workers ready and able to move off the land in pursuit of jobs, and to move again whenever necessary. Thus the extended family gradually shed its excess weight and the so-called "nuclear" family emerged—a stripped-down, portable family unit consisting only of parents and a small set of children. This new style family, far more mobile than the traditional extended family, became the standard model in all the industrial countries.

Super-industrialism, however, the next stage of eco-technological development, requires even higher mobility. Thus we may expect many among the people of the future to carry the streamlining process a step further by remaining childless, cutting the family down to its most elemental components, a man and a woman. Two people, perhaps with matched careers, will prove more efficient at navigating through education and social shoals, through jobs changes and geographic relocations, than the ordinary child-cluttered family. Indeed, anthropologist Margaret Mead has pointed out that we may already be moving toward a system under which, as she puts it, "parenthood would be limited to a smaller number of families whose principal functions would be child-rearing," leaving the rest of the population "free to function—for the first time in history—as individuals."

A compromise may be the postponement of children, rather than childlessness. Men and women today are often torn in conflict between a commitment to career and a commitment to children. In the future, many couples will sidestep this problem by deferring the entire task of raising children until after retiremet.

This may strike people of the present as odd. Yet once childbearing is broken away from its biological base, nothing more than tradition suggests having children at an early age. Why not wait, and buy your embryos later, after your work career is over? Thus childlessness is likely to spread among young and middle-aged couples; sexagenarians who raise infants may be far more common. The post-retirement family could become a recognized social institution.

Bio-Parents and Pro-Parents

If a smaller number of families raise children, however, why do the children have to be their own? Why not a system under which "professional parents" take on the childrearing function for others?

Raising children, after all, requires skills that are by no means universal. We don't let "just anyone" perform brain surgery or, for that matter, sell stocks and bonds. Even the lowest ranking civil servant is required to pass tests proving competence. Yet we allow virtually anyone, almost without regard for mental or moral qualification, to try his or her hand at raising young human beings, so long as these humans are biological offspring. Despite the increasing complexity of the task, parenthood remains the greatest single preserve of the amateur.

As the present system cracks and the super-industrial revolution rolls over us, as the armies of juvenile delinquents swell, as hundreds of thousands of youngsters flee their homes, and students rampage at universities in all the techno-societies, we can expect vociferous demands for an end to parental dilettantism.

There are far better ways to cope with the problems of youth, but professional parenthood is certain to be proposed, if only because it fits so perfectly with the society's overall push toward specialization. Moreover, there is a powerful, pent-up demand for this social innovation. Even now millions of parents, given the opportunity, would happily relinquish their parental responsibilities—and not necessarily through irresponsibility or lack of love. Harried, frenzied, up against the wall, they have come to see themselves as inadequate to the tasks. Given affluence and the existence of specially-equipped and licensed professional parents, many of today's biological parents would not only gladly surrender their children to them, but would look upon it as an act of love, rather than rejection.

Parental professionals would not be therapists, but actual family units assigned to, and well paid for, rearing children. Such families might be multi-generational by design offering children in them an opportunity to observe and learn from a variety of adult models, as was the case in the old farm homestead. With the adults paid to be professional parents, they would be freed of the occupational necessity to relocate repeatedly. Such families would take in new children as old ones "graduate" so that age-segregation would be minimized.

Thus newspapers of the future might well carry advertisements addressed to young married couples: "Why let parenthood tie you down? Let us raise your infant into a responsible, successful adult. Class A Pro-family offers: father age 39, mother, 36, grandmother, 67. Uncle and aunt, age 30, live in, hold part-time local employment. Four-child-unit has opening for one, age 6–8. Regulated diet exceeds government standards. All adults certified in child development and management. Bio-parents permitted frequent visits. Telephone contact allowed. Child may spend summer vacation with bio-parents. Religion, art, music encouraged by special arrangement. Five year contract, minimum. Write for further details."

The "real" or "bio-parents" could, as the ad suggests, fill the role presently played by interested godparents, namely that of friendly and helpful outsiders. In such a way, the society could continue to breed a wide diversity of genetic types, yet turn the care of children over to mother-father groups who are equipped, both intellectually and emotionally, for the task of caring for kids.

Communes and Homosexual Daddies

Quite a different alternative lies in the communal family. As transience increases the loneliness and alienation in society, we can anticipate increasing experimentation with various forms of group marriage. The banding together of several adults and children into a single "family" provides a kind of insurance against isolation. Even if one or two members of the household leave, the remaining members have one another. Communes are springing up modeled after those described by psychologist B.F. Skinner in *Walden Two* and by novelist Robert Rimmer in *The Harrad Experiment* and *Proposition 31*. In the latter work, Rimmer seriously proposes the legalization of a "corporate family" in which from three to six adults adopt a single name, live and raise children in common, and legally incorporate to obtain certain economic and tax advantages.

According to some observers, there are already hundreds of open or covert communes dotting the American map. Not all, by any means, are composed of young people or hippies. Some are organized around specific goals—like the group, quietly financed by three East Coast colleges—which has taken as its function the task of counseling college freshmen, helping to orient them to campus life. The goals may be social, religious, political, even recreational. Thus we shall before long begin to see communal families of surfers dotting the beaches of California and Southern France, if they don't already. We shall see the emergence of communes based on political doctrines and religious faiths. In Denmark, a bill to legalize group marriage has already been introduced in the Folketing (Parliament). While passage is not imminent, the act of introduction is itself a significant symbol of change.

In Chicago, 250 adults and children already live together in "family-style monasticism" under the auspices of a new, fast-growing religious organization, the Ecumenical Institute. Members share the same quarters, cook and eat together, worship and tend children in common, and pool their incomes. At least 60,000 people have taken "EI" courses and similar communes have begun to spring up in Atlanta, Boston, Los Angeles and other cities, "A brand-new world is emerging," says Professor Joseph W. Mathews, leader of the Ecumenical Institute, "but people are still operating in terms of the old one. We seek to reeducate people and give them the tools to build a new social context."

Still another type of family unit likely to win adherents in the future might be called the "geriatric commune"—a group marriage of elderly people drawn together in a common search for companionship and assistance. Disengaged from the productive economy that makes mobility necessary, they will settle in a single place, band together, pool funds, collectively hire domestic or nursing help, and proceed—within limits—to have the "time of their lives."

Communalism runs counter to the pressure for ever greater geographical and social mobility generated by the thrust toward super-industrialism. It presupposes groups of people who "stay put." For this reason, communal experiments will first proliferate among those in the society who are free from the industrial discipline—the retired population, the young, the dropouts, the students, as well as among self-employed professional and technical people. Later, when advanced technology and information systems make it possible for much of the work of society to be done at home via computer-telecommunication hookups, communalism will become feasible for larger numbers.

We shall, however, also see many more "family" units consisting of a single unmarried adult and one or more children. Nor will all of these adults be women. It is already possible in some places for unmarried men to adopt children. In 1965 in Oregon, for example, a thirty-eight-year-old musician named Tony Piazza became the first unmarried man in that state, and perhaps in the United States, to be granted the right to adopt a baby. Courts are more readily granting custody to divorced fathers, too. In London, photographer Michael Cooper, married at twenty and divorced soon after, won the right to raise his infant son, and expressed an interest in adopting other children. Observing that he did not particularly wish to remarry, but that he liked children, Cooper mused aloud: "I wish you could just ask beautiful women to have babies for you. Or any woman you liked, or who had something you admired. Ideally, I'd like a big house full of children—all different colors, shapes and sizes." Romantic? Unmanly? Perhaps. Yet attitudes like these will be widely held by men in the future.

Two pressures are even now softening up the culture, preparing it for acceptance of the idea of child-rearing by men. First, adoptable children are in oversupply in some places. Thus, in California, disc jockeys blare commercials: "We have many wonderful babies of all races and nationalities waiting to bring love and happiness to the right families . . . Call the Los Angeles County Bureau of Adoption." At the same time, the mass media, in a strange non-conspiratorial fashion, appear to have decided simultaneously that men who raise children hold special interest for the public. Extremely popular television shows in recent seasons have glamorized womanless households in which men scrub floors, cook, and, most significantly, raise children. *My Three Sons, The Rifleman, Bonanza* and *Bachelor Father* are four examples.

As homosexuality becomes more socially acceptable, we may even begin to find families based on homosexual "marriages" with the partners adopting children. Whether these children would be of the same or opposite sex remains to be seen. But the rapidity with which homosexuality is winning respectability in the techno-societies distinctly points in this direction. In Holland not long ago a Catholic priest "married" two homosexuals, explaining to critics that "they are among the faithful to be helped." England has rewritten its relevant legislation; homosexual relations between consenting adults are no longer considered a crime. And in the United States a meeting of Episcopal clergymen concluded publicly that homosexuality might, under certain circumstances, be adjudged "good." The day may also come when a court decides that a couple of stable, well educated homosexuals might make decent "parents."

We might also see the gradual relaxation of bars against polygamy. Polygamous families exist even now, more widely than generally believed, in the midst of "normal" society. Writer Ben Merson, after visiting several such families in Utah where polygamy is still regarded as essential by certain Mormon fundamentalists, estimated that there are some 30,000 people living in underground family units of this type in the United States. As sexual attitudes loosen up, as property rights become less important because of rising affluence, the social repression of polygamy may come to be regarded as irrational. This shift may be facilitated by the very mobility that compels men to spend considerable time away from their present homes. The old male fantasy of the Captain's Paradise may become a reality for some, although it is likely that, under such circumstances, the wives left behind will demand extramarital sexual rights. Yesterday's "captain" would hardly consider this possibility. Tomorrow's may feel quite differently about it.

Still another family form is even now springing up in our midst, a novel child-rearing unit that I call the "aggregate family"—a family based on relationships between divorced and remarried couples, in which all the children become part of "one big family." Though sociologists have paid little attention as yet to this phenomenon, it is already so prevalent that it formed the basis for a hilarious scene in a recent American movie entitled *Divorce American Style.* We may expect aggregate families to take on increasing importance in the decades ahead.

Childless marriage, professional parenthood, post-retirement child-rearing, corporate families, communes, geriatric group marriages, homosexual family units, polygamy—these, then, are a few of the family forms and practices with which innovative minorities will experiment in the decades ahead. Not all of us, however, will be willing to participate in such experimentation. What of the majority?

The Odds Against Love

Minorities experiment; majorities cling to the forms of the past. It is safe to say that large numbers of people will refuse to jettison the conventional idea of marriage or the familiar family forms. They will, no doubt, continue searching for happiness within the orthodox format. Yet, even they will be forced to innovate in the end, for the odds against success may prove overwhelming.

The orthodox format presupposes that two young people will "find" one another and marry. It presupposes that the two will fulfill certain psychological needs in one another, and that the two personalities will develop over the years, more or less in tandem, so that they continue to fulfill each other's needs. It further presupposes that this process will last "until death do us part."

These expectations are built deeply into our culture. It is no longer respectable, as it once was, to marry for anything but love. Love has changed from a peripheral concern of the family into its primary justification. Indeed, the pursuit of love through family life has become, for many, the very purpose of life itself.

Love, however, is defined in terms of this notion of shared growth. It is seen as a beautiful mesh of complementary needs, flowing into and out of one another, fulfilling the loved ones, and producing feelings of warmth, tenderness and devotion. Unhappy husbands often complain that they have "left their wives behind" in terms of social, educational or intellectual growth. Partners in successful marriages are said to "grow together."

This "parallel development" theory of love carries endorsement from marriage counsellors, psychologists and sociologists. Thus, says sociologist Nelson Foote, a specialist on the family, the quality of the relationship between husband and wife is dependent upon "the degree of matching in their phases of distinct but comparable development."

If love is a product of shared growth, however, and we are to measure success in marriage by the degree to which matched development actually occurs, it becomes possible to make a strong and ominous prediction about the future.

It is possible to demonstrate that, even in a relatively stagnant society, the mathematical odds are heavily stacked against any couple achieving this ideal of parallel growth. The odds for success positively plummet, however, when the rate of change in society accelerates, as it now is doing. In a fast-moving society, in which many things change, not once, but repeatedly, in which the husband moves up and down a variety of economic and social scales, in which the family is again and again torn loose from home and community, in which individuals move further from their parents, further from the religion of origin, and further from traditional values, it is almost miraculous if two people develop at anything like comparable rates.

If, at the same time, average life expectancy rises from, say, fifty to seventy years, thereby lengthening the term during which this acrobatic feat of matched development is supposed to be maintained, the odds against success become absolutely astronomical. Thus, Nelson Foote writes with wry understatement: "To expect a marriage to last indefinitely under modern conditions is to expect a lot." To ask love to last indefinitely is to expect even more. Transience and novelty are both in league against it.

Temporary Marriage

It is this change in the statistical odds against love that accounts for the high divorce and separation rates in most of the techno-societies. The faster the rate of change and the longer the life span, the worse these odds grow. Something has to crack.

In point of fact, of course, something has already cracked—and it is the old insistence on permanence. Millions of men and women now adopt what appears to them to be a sensible and conservative strategy. Rather than opting for some offbeat variety of the family, they marry conventionally, they attempt to make it "work," and then, when the paths of the partners diverge beyond an acceptable point, they divorce or depart. Most of them go on to search for a new partner whose developmental stage, at that moment, matches their own.

As human relationships grow more transient and modular, the pursuit of love becomes, if anything, more frenzied. But the temporal expectations change. As conventional marriage proves itself less and less capable of delivering on its promise of lifelong love, therefore, we can anticipate open public acceptance of temporary marriages. Instead of wedding "until death us do part," couples will enter into matrimony knowing from the first that the relationship is likely to be short-lived.

They will know, too, that when the paths of husband and wife diverge, when there is too great a discrepancy in developmental stages, they may call it quits—without shock or embarrassment, perhaps even without some of the pain that goes with divorce today. And when the opportunity presents itself, they will marry again . . . and again . . . and again.

Serial marriage—a pattern of successive temporary marriages—is cut to order for the Age of Transience in which all man's relationships, all his ties with the environment, shrink in duration. It is the natural, the inevitable outgrowth of a social order in which automobiles are rented, dolls traded in, and dresses discarded after one-time use. It is the mainstream marriage pattern of tomorrow.

In one sense, serial marriage is already the best kept family secret of the techno-societies. According to Professor Jessie Bernard, a world-prominent family sociologist, "Plural marriage is more extensive in our society today than it is in societies that permit polygamy—the chief difference being that we have institutionalized plural marriage serially or sequentially rather than contemporaneously." Remarriage is already so prevalent a practice that nearly one out of every four bridegrooms in America has been to the altar before. It is so prevalent that one IBM personnel man reports a poignant incident involving a divorced woman, who, in filling out a job application, paused when she came to the question of marital status. She put her pencil in her mouth, pondered for a moment, then wrote: "Unremarried."

Transience necessarily affects the durational expectancies with which persons approach new situations. While they may yearn for a permanent relationship, something inside whispers to them that it is an increasingly improbable luxury.

Even young people who most passionately seek commitment, profound involvement with people and causes, recognize the power of the thrust toward transience. Listen, for example, to a young black American, a civil-rights worker, as she describes her attitude toward time and marriage:

"In the white world, marriage is always billed as 'the end'—like in a Hollywood movie. I don't go for that. I can't imagine myself promising my whole lifetime away. I might want to get married now, but how about next year? That's not disrespect for the institution [of marriage], but the deepest respect. In The [civil rights] Movement, you need to have a feeling for the temporary—of making something as good as you can, while it lasts. In conventional relationships, time is a prison."

Such attitudes will not be confined to the young, the few, or the politically active. They will whip across nations as novelty floods into the society and catch fire as the level of transience rises still higher. And along with them will come a sharp increase in the number of temporary—then serial—marriages.

The idea is summed up vividly by a Swedish magazine, *Svensk Damtidning,* which interviewed a number of leading Swedish sociologists, legal experts, and others about the future of man-woman relationships. It presented its findings in five photographs. They showed the same beautiful bride being carried across the threshold five times—by five different bridegrooms.

Marriage Trajectories

As serial marriages become more common, we shall begin to characterize people not in terms of their present marital status, but in terms of their marriage career or "trajectory." This trajectory will be formed by the decisions they make at certain vital turning points in their lives.

For most people, the first such juncture will arive in youth, when they enter into "trial marriage." Even now the young people of the United States and Europe are engaged in a mass experiment with probationary marriage, with or without benefit of ceremony. The staidest of United States universities are beginning to wink at the practice of co-ed housekeeping among their students. Acceptance of trial marriage is even growing among certain religious philosophers. Thus we hear the German theologian Siegfried Keil of Marburg University urge what he terms "recognized premarriage." In Canada, Father Jacques Lazure has publicly proposed "probationary marriages" of three to eighteen months.

In the past, social pressures and lack of money restricted experimentation with trial marriage to a relative handful. In the future, both these limiting forces will evaporate. Trial marriage will be the first step in the serial marriage "careers" that millions will pursue.

A second critical life juncture for the people of the future will occur when the trial marriage ends. At this point, couples may choose to formalize their relationship and stay together into the next stage. Or they may terminate it and seek out new partners. In either case, they will then face several options. They may prefer to go childless. They may choose to have, adopt or "buy" one or more children. They may decide to raise these children themselves or to farm them out to professional parents. Such decisions will be made, by and large, in the early twenties—by which time many young adults will already be well into their second marriages.

A third significant turning point in the marital career will come, as it does today, when the children finally leave home. The end of parenthood proves excruciating for many, particularly women who, once the children are gone, find themselves without a *raison d'être*. Even today divorces result from the failure of the couple to adapt to this traumatic break in continuity.

Among the more conventional couples of tomorrow who choose to raise their own children in the time-honored fashion, this will continue to be a particularly painful time. It will, however, strike earlier. Young people today already leave home sooner than their counterparts a generation ago. They will probably depart even earlier tomorrow. Masses of youngsters will move off, whether into trial marriage or not, in their mid-teens. Thus we may anticipate that the middle and late thirties will be another important breakpoint in the marital careers of millions. Many at that juncture will enter into their third marriage.

This third marriage will bring together two people for what could well turn out to be the longest uninterrupted stretch of matrimony in their lives—from, say, the late thirties until one of the partners dies. This may, in fact, turn out to be the only "real" marriage, the basis of the only truly durable marital relationship. During this time two mature people, presumably with well-matched interests and complementary psychological needs, and with a sense of being at comparable stages of personality development, will be able to look forward to a relationship with a decent statistical probability of enduring.

Not all these marriages will survive until death, however, for the family will still face a fourth crisis point. This will come, as it does now for so many, when one or both of the partners retires from work. The abrupt change in daily routine brought about by this development places great strain on the couple. Some couples will go the path of the post-retirement family, choosing this moment to begin the task of raising children. This may overcome for them the vacuum that so many couples now face after reaching the end of their occupational lives. (Today many women go to work when they finish raising children; tomorrow many will reverse that pattern, working first and child rearing next.) Other couples will overcome the crisis of retirement in other ways, fashioning both together a new set of habits, interests and activities. Still others will find the transition too difficult, and will simply sever their ties and enter the pool of "in-betweens"—the floating reserve of temporarily unmarried persons.

Of course, there will be some who, through luck, interpersonal skill and high intelligence, will find it possible to make long-lasting monogamous marriages work. Some will succeed, as they do today, in marrying for life and finding durable love and affection. But others will fail to make even sequential marriages endure for long. Thus some will try two or even three partners within, say, the final stage of marriage. Across the board, the average number of marriages per capita will rise—slowly but relentlessly.

Most people will probably move forward along this progression, engaging in one "conventional" temporary marriage after another. But with widespread familial experimentation in the society, the more daring or desperate will make side forays into less conventional arrangements as well, perhaps experimenting with communal life at some point, or going it alone with a child. The net result will be a rich variation in the types of marital trajectories that people will trace, a wider choice of life-patterns, an endless opportunity for novelty of experience. Certain patterns will be more common than others. But temporary marriage will be a standard feature, perhaps the dominant feature, of family life in the future.

The Demands of Freedom

A world in which marriage is temporary rather than permanent, in which family arrangements are diverse and colorful, in which homosexuals may be acceptable parents and retirees start raising children—such a world is vastly different from our own. Today all boys and girls are expected to find life-long partners. In tomorrow's world, being single will be no crime. Nor will couples be forced to remain imprisoned, as so many still are today, in marriages that have turned rancid. Divorce will be easy to arrange, so long as responsible provision is made for children. In fact, the very introduction of professional parenthood could touch off a great liberating wave of divorces by making it easier for adults to discharge their parental responsibilities without necessarily remaining in the cage of a hateful marriage. With this powerful external pressure removed, those who stay together would be those who wish to stay together, those for whom marriage is actively fulfilling—those, in short, who are in love.

We are also likely to see, under this looser, more variegated family system, many more marriages involving partners of unequal age. Increasingly, older men will marry young girls or vice versa. What will count will not be chronological age, but complementary values and interests and, above all, the level of personal development. To put it another way, partners will be interested not in age, but in stage.

Children in this super-industrial society will grow up with an ever enlarging circle of what might be called "semi-siblings"—a whole clan of boys and girls brought into the world by their successive sets of parents. What becomes of such "aggregate" families will be fascinating to observe. Semi-sibs may turn out to be like cousins, today. They may help one another professionally or in time of need. But they will also present the society with novel problems. Should semi-sibs marry, for example?

Surely, the whole relationship of the child to the family will be dramatically altered. Except perhaps in communal groupings, the family will lose what little remains of its power to transmit values to the younger generation. This will further accelerate the pace of change and intensify the problems that go with it.

Looming over all such changes, however, and even dwarfing them in significance is something far more subtle. Seldom discussed, there is a hidden rhythm in human affairs that until now has served as one of the key stabilizing forces in society: the family cycle.

We begin as children; we mature; we leave the parental nest; we give birth to children who, in turn, grow up, leave and begin the process all over again. This cycle has been operating so long, so automatically, and with such implacable regularity, that men have taken it for granted. It is part of the human landscape. Long before they reach puberty, children learn the part they are expected to play in keeping this great cycle turning. This predictable succession of family events has provided all men, of whatever tribe or society, with a sense of continuity, a place in the temporal scheme of things. The family cycle has been one of the sanity-preserving constants in human existence.

Today this cycle is accelerating. We grow up sooner, leave home sooner, marry sooner, have children sooner. We space them more closely together and complete the period of parenthood more quickly. In the words of Dr. Bernice Neugarten, a University of Chicago specialist on family development, "The trend is toward a more rapid rhythm of events through most of the family cycle."

But if industrialism, with its faster pace of life, has accelerated the family cycle, super-industrialism now threatens to smash it altogether. With the fantasies that the birth scientists are hammering into reality, with the colorful familial experimentation that innovative minorities will perform, with the likely development of such institutions as professional parenthood, with the increasing movement toward temporary and serial marriage, we shall not merely run the cycle more rapidly; we shall introduce irregularity, suspense, unpredictability—in a word, novelty —into what was once as regular and certain as the seasons.

When a "mother" can compress the process of birth into a brief visit to an embryo emporium, when by transferring embryos from womb to womb we can destroy even the ancient certainty that child bearing took nine months, children will grow up into a world in which the family cycle, once so smooth and sure, will be jerkily arhythmic. Another crucial stabilizer will have been removed from the wreckage of the old order, another pillar of sanity broken.

There is, of course, nothing inevitable about the developments traced in the preceding pages. We have it in our power to shape change. We may choose one future over another. We cannot, however, maintain the past. In our family forms, as in our economics, science, technology and social relationships, we shall be forced to deal with the new.

The Super-industrial Revolution will liberate men from many of the barbarisms that grew out of the restrictive, relatively choiceless family patterns of the past and present. It will offer to each a degree of freedom hitherto unknown. But it will exact a steep price for that freedom.

As we hurtle into tomorrow, millions of ordinary men and women will face emotion-packed options so unfamiliar, so untested, that past experience will offer little clue to wisdom. In their family ties, as in all other aspects of their lives, they will be compelled to cope not merely with transience, but with the added problem of novelty as well.

Thus, in matters both large and small, in the most public of conflicts and the most private of conditions, the balance between routine and non-routine, predictable and non-predictable, the known and the unknown, will be altered. The novelty ratio will rise.

In such an environment, fast-changing and unfamiliar, we shall be forced, as we wend our way through life, to make our personal choices from a diverse array of options. And it is to the third central characteristic of tomorrow, *diversity*, that we must now turn. For it is the final convergence of these three factors—transience, novelty and diversity—that sets the stage for the historic crisis of adaptation. . .

7 FEMININITY: 2000

by Carol Rinzler

AT FIVE O'CLOCK in the afternoon of January 2, 2000, Nora Jones-Cohen, twenty-five and in her second year as a lawyer with the venerable firm of Abzug, Chisholm & Holtzman, throws several briefs into her Vuitton briefcase (some things will endure) and takes the helitrain up from Forty-second and Third to her one-bedroom apartment on East Sixty-first Street. She wearily taps the heat-sensitive patternboard of her apartment door with her index finger: one short, two long, three short, one long, one short, one long. Nobody carries keys anymore—and robberies are infrequent—but, since the night when she came home bombed at two in the morning and struggled for two hours unable to remember any combination other than that to her parents' brownstone, she has carried the combination in code right next to her Completecreditcard (the only credit card she, or anyone for that matter, carries).

The door closes gently behind her and she goes to the bar-console in the living room, sets the controls for vodka-martini-straight-up-with-a-twist-on-the-side (some things never change) and pushes a button. With her drinks, the console is also programmed to deliver three pills: weight control, beauty-complex I, and brain stimulator.

Nora eschews tranquilizers, mood elevators and hallucinogens, and so it isn't surprising that she settles down into her overstuffed D/R sofa (an antique inherited from her grandmother) feeling somewhat depressed. It has been a long day.

This is a new year, a new millennium . . . and did she begin it well by telling George on New Year's Eve that she didn't want to consider Marriage I? Perhaps she is heading for a lonely life. After all, she certainly likes him; they get on awfully well in bed—that is, since she'd gotten him to attend sex-counseling with her—and at age twenty-eight George shows every sign of rising to the top of his field—advertising, with the Wells & Trahey agency. They are both not only passionately involved in their careers, but they also share outside interests: Mozart, Midler (now middle-aged and still electrically vital) and Doc Watson (whose music has become wildly popular twenty-six years after his death); horseback riding, sky-diving and ultra-violet apartment gardening; antiquing and traveling (and when they'd gone off for that long weekend to the Moon, there was no question that they were compatible under the worst circumstances—for three days, the air conditioning in their room was off and the depressurization was down to sixty percent).

Still, at the risk of loneliness, she has no intention of getting seriously involved in a "cemented" relationship. At this point, all that truly consumes her is cementing her career, and that's what she'll concentrate on for the next several months. Perhaps it will be best for the two of them if they wait. (An old cliché that Nora rather likes.)

Enough philosophizing; it's been a long day. Nora settles down to more practical matters. Like hunger. She dials herself a shrimp cocktail, a rare steak, salad (with vinegar and oil on the side) and a dish of pink-bubblegum ice cream. Thank God for weight-control pills, she thinks for the ten-thousandth time. Until they'd come along five years ago, she'd had to fight an awful tendency to run ten pounds overweight.

Too bad that the console isn't programmed for anything other than steak; she's getting very bored with it. But programs cost money and she'd rather save it for trip or to buy more *Ms.* Magazine stock. She'd bought in last year just before the news that they were going to acquire Hearst broke, and she saw it triple in five months.

While waiting for dinner, Nora sits down to read the new issue of *Vogue*. Apparently, designers have rediscovered the Seventies, and the clothes are loose and flowing, softly colored and tend to run to ruffles and long skirts. This definitely appeals to the romantic in Nora, who's awfully sick of the straight, practical lines so prevalent for the last five or so years. And she's really had it with vinyl, ultrasuede and sisal. There is also a feature on the "one-piece"—a new method of dressing up in only a single piece of fabric that need not be sewn: the trick, the art in fact, is in knotting, and the variety of styles is practically infinite. Both men and women are able to use the "one-piece," and the *Vogue* feature presents the Kennedys modeling—Senator John F. Kennedy, Jr. is shown posing in some undeniably masculine, conservative styles, and Caroline is quoted as saying that even her mother is taken with the notion.

In this mood, Nora decides now is as good a time as any to give the house the three-weeks-overdue, thorough monthly cleaning. She goes to the service board in the kitchen and starts to program the buttons that will remove all dust from the house, defrost the refrgerator, scour the bathtub, clean the medicine chest, linen closet and cabinets. While the surfaces are being dusted, Nora hangs up all her clothes, puts books back on their shelves, unpacks laundry and makes her bed. Within two hours all is neat and thoroughly clean, and Nora feels terrific. She only wishes she could get it together to do this once a month. She only wishes she had a maid.

At eleven o'clock, Nora removes her make-up with Revlon's "facial duster" (which works on the simple principle of the vacuum cleaner, and also includes a moisturizer), jumps into the sauna/shower and then watches a bit of the Mason Reese Tonight Show on the life-size TV screen in her bedroom. At midnight, twenty-five-year-old Nora Jones-Cohen turns off TV and lights, flips on the vibrator and falls asleep.

President, publisher, neurosurgeon, tree surgeon, senator or housewife, no matter how the employment situation may have improved in twenty-five years most of us will still be wondering, around four o'clock, what button we will push on the kitchen console to deliver up dinner; most of us will still be considering, around eleven o'clock in the morning, whether we should grab a sandwich and buzz over to Saks to pick up a new number for Friday night; most of us will still be trying to think of someone we know on the board of Happy Hours Nursery School who can get our two-year-old in; most of us will still be struggling with the problem of whether we should spay the dog, save the marriage, shorten the skirt or say "yes" to the proposition. More will be the same than will be different.

Yet the old definitions of femininity are already eroding, as a career becomes an increasingly viable option, and the feminine functions of housewifing and mothering are shared more and more by husbands and fathers. There will always be women who value their ability to make chocolate mousse and sew their own clothes; but I think that for the mass of educated, middle-class women, far less loss or guilt will be felt because of an absence of some domestic ability, and since it will simply be less onerous, because of technological developments, to get the stupid little encumbrances of life—meals, housework, mending clothes—out of the way, far less of ourselves and our satisfaction with ourselves will be invested in it.

The definition of femininity that we will accept in the year 2000, will be, I hope simply: the quality of functioning as, and liking oneself as, a woman. The definition of "femininity" will be, I hope, much closer to the definition of "humanity." But no one can possibly be brought up asexual. The two-hundred-pound crane operator who enters weight-lifting contests in her spare time can be every bit as feminine as the contented housewife whose highest intellectual achievement is to design her own needlepoint. I do think that to like ourselves as women we must have some happy combined emotional and sexual commerce with men—we must find some happiness and satisfaction in loving and being loved by a man.

I realize that in structuring such a definition of femininity, I am denying possession of that quality to homosexual women and to women who have chosen to read any sort of love relationship with men out of their lives. But if one cannot call lesbians feminine, neither can one assume that they are any less content or less ecstatic, or less miserable, than heterosexual women.

Nor am I saying that it is necessarily better to be feminine or to be dependent on men for emotional satisfaction. Is there one of us who has not, at the end of a devastating love affair or in the midst of an intolerable marriage or even as adolescents waiting for the phone to ring, condemned the male sex, wished that she could do without them, sworn never to get involved again? And yet, most of us, if we are honest with ourselves, do not feel entirely satisfied with life—no matter how well things may be going in other areas—unless we are in some facet, however subtle, of the state of love. What I think we shall get away from is the extremity of our dependency on love, and its importance in defining ourselves as "feminine."

We will, I think, have some outside help from society: with improvement in jobs for women, more personal satisfaction will be invested in work. We simply won't *need* love so much to get it off, as it were. Similarly, sexual freedom, which most of us over thirty cannot quite seem to get the hang of, should rest rather more lightly on the shoulders (or pelvises) of our daughters. (I confess that I harbor a small, hopeful suspicion that the gung-ho sexuality of the Sixties may settle down to a point of balance; I really can't face up to the idea of my daughter having a different partner every night.) In any case, growing up without ever having thought of abortion as anything other than an inconvenience should make a world of difference.

Of course, there will always be those of us who will cling to the notion of loving and being loved by a man, being defined by him, building a life around him and children. And why ever should the option be closed? In twenty-five years, though, I think that young women will be no more driven to that excessive dependency than are today's young men; that the balance for those women will be considerably healthier. Those of us who are still carrying the accretions of being raised in the Forties or Fifties have every reason to hope we will be able to realize the importance of placing love somewhat lower in the order of priorities.

And what will become of the expressions of femininity—the flirting, the posturing, the little frills that we learned to present so well for much of our adult lives and have spent the last five years unlearning? I think they will come back—are coming back and probably should come back because they're fun. But, again, in a far more balanced way. If we are still capable of dealing with men as women when we wish to, we are now capable of dealing with men as people, which we were previously rarely able to. Beginning relationships with men on a basis of mutual respect has, I think, yet another advantage. It increases the possibility of a love or a marriage that has its grounding in respect and I do not think anyone could wish for more than that.

2

*On Her Working
Choices and Rights*

8 WAGES OF WRATH: WOMAN'S RELATIONSHIPS IN THE WORKING WORLD

by Nora Sayre

THERE WAS OFTEN SOMEONE CRYING in the ladies' room. Sobs or gasps (and sometimes retches) came jerking out of those grim cabinets, while others swiftly swallowed pills, choked, sighed, and recombed their hair—to prolong that moment known as "away from your desk." Due to some spasm of corporate economy, there were no towels of any kind, so we had to dry our hands on thin, dissolving toilet paper. My sense-memory of working at one of New York's choicest women's magazines has always been peeling those wet wisps of paper from my palms and fingers, as the notes of weeping receded down the hallway, while I reluctantly walked back to my office, bracing myself for a fresh burst of violence —plus collective confusion, paranoia, and fatigue. Recently, I admitted to a former colleague that the experience was the only one in my life which seems just as bad in retrospect as it did at the time. "Even worse," she said, in accents of awe.

My job was a good one. (Veterans had warned me not to take it, but I'd shrugged off their sordid accounts as exaggerations.) Being in the features department meant seeing plays and movies, reading some of the season's best books, interviewing luminaries, investigating the development of a new museum or Italian architecture or Scandinavian design, and . . . writing. But each day's ferocity was distilled from working for the kind of person who mistakes sadism for authority, or hysteria for energy. Male or female, these quite classical bone-crunchers differ only in their compulsion to disembowel their own—or the opposite—sex. The identifying trait is to swell like a frog with rage; veins in the throat and forehead often stand out thickly. The nose looks as though it may burst. (As in some other firms, the company-founder believed that employees work best when they are extremely nervous. Hence there should be one ogre in every department. But the hours and days lost in illness should have conveyed the waste in productivity. Quite a few on the staff automatically spent their weekends in bed.) At any rate, our employer zapped our vitals by being (quite triumphantly) unable to give directions: to merely say what she wanted us to do. Unfortunately, some women still lack this ability: it's a deficiency of upbringing and education, which determines that women shouldn't be executives. But anger accelerates from not being understood: the flush of frenzy reveals the frustration of making almost no sense at all. An average morning could begin with the furious question:

"*What* are you *doing* here?"

"Why . . . I just came to work."

"You're not supposed to *be* here! You know perfectly well that you should be down . . . down . . . *down* there . . . Down there! Now!"

"Down?"

"Yes, you're interviewing what's his name, what's-his-name . . . *What's* his *name?*"

"I don't know." (Evidently, an appointment has been made without one's knowledge. This happens constantly. Explanations are useless.) "Nobody told me."

"They *did.* I *did.* Why are you standing there? You think you're a *guest* in this department?"

"Where am I supposed to be?" (Patience and cunning.)

"You know! You know! You know *perfectly* well! Get on *down* there . . . How can you? And Danes are always so punctual. And Oliver's on the roof."

Oliver is an eminent photographer, but who's the Dane on the roof? Ten more minutes of ardent detective work extract a reference to the Congo. So if Danish means Swedish—sometimes it means German around here—the victim may be Dag Hammarskjöld, since the UN is downtown from this office. A photographic session on the roof? A heart-bursting race to the UN and into the building and up in the elevator reveals what tourists often learn: the guards don't want you to go on the roof. No trace of Oliver. Next, a conference with the dignitary's secretary, who gently explains that no such appointment was ever made, "And besides, he's in Geneva/ at a conference/dead/retired a year ago." A call to Oliver confirms some of these regretable facts, but it's crucial to check the first assumption carefully.

"You mean you never heard a word about this?"

"*No.*"

"You're sure?"

"Very sure. And I'm actually on vacation—as they *ought to know*. I only came in town to look for a tie."

Back to the office, armored for the abuse which no rational defense can forestall. It will be one's own fault that the great man was croaked or absent, or that no one ever called him. Still, there's a hideous suspicion: should it have been the Stock Exchange? Maybe the Aquarium. One clings to a few securities in life: it can't be the Guggenheim, that's uptown.

Some experts believe that a spell in a women's office is an inevitable chapter in most young women's lives: a bath of fire that many professionals must pass through. Of course there are more writing or editing jobs open to women in this area than in the news or feature magazines which still imply that women can't write because their biological clocks are full of fudge, or because "they can't think conceptually." But almost every young woman I've met who's served on an all-female staff has found it just as mangling as I did. From the initial astonishment of the application form, which inquired, "Have you ever tried to overthrow the American government?" (no, but I'd love to), to the first day's intimate physical ("Have you ever had a miscarriage?"), to being savagely called *"Darling"* and *"Sweetie"* (and Pam and Jane and Doris) because one's name was punctually forgotten, dignity dissolved and the intestines howled.

It was useless to fight the employer—or to refuse to fight. Once, as I waited silently for a bottomless tantrum to subside, my editor flung herself hard against her desk—not quite cracking a rib, as I'd hoped—and yelled, "Don't-just-stand-there-being-*polite!*" Colleagues wove a landing net of sympathy; when office morale is in rags, there are gusts of desperate jokes and nervous laughter as partners in suffering try to cheer each other. Since then, I've always measured the health of a department or an organization by the character of its humor: compulsive clowning or rapid, forlorn gags mean that the staff is reduced to childishness in secret defiance of a loathed parent figure. Usually, in offices where demoralization thrives, the employee is treated as a (good or bad) child.

Quite a few of my nicest colleagues had grim reasons for needing the money which shackled them to the magazine: expensive divorces, hospital bills, sick parents or children, drunk or unemployable husbands. So some felt trapped. (And it's still not acknowledged that most women don't work for fun, any more than men do.) As in the worst offices, many revealed too much about their personal problems, which made it awkward to deal with them professionally later: How can you ask me to check those proofs when you know I've just had an abortion/lost my lover/been kicked out by my shrink? Some have since remarked that the office was destructive to their private lives: shredded nerves and humiliations made them testy and dyspeptic with their families or their boyfriends; the stark self-control needed on the job meant overreaction to irritations at home. And, while men have long been excused for anger after "a bad day at the office," no such understanding has yet been granted to women.

Meanwhile, we all paid for the days when those above us were ripping one another apart. As they reveled in the mutual humbling process, we were lacerated by their brawls about the approach to Degas, vermeil, Sophia Loren, or Robbe-Grillet. (We'd keep rewriting our captions while each editor gleefully condemned the adjectives which had been requested by the others. Among enemies, the loser could become a stretcher-case: "Read this for me, uh, sweetie, my mind's all gone today"—which was true.) Reshaping senior colleagues' work was sometimes part of the freshman hazing system: during my first week, I wrestled with an older editor's account of her trip to Moscow. My favorite sentence was: "If you care about thickness, take Nescafé and towels."

Reeling out of the office, detailing my horrendous days to friends, I was rewarded by cascades of male laughter. While I protested that it wasn't just a barrel of yuks—that in fact, my office mirrored many of the degrading experiences that we'd heard from men in advertising and news magazines or from those who worked for Lyndon Johnson—some of my male schoolmates startled me by repeating how much they approved of my job: more so than of the straight reporting and reviewing I'd previously done. They insisted that my position was glamorous, even though I told them it was tacky and brutalizing. And some men seemed rather relieved that I was now out of their own field: of valid writing. Most asked eagerly if there were lots of lesbians on the staff. I said I didn't know, and anyway, the dump was desexing for everyone. They seemed disappointed about the lesbians, but urged me to stick with the job: "It must be good discipline—mustn't it?"

Over the decades, the magazine has published many fine articles and stories, as anthologies can prove. However, the staff-written text is adored by satirists, and pieces by the non-famous were often grotesquely restyled for "reader appeal." (I once spent a hilarious two hours helping a writer—whose essay I'd commissioned—to insert lots of clichés and repetitions, so that the editors would cut them without mutilating the rest of the piece. It worked beautifully.) As with many other publications, the stylistic level had to sink when fashion magazines ceased to be aimed at the consumers, and were directed at the manufacturers—actually, written to attract and satisfy the advertisers.

The attitude toward the readers mingled flattery with contempt. The technique was to tickle their vanity by suggesting that they were bright—to pretend to assume that they were actually interested in Cocteau, Zen, the paintings of Emil Nolde, Milan's Piccolo Teatro, or the works of Marguerite Duras. However, they were expected to be stupid. Every reference had to be explained: Nixon or Wilde could not be mentioned without a first name and an identification slip. Each idea had to be pitched down to basement level, even though the language was contorted. "Ideas" indeed were frantically sought: the editors kept lists of titles in hopes that someone would invent a fitting topic. One author, offered the title "What To Use Instead Of Money," finally wrote an essay on the joys of the five senses.

Throughout, a brief snort of great works of art was considered sufficient for the subscribers, who were usually addressed as "You" ("You and the Atom," "You and Picasso"), in order to plug them into a subject that was presumably baffling for them. Meanwhile, art was mainly advertised through personalities—by portraits and paragraphs that skimpily summarized the work and underlined the life style of the practitioner. "Find a phrase for it!": the habit of *reductio ad absurdum* meant trying to tease language into little headlines—the slogan mentality which tends to curdle the readers' minds. Here, I should hastily add that I like fashion magazines; looking at pictures of clothes is good for the soul, and a wild text bestows a pleasurable jolt. But having to package poetry and sculpture and snips of history as though they were blouses or scarves or shoes felt like a binge of perversion—especially if the readers were such idiots as we were told. Moreover, they had to be protected: I was once ordered to describe a movie about a black man and a white woman as "a sensitive account of an unhappy love affair."

But the clanking irony was that our fat and fatuous paragraphs were seriously regarded as *good writing*. At first, I'd (wrongly) imagined that parodying the magazine's style would produce what was required. But we were made to rewrite until the final word salad would have shamed an autistic child. The demand for "passionate" copy meant that we had to use words like "ebullient," "irrepressible," and "kicky" as often as possible. "Swerve," "veer," "sinewy," and "slithery" kept our pages effervescent—another favorite. "Implacable" also gained points, but I never knew why. Ideally, personalities were "amusing," or, failing that, "amusable"—which was even applied to Queen Sirikit of Thailand. Wit and wisdom often went together. Three adjectives were the norm for characterization: thus, "bubbling, valiant, enduring" (an octogenarian actress), "austere, important, young" (Jasper Johns), "tiny, mercurial, young" (Elizabeth Ashley), "witty, beautiful, stubborn" (Mrs. Patrick Campbell). Marianne Moore was "gentle but not sloppy," Cornelius Ryan was "a gentle, bursting man," in contrast to "a bouncy, friendly, internationally famous astronomer." Only David Merrick won the space race: "a soft-spoken, good-looking, stage-struck, enterprising, single-minded, aggressive, rattrap-minded lawyer."

Novels were harder to nail neatly: "revolting, horrifying, funny" *(Naked Lunch)*, or "a big, laughing, hoaxy book" *(Catch 22)*, unless you could rise to the inspiration of describing Sybille Bedford's *A Favorite Of The Gods* as "crisp and unsatisfying, like eating Cracker Jacks in bed." Once, praising an exceptional first novel, I found that none of my tributes were acceptable to my editor until I despairingly invented the phrase, "the cool bloom of his style." It took hours to recompose a finally approved passage like this one: "A loving grandmother with ash-blond-grayish hair and eyes the color of hazlenuts, she is right now finishing some works in mechanics and probability theory ... As a scientist and a woman, she has a life rich in great experiences and full of rewards." And it's not easy to arrive at: "His intellect is all in his cuticle where it hurts."

Today, as I sift through recent issues of the magazine, I'm feverishly grateful that I didn't have to write about "the feeling of relief at storing away the 'sixties and jouncing into the 'seventies," or refer to "the clangour of the Vietnam war," or describe a TV series as "marvelous, chatty, a window opened by a man whose mind is an orchard of plums."

Naturally, the solution to a maiming job is to leave it, as many of us did. (It took less than a month to realize that a good salary makes no amends for deploring your work.) But several ugly questions lurch out of the closet of experience. First: what (the devil) were we giving women to read? The magazine showed them marvelous clothes and some magnificent photographs. But our features department betrayed a bale of potentially good material. The well-educated may ignore the kiss-off approach to culture, but it's disturbing to think of its effect on those whose backgrounds are meager—the many starvelings whom this country schools so badly. Second: why are some women so horrible to women? In my office, the old knee-jerk answers of envy and competition didn't apply: the (already successful) tyrants weren't imperiled by those whom they reduced to hamburger. Perhaps the mere guilt of being female—fighting the instincts of inferiority—makes certain women despise others and want to punish them. Perhaps the yelling and threatening was merely a tradition of behavior—the way some women think that they should treat one another. Finally, one has to rehash the familiar fact that so much of our whole office system functions abominably. Granted that many departments are structured to make people dislike each other and to prevent work from being done, all that uproar seems like part of our rotting national heritage: toiling without questioning, accepting the product as the same old sausage comes grinding out of the exhaust.

Postscript, 1974: When I wrote this essay in 1970, I was evoking the bad old days of the early Sixties—long before most consciousnesses were raised. And of course I was examining a rather extreme situation: a magazine that was already losing its purpose and its power. But I've never seen women act this way in any other professional context. Hence it was my intention to shame the employers who positively encouraged women to behave badly toward one another. Also, plenty of men can recognize the habits of large corporations, which approve of games and in-fighting within the staff: what passes for healthy competition merely wastes time and ruins stomachs. And that kind of thinking could become as obsolete as many of the magazines and garments and technologies that we know now.

Naturally, the question of how women treat other women has been as crucial to feminists as how women are treated by men or by society. Due to the women's movement, women's relationships in offices have already altered enormously: we've all appreciated the sense of mutual support, of professional problems shared, which was hardly abundant some ten years ago. In numerous offices, the women's groups that have put pressure on management to hire and promote more women have enabled a number of us to advance in a way that we owe quite directly to other women.

Yet we still haven't fully coped with the fact that some women were raised and trained to be hostile toward others. The notion that women are natural enemies is still pleasing to many men—and women who put down their own sex are thought more loyal to men. Also, a few women continue to flatter their reactionary employers by deriding the questions of equality—by insisting that women who don't advance professionally are simply lacking in talent or skill.

In the next twenty-five years, when everyone will have to battle all the harder for survival, to earn a living, simply to hold a job, we can't quite expect that human nature will become celestial. But since many women professionals' ways of dealing with one another have improved so greatly in the last few years, it seems reasonable to be very optimistic about the way we'll be working with each other in the year 2000.

9 THE IMPACT OF THE MID-TWENTIETH CENTURY MOVEMENT FOR SEX EQUALITY IN EMPLOYMENT ON THREE CONTEMPORARY ECONOMIC INSTITUTIONS*

by Caroline Bird

SOME OF MY FELLOW-HISTORIANS here may be wondering why I have chosen to resurrect the sex equality movement of the late 1960s. Its objectives have been so fully realized in the past ten years, and the arguments on both sides sound so irrational today, that most serious students of history have relegated the whole episode to antiquarians and connoisseurs of the near past. My own interest may, indeed, seem old-fashioned to professional historians of the 21st century who can no longer afford the leisurely study of forgotten causes that was possible as recently as forty years ago.

I address myself to the now-forgotten "Women's Liberation Movement," only because I believe that the contemporary scene, and particularly the speed and volatility of change which is its most puzzling characteristic, owes much more to "Women's Lib," as it was pejoratively called, than has been generally recognized. Indeed, the very foolishness of the arguments advanced by otherwise intellectually-respectable oppon-

* A paper presented at the 2001 Annual Meeting of the American Historical Association.

ents of the movement in the 1960s proves how well these opponents and the established authorities recognized that true sex equality in employment would undermine the whole fabric of existing economic and social relationships.

The opponents were right. The series of fundamental economic reforms which have assured every citizen freedom of employment choice and, in the process, radically altered not only the system of producing and distributing goods and services but also the kinds of goods and services available were inevitable once our society attempted to put into practice the noble and long-held ideal of equality of opportunity.

It is easy to see, in retrospect, that "equality of opportunity" was as threatening as Christianity to the old social order, especially to the family, which enforced that social order. It is more instructive to trace exactly how the old system was undermined. In this paper I shall consider the impact of the campaign for sex equality in employment on three contemporary institutions conspicuously absent when the National Organization for Women was founded in 1967. They are:

1. The National Employment Exchange System set up in 1979, which now assures freedom of occupational choice for all those who wish to supplement their subsistence income with paid employment.

2. The Neighborhood Play Group System set up in 1977, which offers every person sixteen years of age and over an opportunity to spend as much time as desired at hours of his or her own choosing with children resident nearby.

3. The Minimum Income Security System inaugurated when the Internal Revenue Service absorbed the welfare system in 1980, under which every resident is assured subsistence income payable in antitaxes for those whose incomes fall short of the legally established minimum.

The open system of production and consumption seems so obvious now, that it is difficult to trace it to sex equality. Blacks and the non-academic were just as oppressed as women, and the logic of equality of opportunity for them was just as threatening to the old coercive society. Yet the old regime managed to survive the Civil Rights Movement for race equality by opening the doors to a few leaders of these segregated minorities and coopting the rest. The middle-aged male WASPs who operated the economic system in their own interest found their own women a more formidable obstacle.

This doesn't mean that "Women's Lib" was the only force which established the civil right to a job of one's own choosing—a civil right now held as sacred as the right to a sex life of one's own choosing.

Indeed, it may come as a surprise to younger members of this audience to learn that neither of these freedoms was regarded as a civil right as recently as the 1950s. I hope only to show that it was the demand of women for sex equality that overturned the coercive economy and speeded establishment of a distribution system insuring equality of *results*.

Before spelling out how sex equality in employment doomed paycheck slavery, let us recall some of the truly oppressive conditions which prevailed within the memory of people still alive. Accustomed as we now are to rapid social change, it will probably come as a surprise to many of you to learn that I myself have not only seen an operating time-clock, but actually "punched" one myself when I worked briefly in a factory one summer during college. And while I never saw classified ad columns headed "Help Wanted, Colored" and "Help Wanted, White," I once myself actually looked for a job in a classified column headed "Help Wanted, Male."

Although posting jobs on the basis of sex sounds merely silly, it is, and even in my youth was, illegal. Discrimination in employment on the basis of race and sex was formally outlawed in 1964, discrimination on the basis of age between forty and sixty-five in 1967, and on the basis of educational status by a series of landmark court decisions beginning with *Griggs vs. Duke Power* in 1971. The minimum age laws barring or "protecting" young people from employment and *requiring* school attendance were still on the books of many states until early in the 1980s. Equal opportunity laws were needed (and when enacted widely flouted) because of a universal belief that employers should consider a job applicant's sex. It was not so much that women were openly turned away when they applied for one of the high-paying "men's jobs"—although that happened. Rather, women were afraid of applying because they were brought up to believe that a man's job would make a woman *sexually* unattractive to men, and since marriage was not only a vocation, but the vocation with the highest pay potential open to women, the risk of repelling men was economic as well as personal. This sounds muddled, but it was perfectly logical when you recall that before the passage of the Equal Rights Amendment the economic responsibility of mates was a one-way street: husbands were legally liable for the support of able-bodied wives, while wives were not generally required to support husbands, even if the husbands were disabled. Before the minimum income guarantees, these support responsibilities were, of course, very important to both sexes.

Imagine a world in which you could reliably guess the sex of everyone on the basis of occupation. In 1970, for instance, all but two percent of engineers and all but eleven percent of physicians were male. An unknown electrician could confidently be referred to as "he," and so could any person known to be a truck driver, dentist, fireman, merchant marine officer, pilot, or university president. Congresswomen were so rare that members of Congress didn't know whether to call Martha Griffiths, the architect of the Equal Rights Amendment "gentle lady" or "gentlewoman" when they would have referred to a male as "gentleman." But if some jobs were exclusively male, others were the province of females. A kindergarten teacher, flight attendant, or nurse could be referred to as "she" and so could the many workers engaged in producing, transmitting, and storing the voluminous paper records which lawyers continued to demand long after electronic information systems were perfected.

For those who care, the Census Bureau continues to publish the sex breakdown of workers in each occupation, and it is not 50/50 for each job classification. The overwhelming majority of physicians are now female, but only a third of the engineers. Historical influences affect today's occupational sex ratios. Thus women monopolize the repair of small electrical appliances, an occupation to which they were attracted during the early days of equal employment opportunity because women were widely believed to excel in a competence labeled "finger dexterity," and they dominate local bus driving because their safety record warranted lower insurance rates for women back when sex was regarded as legitimate actuarial basis for rate-making. These are relics of the widespread rationalization of sex segregation in employment.

Many of these rationalizations were taken quite seriously forty years ago, when sex was regarded as an important predictor of job performance. Sex labelling created interesting anomalies. At a time when almost all hospital nurses were females, males were preferred in psychiatric wards, on the theory that the mentally ill were potentially violent and required male muscular strength to control, even though those engaged in this work knew from personal observation that the mentally ill were seldom violent and were more easily controlled by suggestion than force when they were.

Similarly, the theory that women cannot deal with violence was the basis on which women were long excluded from police forces, or assigned to special, "safe" duty until the equal employment opportunity laws forced police departments to hire them. It was not until women riot control specialists protected Congress from a surprise attack of armed vigilantes opposing the Income Security System in 1980 that women policemen were routinely assigned to deal with dangerous situations. We now know, of course, that the gender of a policeman does not matter one way or another. I cite this reversal merely to show that the erroneous belief that the sex of a person makes a difference in his or her effectiveness was harder to eradicate than the particular difference gender was supposed to make in any specific situation.

The obsession with gender led to many ludricous demands. Laughable as it now seems, a 50/50 breakdown between men and women in every occupation was once regarded as evidence of sex equality in employment, if not its actual goal. During the 1970s an attempt was made to require the larger corporations to promise a certain proportion of jobs to women and blacks; the sexism and racism implicit in these demands were overlooked by the reformers, because objections to the "quota system" came primarily from those who were trying to keep the best jobs for males and whites. Like so many other hard-fought issues, the debate on the quota system was never resolved, but sidetracked by more urgent issues.

During the late 1970s, when equal pay for equal work became the rule, sizable industries were threatened by the defection of women who had accepted modest wages simply because they had to earn money and had been denied access to better-paying work. Young women simply refused to work at the pay offered for "women's jobs." While some of the men displaced by women "invading" men's jobs were forced to take these menial, deadend positions, the initial impact was a labor "shortage" during rising unemployment. By 1978, the United States was experiencing something new to economists: a passive, unorganized strike against the prevailing conditions of work.

It became suddenly and painfully obvious that wages would have to rise in order to maintain services such as telephone information, nursery schools, itemized billing, circulating libraries, bedside hospital care, and cash transactions in retail stores. Shortages and lapses of service alerted even the simplest-minded to the relationship between amenities taken for granted and the quasi-slave labor of women.

It soon became obvious that equal pay for equal work eliminated the goods and services which could not be provided at truly competitive wage scales.

It used to be possible to get someone else to bring your food to you and clean up the dishes after you were through eating in a public restaurant. You sat down at a table, waited until a young woman in a specially designed apron appeared, told her what you wanted to eat, and eventually she brought it. For this service you not only paid a higher price for the food itself, but left a "tip" or pile of small change equivalent to fifteen percent of the total bill for the "waitress." Until the 1960s, very high-priced restaurants employed only males, and the rule, towards the end at least, was that the tip for a "waiter" was always in folding money rather than silver. (The last waiter collapsed at his post in 1975 at the age of 91, leaving an estate of $475,000. The last genuine waitress retired recently from a Schrafft's restaurant operated as a historical exhibit by the Smithsonian Institution in Washington.)

More basic and more serious has been the virtual disappearance of an occupation which employed more than three million women at the Census of 1970. This is the job of "stenographer–secretary." Women denied the opportunity to make decisions in business frequently chose to attach themselves to men who did make decisions. They were called "secretaries," and there were so many highly educated women in this situation (educators welcomed women as college students long before employers welcomed them in professional capacities) that the lowliest middle manager could afford his own "girl." These office servants took down a man's dictation in shorthand, typed his letters, filed his papers, answered his phone, welcomed his visitors, and performed the gamut of personal services—including general emotional reassurance—expected of Nineteenth-Century butlers to the British landed gentry. At the Census of 2000, while some several million women called themselves secretaries, only a few thousand persons reported their occupation as "secretary." Many of these were, of course, males, and all of them commanded salaries so elevated that only a handful of business and government leaders could afford their services.

The end of the secretarial job came much more quickly than expected. Equal employment opportunities speeded adoption of contemporary electronic systems of data handling, removing the dictation and filing which had long been the excuse for providing decision-making males with female office servants. For a time, secretaries and their bosses attempted to justify their relationship on the ground that "more was involved" than paperwork management. This did not last. With few exceptions, secretaries able to do the work of their bosses were unwilling to remain secretaries, and bosses attempting to replace them when they left quickly discovered that it wasn't worth having any other kind around.

Freedom of occupational choice has greatly reduced the number of persons following some occupations, but it has eliminated very few entirely. Just as there are some secretaries left, there are some "housepersons," as the Census category has been renamed. More than half the married women of 1970 reported themselves "housewives"; at the Census of 2000, two percent of persons over sixteen said they were "housepersons," about the same proportion as reported themselves farmers. These "housepersons" were almost all women who perpetuated the early Twentieth-Century practice of designating the wife as a full-time unpaid home servant by taking employment with a husband who could satisfy the Internal Revenue Service that a standard of consumption more elaborate than he could maintain unaided was a deductible business expense in his profession. These deductions have, as you know, been under challenge. IRS is a pocket of survivors of the old regime and has been slow to close this loophole.

The argument which deterred women from demanding sex equality in employment was that it would force women to work like men. This fate sounded so oppressive that polls of the 1960s and 1970s turned up more men than women favoring the Equal Rights Amendment, which equalized the obligations of spouses to support each other. By 1980, it became clear that sex equality was working the other way around: men were adopting the employment patterns of married women. Relieved of their sole responsibility to support women and children, men withdrew from paid employment for family and personal reasons, opted for volunteer community service, and demanded flexible schedules, short hours, and meaningful work. Especially after the Portable Pension Act and the

Income Security System, men switched employers and occupations for reasons that their fathers would have found whimsical if not downright irresponsible. Employers who had discriminated against women because they were "less committed" to paid employment soon found that men who did not "have" to work were even less willing than women to stick with dull, unrewarding, and dehumanizing jobs.

It is difficult in retrospect to see how anyone was willing to stand for the working conditions of the 1950s and 1960s—difficult unless you recall the longer perspective of history which includes the institution of galley slavery in classical times. Suffice it to say that the stick has always been the main reliance of work discipline. Indeed, it was counted a great humanitarian advance when the actual flogging stick was replaced by the threat of starvation and finally of social ostracism.

When men had to support women in order to enjoy sexual relations, they sold a part of their lives—normally five eight-hour shifts a week—for the money required to support themselves and "their" women and children. Working hours were "company time," and employers regulated what employees did on it more precisely than slaveholders on some early Nineteenth-Century Southern plantations. Before the 1970s, workers on company time were supposed to confine their conversation to company business unless an extraordinary personal emergency, such as death or serious illness in the family, intervened. They were not supposed to move from their work stations and, sometimes, permission had to be obtained to visit the toilet.

Work was concentrated in huge workshops—great high-rise office buildings or sprawling factories organized for armies of specialized workers. Nonworkers were excluded from the workplaces, and armed guards were often posted at gates to admit only those authorized to enter. This meant that children did not see their parents work, as many now do in our smaller workshops and homes, and since there were no neighborhood play centers in the parks, children had to be cared for while their parents worked by paid so-called "babysitters," whose job was merely to "sit" with a child. The huge workshops were located centrally, so that most workers had to travel for an hour or more a day from their homes, creating huge traffic tie-ups during what was considered "leisure time" because it was not paid "company time." At the work place, workers were subject to minute regulations of speech, behavior, hair style and clothing.

Working uniforms, formal and informal, were very important in the days when a man's job determined the respect paid him (and his wife as well). Jobs were divided into "blue collar" and "white collar." A "white collar" job was one that did not involve getting dirty, and carried higher prestige even though the army of "white collar" clerks required during the last years of paper records was generally paid less than the dwindling ranks of "blue collar" craftsmen and mechanics trained to keep machinery running. The white shirt, clean every day, was a powerful status symbol, worth many dollars a week in wages to workers whose parents had worn blue collars.

For those who have never seen one, the white shirt (later subdued colors were permitted in some establishments) was a rather complicated garment made of cotton, with many seams. In order to make the surfaces smooth after each washing, handworkers had to press each part with a hot iron. Although machines were invented to do part of the work, the whole idea of the white shirt was that it required the handwork of an ironer. Ironing shirts provided paid employment for women whose husbands, if any, were unable to support them and their children.

Men who aspired to the modest respect of their neighbors had to endure this regimen of work all the years of their adult lives, typically from the age of eighteen, when most left full-time schooling, to sixty-five, when they were eligible for a Social Security pension. The normal course was for a man to work as many of his working years as possible with one employer. Especially toward the end of the old regime, employers were forced to relieve the monotony—as slaveholders had been forced to alleviate discipline—in order to get any work done at all. Two-week vacations, which were common in the 1950s, were gradually lengthened, and the number of paid holidays increased. Only women workers quit when they were tired of a job or, as more often happened, were fired because they had been assigned to seasonal or intermittent work. Before the Minimum Income law, men did not dare to quit unless they were reasonably sure of getting a comparable or better job.

Why did they put up with it? It is not fair to say that men who quit would have starved. A bewildering welter of welfare provisions provided the capability of subsistence for the unemployed, although the provisions were so complicated and obscure that only a small percentage of those eligible availed themselves of the welfare payments due them. There had been, of course, a Social Security System since the 1930s, and it was gradually extended during the 1960s and 1970s. It provided primarily a retirement pension based on the hours and earnings an individual had accrued during his working life, and the highest pensions were slightly below the minimum subsistence now available to everyone of every age and sex. However, Social Security was given out not to individuals, but to *families*. A married woman who earned all her life received no more Social Security on retirement than she might have received through her husband's Social Security account. Until late in the 1970s, the Social Security system reinforced the social coercion of men to earn. Being "out of work" was a disgrace rather than a deliberate choice of leisure, and highly paid jobs were the most respected and the easiest rather than the most unpleasant and difficult.

Equal opportunity exploded the myth that the productivity of the job depended on getting exactly the right person to do it. Even during the heyday of the "personnel man" in the labor-short 1950s, the shrewdest executives distrusted scientific selection methods. Those who recalled the performance of untrained workers in World War II suspected that the conditions of work, and the worker's motivation to get the job done, were far more important than anything you could tell about a candidate by looking at him, testing him, or talking with him. Equal opportunity policies put these suspicions to the test by forcing employers to give blacks, women, chicanos, high school dropouts, and candidates normally regarded as too young or too old a chance to prove themselves on the job.

So long as desirable jobs always went to middle-aged male WASPs, it was easy to fall into the error of assuming that ceremonial duties, such as presiding over committee meetings, required extraordinary qualifications, including the "right" family background. In the days before children were exposed to many different adults while learning to talk, "family background" was easily determined by differences of speech signaling the education and income of parents. Under these circumstances, the duller WASPs failed to see that they were often hired to do nothing at all.

Explosion of these myths so disorganized the job market that the Federal Government had to take over the function of matching applicants and jobs in order to avert chaos. Let us turn now to the events leading to the adoption of our present National Employment Exchange System.

The National Employment Exchange System

Equal opportunity laws went unenforced for almost a decade after they were enacted in the early 1960s. Indeed, many women agreed with employers that they were not "qualified" because they had not been allowed to get the field or executive experience required for top jobs.

The first real challenge to the personnel selection system was a Supreme Court decision of 1971 that went unnoticed for years. In *Griggs vs. Duke Power Company,* the Supreme Court decided that the Duke Power Company had no right to demand a high school diploma of applicants for the job of office boy because this requirement ruled out most black applicants without predicting competence on the job. The position of the court was that an office boy didn't have to have a high school diploma, and that the diploma was required only to screen out blacks in violation of the Civil Rights Act of 1964, which prohibited discrimination in employment on the basis of race, religion, national origin, and sex.

Personnel administrators shuddered at the sweeping Griggs doctrine. They knew that there was little proof that the many requirements they had set up to screen out applicants actually predicted competence, all other things being equal. "Validation" that males really did better than females, or whites than blacks, was not only lacking, but impossible to get until enough blacks and women were put into the jobs on an equal basis with the whites and males then occupying them. Only the largest and most vulnerable companies went to the expense of "validation" and results were so ambiguous that they quietly dropped the dubious requirements.

As the 1970s wore on, women won many suits against big companies for back pay under the equal opportunity laws, leading to massive recruitment of women in job categories dominated by men. And as women learned how to sue, women college professors denied academic promotion began to claim, in court, that the requirement of a doctoral degree for purely teaching assignments was as discriminatory as the requirement of a high school diploma for the job of office boy in some states, for fewer women than men had been admitted to graduate school and held the Ph.D. required by colleges for professional rank. A few highly publicized cases triggered a general review of hiring requirements.

Before *Griggs,* blacks and women had accepted the prevailing requirements for candidates and attempted to "qualify" by securing more special training, at their own expense, than male WASP competitors and by generally "working twice as hard" and proving themselves "twice as competent" as the candidates who "looked" right. But when the university women challenged the relevance of academic requirements for promotion and collected damages from Harvard and the University of California at Berkeley, women in the corporations began to challenge many other job requirements as well.

Competition for jobs during the Deep Depression of the late 1970s made it possible for employers to demand higher and higher qualifications from applicants. As teaching jobs dwindled, for instance, high schools could require Ph.Ds for the simplest positions. Resuming the pattern of the Depression of the 1930s, women married later and many more women college graduates applied for medical and law schools. Women denied access suspected discrimination on the basis of sex, and following *Griggs,* some of them charged that the traditional medical and legal institutes discriminated against women because they concentrated intensive day and night training during the peak child-bearing years. Couldn't medical and legal training be organized on a slower schedule, one that allowed a woman student to defer training while she had a baby? Experiments at several of the best medical schools proved that physicians trained on a slower schedule compatible with maternity were equally if not more effective than those pushed through rapidly. As a matter of fact, the *timetable* of training proved far less influential in physicians' competence than the conditions under which they practiced.

During the late 1970s Depression, candidates turned down for hiring and promotion took to the courts. After a decade of struggle and a few bruising damage awards, the most enlightened and vulnerable employers gave up the attempt to fill jobs on the basis of age or education or experience, and selected job candidates by lot or on a "first come, first hired" basis. The attempt, at first, was to validate the traditional employment standards by allowing blacks, women and oldsters to try and fail. Turnover was high. But so many succeeded that the employers stopped trying to predict competence by these outmoded criteria.

Although arbitrary, and inequitable, the old system of allocating the desirable jobs on the basis of demography had the signal virtue of preserving order. Applicants without the "right" background were easily convinced that they were not qualified and settled, with only nominal grumbling, for the large number of menial jobs which could never return in productivity more than a subsistence income—jobs which, for the most part, have since disappeared. The transition to a more rational and equitable economy would have been difficult even under conditions of a rising demand for labor in productive work. As it happened, the credentialing system lost its credibility in the midst of a Depression which reminded older policymakers of the crisis leading to the election of Franklin Delano Roosevelt in 1932.

Queues of applicants assaulted employers suspected of needing help. In order to function at all, many organizations kept job openings secret, particularly jobs for which clerical workers, mostly women, had a right to consideration under the equal opportunity laws. Passage of the Equal Rights Amendment to commemorate the Bicentennial in 1976 did not, as its opponents had argued, throw dependent wives onto the employment market. Even those whose husbands held on to their jobs were moved to seek paid employment in order to keep up with rising prices, and enough of them used the anti-discrimination laws to make it impractical for large-scale employers to exploit the willingness of wives to work by offering them lower pay and fringe benefits. In the pinch, many employers found that it was cheaper to eliminate do-nothing jobs rather than fill them at equal-pay wages, and many jobs went unfilled in spite of unemployment.

Democrats, then a majority in Congress, demanded that the Ford administration launch a massive make-work project. Committed to balancing the budget, President Ford insisted on letting wages find their market level. As protests mounted, radical elements in the Democratic Party demanded equality not merely of opportunity—for that had failed to redress imbalances—but "equality of results." A majority of both Houses passed a bill providing a minimum income for every resident of the country, but the bill failed to get the two-thirds support required to override President Ford's veto. Democrats brought the issue to the country and gained significantly in the elections of 1978.

The National Employment Exchanges of 1979 were designed strictly as an emergency measure. To cope with "imbalances" and "imperfections" in the employment market, all employers were required to hire through a network of employment agencies set up by the Federal Government to insure the orderly and equitable allocation of available work. In order to appease the left-wing Democrats, the employment service was instructed to disregard qualifications which employers could not validate as relevant to job performance and to fill all positions on the "first come, first hired" basis which the largest and most vulnerable employers had already adopted.

The impact was sharp and unpredictable. Studies mounted by the employment service disclosed that part-time workers were as productive in most tasks as full-time workers, and in many cases even more so. Other studies demonstrated that productivity could be raised by permitting certain kinds of employees to work their own hours rather than hours scheduled by the employer.

The Federal Employment Service, manned by veteran civil servants, became the champion of workers "cooled out" by arbitrary requirements of every kind. When employees complained that they were denied promotions or jobs because they did not have the years of experience employers required, the "Federals" mounted some demonstrations which showed that a realistic training period followed by six months of apprenticeship on the job fitted most workers for duties heretofore regarded as "highly skilled."

The Neighborhood Play Group System

The biggest obstacle to equal employment of women was the fear that the family would come unstuck and children would suffer. This twisted logic depended on two assumptions we now know to be false: first, every child needs the twenty-four-hour presence of one person, preferably the biological mother for at least six and ideally many more years; second, mothers wouldn't stay with their children if allowed any but the dullest and least rewarding alternatives. Mothers were supposed to care physically for children, while fathers were expected merely to provide financial support. This division of labor was not based on ignorance of the way children are conceived. The male role in procreation was known, in the 1950s, even to the last remaining human primitive. Information on reproduction was scientifically provable, but reasoning about the data remained magical. A baby was held to belong, both as property and responsibility, to the woman who brought it into the world, even though that woman was not allowed to decide whether to bear an unborn child.

More strongly even than men, women believed that their anatomy destined them to exclusive responsibility for child care and home maintenance. As more of the needs of children had to be met by money purchases, women sought employment outside of the home, while continuing to believe that they owed their children nontransferable, twenty-four-hour care. So many tried to compromise by dividing their time between home and job that employers did not have to pay full rates to women whom they permitted to work "part-time"—that is, less than the seven- or eight-hour day then required of all "full-time, regular" employees. Before National Employment Service research proved otherwise, they were able to justify this lower rate on the ground that part-time workers were less productive than full-time workers.

Mothers forced to work campaigned for improved, Federally funded day care centers where children could play while their mothers worked. The proposal aroused intense controversy. The first provisions for the care of preschool children were intended to enable mothers on welfare to support themselves. Mothers who could possibly afford to stay with their children were regarded as unnatural for choosing employment instead, even though the richest women put their preschool children in "nursery school," organized to give very small children wider experiences, both social and physical, than was generally available in small homes.

Federal funding for improved, professionally staffed day care centers became a priority demand of the women's movement of the 1970s. The Johnson and Nixon administrations considered national programs, but the proposals were postponed, and finally abandoned when the Ford administration attempted to fight the stagflation-depression of 1975-76 by cutting Government expenditures. Meanwhile, as more and more mothers were forced to seek paid employment, organized women supported Congressional candidates who promised to vote for day care centers.

The Neighborhood Play Group Act of 1977 was one of President Ford's brilliant legislative compromises with the liberal Democratic Congress elected in 1976. Instead of funding professionally staffed day care centers as an extension to the school system, the administration proposed that the Federal Government provide physical space and equipment to neighborhood groups which could find enough volunteers to supervise informal "play groups." In order to minimize Federal "control" of local child care practices, the physical facilities were set up and maintained by the National Park Service and were assigned for operation to local groups, which were required to meet only the broadest and simplest safety and health requirements. Expense and Federal involvement was minimal, and the designers of the program did not expect that the National Park Service would be overloaded with requests from neighborhood groups. Conservatives supported the bill because they were sure that few neighborhoods would ask for play groups, proving that day care was of interest only to a small, noisy part of "unnatural" mothers.

We all know how wrong they were. Cut loose from the oppressive and expensive school system, the facilities set up modestly on land rented and bought by the Park Service became favorite gathering spots for adults, too. With no set program and no educational theories to implement, children and adults were left to interact on their own. Childless adults and parents of grown children made friends with individual youngsters, often taking them on trips to their homes or work places. Older children taught games to younger children and helped them build simple playground equipment. If requested, the National Park Service supplied tables and chairs and let concessions for soft drinks so that adults could gather and play adult games while watching the children. Well-to-do neighborhoods raised funds to install skating rinks, sports fields and entertainment facilities not provided under the modest Park Department budgets. Any safe facility or activity could be authorized, providing it met the minimum requirements. One of the most popular facilities turned out to be the nursery for infants under one year maintained under the care of a volunteer trained in baby nursing at the local hospital. In most neighborhoods, adult males as well as girls and women were usually on hand to help in the nursery, and a large number of older men went to the trouble of qualifying so that they could take a turn as nursery supervisor.

Some observers believe that the Neighborhood Centers succeeded because of the gasoline shortage which kept adults close to home. Others say that the sharply declining birth rate of the 1970s and the rise in the proportion of single, childless adults made children more precious than they were in the 1950s, when families were burdensomely large. Our own view is that the availability of safe, cheap, informal, and nearby child care around the clock relieved the pressure on parents so that they could interact with their own and other children in a more spontaneous way. There were, of course, problems. In order to protect children, professional Child Advocates were funded for every Neighborhood Play Group, charged with responsibility for choosing and training the volunteers who actually operated the play groups. Eventually, of course, when a full Children's Bill of Rights was voted in 1990, the corps of Child Advocates in service all over the country took on formal responsibility for defending the new rights of children against parents, schools, employers, and other adults. Just as sex desegregation followed race desegregation, so age desegregation turned out to be a local outcome of sex desegregation.

The Minimum Income Security System

Although it is the foundation of the open economy of the twenty-first century, the Minimum Income Security System was the hardest-fought and the last of the reforms triggered by the campaign for sex equality in employment. Indeed, it could be argued that an expanding economy could have provided equal pay and job access to the millions of underpaid and underemployed women of the 1960s without changing the old system under which individuals had to support themselves completely on the money they or their families could earn by work or from the investment of private capital. The historical facts are, however, that private employment could not take care of the underemployment and manpower dislocations dramatized by the Depression of the late 1970s. Because they were marginal, temporary, and disadvantaged workers, women suffered more from the slow growth and unemployment of the Depression just at a time when their legal claims to equal treatment were being recognized by courts and employers. This gave them a tactical advantage in the reorganization which brought the Democrats to power in 1980, and had much to do with the nomination and election of our first woman president.

It is perhaps too sweeping to say that all income had to be earned in the 1970s. Ever since the New Deal of the 1930s, there had been a modest Social Security System which worked to transfer funds from income producers to those unable to earn. Every state and many cities as well had welfare systems which had grown up to take care of the blind, of disabled or orphaned children, of the unemployed, the unemployable, or the merely ill. But under the old regime, a person could claim unearned income only by virtue of some circumstance that made it impossible for him to earn his keep, and substantial numbers of those entitled to unearned transfer income were dissuaded from claiming it by the heavy stigma attached to "relief," "the dole," "welfare" or "charity."

The welfare system was makeshift and expensive even in good times. One of its most troublesome assumptions was that aid should go to families rather than individuals. This meant that welfare officials were supposed to track down absent husbands before awarding welfare to deserted wives, and it left dependent children without protection against the misuse of welfare allowances, made on their behalf, by their parents. As it turned out, it was discrimination against women in employment which made the family system of rescuing the unemployed unworkable.

During the 1970s, the proportion of families headed by women increased every year. There were many reasons. Divorce was rising as women refused the family role that was becoming uneconomic and untenable. And at the bottom of the income pyramid, fathers were deserting their families in order to make them eligible for welfare. An increasing proportion of the unemployed and those underemployed at less than a living wage were single women who were limited to poorly paid, deadend "women's work," or the low pensions based on this work under the contributory Social Security System designed by President Franklin D. Roosevelt. At first, unemployment hit hourly male workers hardest and particularly teenagers. But by 1973, Wilma S. Heide, President of the National Organization for Women could declare, "Poverty is a woman's issue." And as the Depression deepened, office managers and affluent housewives learned to do without the servants they had formerly hired to do the duller and dirtier office and household chores.

There had been several attempts to reform the unwieldy welfare system as early as the Johnson administration. Scandals, breakdowns, and the appalling rise in the cost of maintaining the income of the unemployed made welfare reform the priority political issue of the late 1970s. Less well known is the fact that women who had learned the political ropes in the fight for enforcement of the equal opportunity laws joined with conservatives to draft the Income Security Act of 1980.

The Income Security Act was a brilliant political compromise. It appealed to conservatives because it eliminated thousands of Federal civil servants by turning the Social Security System over to the Internal Revenue Service and doing away with the scores of Federal, state and local welfare programs to the blind, the unemployed, the old, the young, and other special groups.

It appealed to liberals because it was a move toward their demand for "Equality of Results." It put an income floor under everyone, eliminating at a single stroke some of the worst labor exploitation. In my youth, for instance, lettuce was not a hobby crop, but a staple served with every dinner, winter and summer. It was generally available only because poor workers had to take such "stoop" work in order to survive.

Finally and deliberately less publicized: it appealed to feminists because it made aid available not on the old family basis which locked women into their subordinate role in employment as well as in the home, but on an individual basis. Conservatives and liberals alike didn't particularly like this feature of the act, but its adoption simplified administration and saved so much money that the individual basis for the minimum income prevailed.

Beginning with the calendar year 1981, everyone in the United States was required to file an income tax return, whether the person had income or not. Child Advocates serving the Neighborhood Centers, and others specially hired for the purpose, assisted children over twelve and certified the return prepared by parents for their younger children. Those who had less income than the amount that was certified necessary for minimum subsistence by the Bureau of Labor Statistics—in 1981 it was $5,000—received a check from the Government for the difference. Those who had income over that level paid regular income taxes. Any deficit or surplus was transferred to general tax funds. The minimum income of children went to their parents, but it could, with the permission of the Child Advocate, be assigned to other guardians if the circumstances warranted. As for spouses, the system dispensed completely with the complicated body of public and welfare law requiring husbands to support wives.

Employers were intuitively against the Income Security System. They predicted that it would be impossible to get enough people to work if subsistence was generally subsidized. But blacks, women, welfare recipients, and millions of ordinary people who were afraid to quit unrewarding jobs joined the campaign for "Equality of Results" and the Act was finally passed.

Its impact has been unexpected. The workers who quit were not the most disadvantaged but the clerical workers and factory operatives, and most of them were quite willing to go back to work after a few months. For the most disadvantaged, the so-called unemployables, the minimum income meant a chance at a middle-class standard of living, and since this had always entailed regular work, many of the chronically poor were encouraged to look for a job. Because turnover was high, many were given a chance at the clerical and blue-collar service jobs vacated by the bored.

There was no wholesale or dramatic drop in labor force participation. The big change was in the composition of the paid labor force. There were more women and fewer men working for money. Many oldsters stayed on after what had been called retirement age, and many youngsters went to work instead of or before college. There was much more job changing and most people tried more than one career in the course of their working lives. New institutions were set up to deal with the new volatile labor force. Residential colleges were converted into adult training centers with continuous courses in job skills and permanent floating discussion groups in art, history, literature, and other liberal arts which attracted persons of every age who became interested in the subject at the time.

Pay scales reflected job conditions and the intrinsic appeal of work. Pay scales for garbage collection had been rising through the 1970s, because fewer people were willing to do this unpleasant and actually dangerous work. In 1974, for instance, New York City garbage men were being paid almost twice as much as many New York City schoolteachers. By 1985, the city had to pay such high wages to get garbage collected that it became economic to install the present system of rubbish collection through underground forced-air tunnels similar to the sewerage system.

Volunteer work engages the time of a larger proportion of the population than when it was relegated to the spare time of housewives. Men and women of all ages are available to staff hospitals and talk with the lonely and troubled. A large number opt, for months on end, to volunteer in the Children's Play Groups. Almost everyone becomes an amateur teacher of his special skill either formally in the regular school system, or informally in the play center. Studies of teaching effectiveness have shown that the enthusiasm of volunteer teachers is more important than the pedagogical methods once taught them in teachers college.

Early feminists used to argue that the liberation of women would liberate men, too. Adult males of the 1960s tended to dismiss the sentiment as pretty but impractical. And even today, men do not fully realize how much they owe to the sex equality movement of the 1960s.

10 WOMEN IN THE ARTS: INSIGHTS INTO THE CULTURAL IMPACT OF WOMAN'S ROLE IN THE CREATIVE ARTS

A Compendium

THE IDEAS EXPRESSED in this chapter are a cross-section of replies to a questionnaire which was sent to women involved in the arts: painting and sculpture, art history, architecture and design, theater, dance and music. The limits of space preclude printing all the responses, including many very fine ones, but we believe that those selected are representative of the whole.

The questions posed were: 1) By the year 2000, what important differences do you see for women in your field? 2) Will this recognition (if your feelings are positive) come from other women, from men and women alike, and/or from critics, judges, foundations, awards, new programs for women? 3) What attitudes must change for women to gain recognition and compensation? 4) What innovations do you expect in the field? 5) What are the negatives? What problems do you see ahead?

CAROLEE SCHNEEMAN *is a painter, kinetic sculptor, filmmaker, writer, pioneer of Happenings and a teacher of art history.*

By the year 2,000 no young woman artist will meet the determined resistance and constant undermining which I endured as a student. Her studio and istory courses will usually be taught by women; she will never feel like a provisional guest at the banquet of life; or a monster defying her "God-given" role; or a belligerent whose devotion to creativity could only exist at the expense of a man, or men and their needs. Nor will she go into the "art world," gracing or disgracing a pervading stud club of artists, historians, teachers, museum directors, magazine editors, gallery dealers—all male, or committed to masculine preserves. All that is marvelously, already falling around our feet.

She will study art istory courses enriched by the inclusion, discovery, and reevaluation of works by women artists: works (and lives) until recently buried away, willfully destroyed, ignored, or reattributed (to male artists with whom they were associated). Our future student will be in touch with a continuous feminine creative istory—often produced against impossible odds—from her present, to the Renaissance and beyond. In the year 2,000 books and courses will only be called "Man and His Image," "Man and His Symbols," "Art History of Man," to probe the source of disease and mania which compelled patriarchial man to attribute to himself and his masculine forebears every invention and artifact by which civilization was formed for over four millennia.

Our woman will have courses and books on "The Invention of Art by Woman," "Woman—The Source of Creation," "The Matriarchal Origins of Art," "Woman and Her Materials." Her studies of ancient Greece and Egypt will reconcile manipulations in translation, interpretation, and actual content of language and symbolic imagery with the protracted and agonizing struggle between the integral, cosmic principles of matriarchy, and the aggressive man-centered cultures gathered as the foundations of Judeo-Christian religion in the Western world.

Fifteen years ago I told my art istory professor I thought the bare-breasted women bull jumpers, carved in ivory or painted in fresco about 1600 B.C. in Crete, could have been made by women depicting women. And I considered that the preponderant neolithic fertility figurines might have been crafted by women for themselves—to accompany them through pregnancy and birth-giving. And I wondered if the frescos of the Mysteries, in Pompeii—almost exclusively concerned with feminine gestures and actions—could have been painted by women. He was shocked and annoyed, saying that there was absolutely no authority to support such ideas. Since then I have given myself the authority to support and pursue these insights. By the year 2000 feminist archeologists, etymologists, egyptologists, biologists, sociologists will have established beyond question my contention that woman determined the forms of the sacred and the functional—the divine properties of material, its religious and practical formations; that she evolved pottery, sculpture, fresco, architecture, astronomy and the laws of agriculture—all of which belonged implicitly to the female realms of transformation and production.

The shadowy notions of a harmonious core of civilization under the aegis of the Great Mother Goddess, where the divine unity of female biological *and* imaginative creation was normal and pervasive, where the female was the source of all living and created images, will once again move to clarify our own conscious desires. The sacred rituals of forming materials to embody life energies will return to the female source.

Our further change will be the assembling of pioneer istorians—themselves discredited or forgotten by traditional masculine authority. In the year 2000, they will be on the required reading lists. What a joy to welcome Helen Diner, J.J. Bachofen, Michelet, Rilke, Gould-Davis, Jane Ellen Harrison, Robert Graves, Jacquetta Hawkes, Ruth Bendict, Robert Briffault, Erich Neumann, Marie de LeCourt, Ruth Herschberger, Bryher, Hays, Minna Mosdherosch Schmidt, Clara E. C. Waters (1904), Elizabeth F. Ellet (1859).

The negative aspect is simply that the young woman coming to these vital studies will never really believe that we, in our desperate groundwork, were so crippled and isolated; that a belief and dedication to a feminine istory of art was despised by those who might have taught it, and considered heretical and false by those who should have taught it. That our deepest energies were nurtured in secret, with precedents we kept secret—our lost women. Now found and to be found again.

ANN SUTHERLAND HARRIS *is professor of art history at the State University of New York at Albany. She speaks here on the subjects of painting and sculpture.*

If the present momentum builds, and women themselves continue to take the initiative—organizing exhibitions, galleries, cooperatives, publishing their own art magazines and contributing feminist articles to existing art publications, then surely women will be better represented in major museums, in important dealers' shows, in major loan exhibitions, in the teaching faculties of college and university art departments, and will receive more serious and regular attention from the critics publishing in influential places. That "if" is important. A generation of hard work will certainly be needed, and the hard work will never end if women painters and sculptors want permanent recognition.

I feel positive that this recognition will initially come from other women, especially a few influential, energetic women critics such as Lucy Lippard and Cindy Nemser, but it will increasingly be shared by the Establishment. Both the pressure from women artists and high-quality work by women artists must be sustained for so long that both will become accepted facts of life. I think that this will happen. The movement so far has brought an extraordinarily large number of talented and original women artists to the attention of the public, though the achievements of the best do not yet get the publicity that they deserve. The belated and insufficient coverage provided by *The New York Times* of the loan show at the Civic Center in Philadelphia is symptomatic of the problems women face.

We are and have long been excited and inspired by the notion of human genius, because even if we ourselves are *not*—and the accomplishments of a genius are a measure of our own inferiority—nevertheless the idea that some human beings have achieved so much is exhilarating and makes us dream and discover some spark of talent that may be in ourselves. When the idea of genius in a woman excites and inspires us with fantasies of human greatness as the idea of genius in a man does now, then women will be recognized and rewarded to the degree that men are. If it is good for some women to devote themselves to great men, providing practical and moral support, then the reverse should be true. Since not all human beings are equally gifted and the most talented need to devote a great deal of time and mental and physical energy to their art, then the role of devoted helper and assistant should he acceptable for both men and women, but I have ambiguous feelings about this, because I'm certain that many women who did devote themselves to men suppressed their own genius by doing so.

As far as innovations are concerned, I would like to see a far higher proportion of people enjoying art, understanding art and buying art instead of cliché reproductions of Van Gogh's *Sunflowers*. Perhaps women will manage to spread art patronage in the feminist community. Many people complain about the marketing of modern art, the power of a few dealers and critics to make a few artists and break the rest. I think the women's movement has brought many women into contact with art—because it is by women—who might not otherwise have gone to see such works. I think it may help to create new patronage. I also think women artists are concerned about humanist content in art and as a result are making works that do not immediately alienate the viewer but instead seek to involve the spectator in shared experiences, and not necessarily female experiences. Women artists also seem to avoid at present being neatly packaged into movements; this is healthy and may help dealers and critics to accept a more variegated picture of "what is happening."

It is already extremely difficult to make a living as an artist. Given that only a small proportion of the general public looks at art at all, and an even smaller proportion covets art enough to collect it, one could say that we have too many artists now. If the women's movement encourages more women to respond to the visual arts, to appreciate them enough to want to own paintings and sculptures instead of big cars and other unnecessary energy-consuming luxuries, then perhaps it will be possible for more artists, female and male, to earn a decent living.

CINDY NEMSER, editor of a feminist art journal, believes that through women's greater participation and recognition, through the much acknowledged sensitivity of women, art will become more related to human needs and will become an essential in everyone's daily life.

MARCIA TUCKER *is a curator at New York's Whitney Museum of Art and an author and teacher in the art field.*

By the year 2000, I hope that women in the arts will find an almost complete absence of discrimination against them and their work. Already, women are beginning to have their work looked at without reference to the person who produced that work—that is, without prejudice. In the museums, many of us already have positions of responsibility; we are now waiting for a woman to become the director of a major musuem in this country. It may not happen for twenty years—but, the handwriting is on the wall. I think that the year 2000 may bring real visibility to our work.

Recognition of excellence must come from the people who set the standards for excellence. In the past, they have always been men, and their criteria have not been broadly based; for example, H.W. Janson's widely used textbook, *History of Art*, does not mention a single woman artist—not Rosa Bonheur, Mary Cassatt, Louise Nevelson, Barbara Hepworth nor Georgia O'Keefe. For Janson, women artists never seem to have existed, and this is a book that deals with the entire history of art in America and Europe from prehistoric cave paintings on. Consequently, women are going to have to reevaluate the standards of excellence imposed on us by men, accepting some and rejecting others, and forming new standards as well. Eventually, the judgments of women *and* men will combine, and the quality of one's work will be the only thing that counts; but the judgments will be made by all of us. They will be, if not correct, at least non-sexist.

HELEN FRANKENTHALER, renowned and widely exhibited painter, comments that recognition for women artists will come from a combined effort from both men and women, and will depend mainly on the quality of each individual artist's work. She sees problems for the future of all art—both by men and women—coming from politics, economics, fashions and tastes, and other areas that have traditionally affected the progress of art.

RACHEL MAINES, Eastern Regional Coordinator for Women and the Arts for NOW, says that, with luck, the arts in general will have become more of a social "backbone" by the year 2000 than they are now, with such as the textile arts held in the same esteem as painting and sculpture.

She feels that we cannot continue dividing up the art forms into fields that are right for women and ones that are right for men. We must be *very* flexible and reach out for more definitions that include such things as needlework, canning and pickling, horticulture and others previously thought to be exclusively "feminine" and not really art forms. That there will be much more environmental art and many more people turning to new kinds of art as jobs in traditional fields become scarcer. Technological art will probably make great advances and become more appealing to the average person.

LUCY LIPPARD is an art critic and author of many books on contemporary art. She helped found the Ad Hoc Women Artists Committee and is active in the Women's Art Registry. Ms. Lippard is confident that by the year 2000 the whole system of how art is *used* will be different; that art will become enmeshed in everyone's lives and this will come about by "new programs for *life*" as a result of more open attitudes toward everything. She feels that progress for the arts and for women in the arts might be hampered by male backlash, conservatism and above all by women giving up or becoming complacent and satisfied with too little before any gains are made.

SUZANNE BENTON *is a sculptor and a theater set designer. She is also National Coordinator of NOW's Women and the Arts Task Force. She said the following about the year 2000:*

Clearly, certain new key elements will make possible a new existence for women in the world at large and the art world—women being allies of each other, real social changes, birth control, child care, ERA, special education, etc.

Ideally, in the year 2000, we shall all be artists. Our daily lives will in large measure take place within an art environment that kindles and keeps glowing the sense of our potential and the path of its fulfillment.

In my involvement in the women's art movement, I see certain similarity in our developing new art forms. The values in our new developing art are:

1. The self as center of expression—being honest about our life experience and conveying this in our art. No more denials of our violation as people.
2. A sharing art, not elitist or untouchable. Women are traditionally communal, and the hierarchic celebration of the few greater men is a system that excludes women.
3. Careful attention to every aspect of presentation. As women we have little help in the many aspects of creating and presenting our art. This emphasis on all aspects, including marketing, will change the form of the art world.
4. Multi-faceted: Many arts are gathering in an expression of how we view the world. Art must regain its unity with daily living and be an expression of our lives.
5. Emphasis on education and sharing knowledge gained.
6. Conscious nurturing of women's talent. Formation of new organizations to foster this, plus a change in attitude toward valuing women's art contribution.

7. New art forms and methods of presentation. When the message has no traditional vehicle for expression (women as self-defined), new vehicles will be developed—new theater, new art.
8. Reawakening our heritage as women artists—Rachel Maines, needlework archivist; Judy Chicago, bringing china painting into the art world.
9. Examining our traditional past through contemporary eyes—my own work, *Ritual Tales of Women of Myth and Heritage;* Adele Aldridge, *Feminist I Ching.*
10. An international network of Women in the Arts—Women's International Arts Festival; International Organization of Women in Art.

MIMI LOBELL *is an architect, an author, a teacher of architecture and an early activist in researching the position of women, who responded to our questions with the following statements:*

New directions: By the year 2000, architecture will be a "woman's profession," because it will be viewed as a close kin to interior decoration. The real action will be in solar system engineering, space stations, and projects like Bill Katavolos' 270-mile-high "buildings" whose structure is stabilized by cables running thousands of miles above the earth where they'll be in stationary orbit. By 2000, women will be free to do whatever they want with the paltry remains on earth, that is, with architecture as we know it.

Women who practice traditional architecture will have the trappings of support but their efforts will not represent the really potent mythologies of the culture (i.e. the male culture?).

To gain recognition, women must either begin to think in these astronomical terms and learn the difficult mathematics, physics, and engineering that they involve; or they must check the ejaculatory, imperialistic, male principle that space engineering represents by creating an alternative which has the same benefits (capturing the imagination, expanding livable space, learning more about the cosmos, etc.) but which stems from the female principle.

I expect people, both men and women, to become interested in the psychic, symbolic, cosmological and mythic forces at work in the balancing of male and female principles. Men must learn to respect what women have to offer, and only through respecting themselves can women also appreciate what men have to offer in a new and meaningful way. When this happens, we will have reached the "millennium." Let's hope it happens by the year 2000.

The problem I see is that the above scenario might not occur and we will continue in mutual exploitation and contempt. From the lessons of the last 2000 years, this works out worst for the women, be they architects or housewives.

The fundamental impact women will make on this cultural change cannot be underestimated. We are moving into an entire world view that comes naturally to women, concerned as it is with the sensual, emotional and symbolic dynamics of life. In many areas women will naturally rise to positions of great power because of their innate familiarity with these realms. I think this won't happen without their conscious efforts, however. But these efforts will take the form of fighting for the principles (the female principles) involved rather than fighting for stop-gap supplications which seek to imitate the male world. This can be seen in architecture through women's efforts to humanize practice, both for the professional and the client. They are seeking nothing less than a fundamental overturn of the ego-oriented star system which intimidates clients and employees and is disastrous for the environment.

MARILYN BOLL *is the founder of the International Woman's Art Festival for the United Nations' International Year of the Woman. When asked the five questions, Ms. Boll answered:*

I certainly hope women will have come into their own on all accounts in the arts. I imagine they will have caused somewhat of a social revolution in that they will have portrayed the true feeling of women. Women will identify with their work and change their self-image. Women will be in positions of power and leadership in the art world as well as in business, academia and government. Therefore, I hope that the artistic endeavors of women will be judged as art in combination with the work of men and there will no longer be a male/female distinction.

Recognition must come from other women. We must support our own. Women must read women authors, attend concerts featuring women composers and have a high regard for and promote the artistic work of women. Women's artistic output and achievements must be publicized. Women's arts should benefit from corporations and foundations who have had their consciousness forcibly raised and are actively seeking to support the work of women artists.

Again, women must help themselves. They must gain self-esteem and have the courage to expose their innermost thoughts and feelings in their art. For those of us viewing the art, the double standard must be eliminated. We cannot be shocked by extreme violence or basic sexuality because it is portrayed or interpreted by a woman. Also, women must be seen as doers not objects, painters not models, playwrights not actresses. It will require a lot of hard work for all women. One of the biggest problems will be to change the attitude of women toward women artists and changing women's image of themselves as "second rate" artists. Getting women into positions of power and influence in all fields will not be easy but it must be done.

MURIEL CASTANIS is an artist, writer, critic and a founder of the Women's Inter-Art Center in New York. She feels that the concept of looking forward twenty-five years is the most important aspect for women artists to realize, because they alone must implement the changes necessary to make themselves a viable part of the art community. It is a common feeling among women that they must work extra hard just to stay in the same place, and so the efforts must be enormous to take meaningful steps forward. Women artists are certainly not getting the recognition needed to support a very difficult and dedicated career.

She continues: since the art world is beginning to be influenced by the new forms women artists are evolving, an art magazine reflecting these new changes would be most helpful—with a woman publisher, of course—and that museums should compensate for their long discrimination against women artists with a yearly show just for women. Also, organizations of women artists must be formed to force changes to make for a healthier, better-balanced art community.

VERNA GILLIS *is a musicologist who teaches at Brooklyn College's New School of Liberal Arts. Her statement about woman's role in the arts, and specifically in music, follows:*

If the women's movement, along with all other important and valid movements, proves to have been truly successful, then she who is a feminist today, by the year 2000, will be a humanist. Women will emerge in the next quarter of a century as important composers and conductors. Women will no longer be restricted to pianos, harps, violins and flutes, but will in fact be playing any and all the instruments that exist. There will be all-women's orchestras, chamber groups, etc. By the year 2000, everyone will have so much more leisure time and proportionately so many more people will have the time to study all aspects of music, and greater numbers of people will be seeking out and attending performances of music. This will be true not only for what we recognize today as classical music, but will also change profoundly in the area of jazz, which today is even less sexually integrated than other musical scenes. Women will be freer to pursue careers in music due to bearing few children and increased assistance on both the spouse level and child-care level. As for the non-Western world, by the year 2000 many of the restricting traditions that cast shame upon women who became musicians and dancers will have changed, making music a valid option for a career—more than knowing how to play the koto or piano as a social grace to entertain one's husband and his guests.

This recognition, which of course I feel great about, will come from everyone and be taken as a matter of course. And I think women and men can only be liberated in a technological society where the roles can be broken down functionally. Attitudes that must change and are changing have to do with men feeling masculine about having their wives work and earn money and not being home all the time. Attitudes about what is masculine or feminine in terms of instruments are already changing, but today how many saxaphone players are women? As women gain power and authority in government, and men and women both become accustomed to directives from women, a woman as conductor will be easier to accept.

Some woman composer will write a menstrual cycle of songs! Men and women composers alike will write music based on space travel!

The negatives I foresee are concerned with the underdeveloped nations and the status of *people* in countries where food and water will become more scarce and survival will be the main concern—and who will be left to sing the funeral laments and birth laments? Since women have always been the professional mourners they should be doing well!

LYNN TAYLOR *is affiliated with the Theatre Dance Collection of New York City.*

Dance is a unique field for women in terms of recognition. We work primarily with homosexual men, who are much more open-minded about sexual roles, since they too are victims of social stigma. This, combined with the fact that modern dance has had great pioneers like Martha Graham, Agnes DeMille, Pearl Primus and Isadora Duncan, seems to have opened up the concert dance field almost completely in terms of equal rights and recognition for women choreographers. However, in terms of leadership in the concert field and equal opportunity in the field of commercial choreography, we have a long way to go.

By the year 2000, more women will head major, established dance companies, will be choreographing in the movie industry and for the Broadway stage where the big money changes hands, and will find more important jobs in the administration and production ends of the business.

I fervently pray that the year 2000 will see the decline of the dancing doll in pink tights image—and of the tits-and-feathers kick-line image of women. Even in the commercial industry there will be a refocusing of attention on the talents and artistry of adult individuals.

The two foundations I have dealt with—The National Endowment for the Arts and the New York State Council on the Arts—have not shown prejudice in the awarding of grants, to my knowledge. Critics are generally unfair and obnoxious without regard for race, creed or sex. There are an equal number of influential women and men critics in New York. I think the significant change, the new recognition, will come from the male producers—and hopefully there will soon be more female producers—in the commercial field, who will slowly but surely give women more chances to be part of the creative mainstream.

Destructive attitudes that must change on the part of these same producers are: a woman may not be able to handle a big pressure situation, she might cry under stress, she might become pregnant at a crucial time in the production schedule, she might be unable to make the social scene which goes hand-in-glove with show business.

Among the innovations I hope to see in the field would be the development of programs in universities across the country which would explore the talents of women, not only in the college but in the college community. This would reach more minority women who may not be able to afford going to college. I also hope to see the influx of more "straight" men into the field of dance. There must be many men who have wanted to dance but suppressed this interest in order to do something more "butch" to satisfy Dad. If sexist attitudes change, they too can be freed from this monstrous suppression. There will also most certainly be more dance companies "for women only" run by women. I hope this need not be a lasting phase for us—the arts are really one of the only communications through which we might eventually share complete understanding with one another. Talented human beings should be able to share their cherished talents regardless of sex.

Side-effects I do not look forward to are: a surge of "women" dances which come not from the heart but because it will be a chic topic, a preoccupation with past wrongs, a perpetuation of bitterness toward men to the exclusion of doing dances which might really motivate men and women to change.

LINDA NOCHLIN *is professor of art history at Vassar College and has written extensively on Nineteenth-Century art. Her article, "Why There Have Been No Great Women Artists," has been widely reprinted.*

I think women and men will be working on entirely equal footing. . . . All the old stereotypical advantages to men are based on self-serving pseudoscience and pseudosociology, and unfortunately, still retained by some women. The whole connection between sex and so-called "creativity" must be reexamined and all our cherished cultural myths about magic potency as related to genius. The mystification surrounding art-making will have to be investigated, along with the underpinnings of the feminine mystique.

MARTHA EDELHEIT *is a painter, a filmmaker and a set designer. What follows is Marty's projection for women's role in the year 2000:*

The "finest" art has always belonged to, and been created for, the chief—king, pope, banker, industrialist. Our institutions change, but slowly. Till now, most institutions—museums, galleries, collectors—have been non-demographic.

Twenty-five years from now I believe that this elitist residue will reflect the demographic structure of the population. If fifty-three percent of the population are women, and eighty percent of the art students are women, then successful, collectable saleable works of art by women will reflect this. As this changes, the value structures will change, and the false categories of "minor," "decorative," "primitive" and "craft" art will enter the pantheon of "fine" art . . . great weaving, jewelry, graphics, pastels, watercolors, pottery, porcelain, etc. (so much of which has been created by women) will no longer be second class.

When women can create their own value judgments, independent of the past strictures of male achievement and approval, when women can accept their own bodies as good, beautiful, valuable . . . when women buy art and value it within their own economic structures . . . then the monetary rewards for beautifully articulated work in any medium will be there. This is changing now with such forms as Navajo rugs.

If women are demographically represented in the leadership of industry and government, then women artists will be able to participate in high economic rewards for their work.

Though I believe recognition for women artists will come from women first, I do not believe that women can truly achieve until they begin to question every category, every automatically accepted value judgment—until they stop mirroring the male past to evaluate what they do. Vast quantities of female mediocrity will have to be produced and exhibited in order for women to produce large quantities of great art. This has always been accepted amongst men, and we must allow it to happen for women. If we judge and censor too hastily we will destroy our potential for the future. The biggest changes will come out of women's involvement in technology. I believe all art will be available to anyone for a small price . . . holographically coded. Only the very rich will accumulate real objects.

Anything, from the ruins of Persepolis to Chinese bronzes, to the latest manipulations of light, space, color, line, volume, will be coded or even created on something the size of toothpicks and will be bought like record tapes or TV. Most "objects" will be destroyed, once they have been coded. The code can then be bought and used at will in any environment. Technology is going to change the very roots and structure of what will be considered art. Moveable type changed the world for most of humanity, instant spatial dream projections will make another revolution.

GLORIA ORENSTEIN is an art critic, writer and teacher of Literature and Women in the Contemporary Arts at Douglas College. Ms. Orenstein believes that more women will take themselves seriously as artists and not consider their creative work as mere pastime, hobby—or, worst of all, inferior. Women will have shows, at first in women's galleries; they will begin to be reviewed and receive the attention and encouragement that men now receive. She feels that women must take themselves and their work seriously—*now*. They must *persevere* no matter what happens; and band together. Women must never do what the male establishment is counting on them to do, and that is to give up. Women must never abandon their work in defeat.

SHEILA DE BRETTEVILLE *teaches at the School of Design at the California Arts Institute and originated the Women's Design Program for the Feminist Studio Workshop. Her answer:*

By the year 2000, those women involved in the design arts, like women in all the other professions, will have greater access to leadership in their field; they will also share equally in the rewards and difficulties that the privilege of leadership has brought to men. In order for women to gain appropriate recognition and compensation, women's ways of contributing will have to be reevaluated. If women are to be able to move into the public sector to have primary responsibility in design, we cannot continue to be thought of as "the second sex," as only viable at home and in private relationships. And the way to overcome this prevalence of wrong-thinking about women, is to train female children to be leaders, doers, and self-determining active persons. Women will have to work for change in attitutdes toward women, will have to be conscious of themselves as women, identify with other women and work to have themselves and all other women be seen as important, creative equals with men. If we work toward recognition and compensation merely as individuals, then attitudes will not change quickly enough. Working together we can bring about the year 2000 before its time!

11 THE CHIEF JUSTICE WORE A RED DRESS

by Doris L. Sassower

As THE CHIEF JUSTICE of the United States rose to deliver the annual State of the Judiciary address to the American Bar Association, she surveyed her audience—bar presidents, judges, law professors, attorneys in public and private practice. She noted with satisfaction the many women on the dais and in the general assemblage—a sharp contrast with A.B.A. meetings she attended as a neophyte, when women were primarily conspicuous by their absence.

Once there had been comments in the press referring to her as the "first woman" Chief Justice, but no one seemed to notice that any more. In the year 2000, equal rights, regardless of sex, had become a way of life, and "lady lawyers" were now just lawyers who happened to be women.

Despite the tumultuous applause, it was a moment of quiet pleasure for her as she recalled the long years of struggle to achieve this poignant moment.

It took almost ten years, but, by 1980, implementation of the Equal Rights Amendment adopted by ratification of the thirty-eighth state some years earlier had all but obliterated the arbitrary sex-based distinctions that had pervaded federal, state and local law. A steady progression of judicial decisions and legislative enactments gave substance to the "Redeclaration of Independence," adopted at the Bicentennial in 1976, that "all men and *women* are created equal."

The fundamental changes affecting men and women in our society which have taken place in the lifetime of all of us here today, she began, constitute a social revolution greater than any other that ever occurred in human history in so short a period of time.

The rise of the women's movement in the 1970s and the strategic decision of its feminist leaders to concentrate upon the law as the key to social progress brought about these changes.

And the most far-reaching of these is the Parental Responsibility Act, enacted less than six years ago. At one stroke, it removed all remnants of the fabric of gender-based laws so inextricably bonded to the rigid sex-role system underpinning our social structure. Women who bore the entire burden of home and child care suffered the disadvantages of dependency as uncompensated domestic workers. Girls, geared toward marriage and motherhood as their primary purposes in life, gave up paid employment outside the home to devote themselves—sometimes temporarily—to the role of full-time homemakers and generally did not pursue professional training or careers.

The Parental Responsibility Act seeks to avoid the problem of a societally-created dependent spouse. One of the cases that arose in the past judicial year, involving a class action challenge to this legislation, illuminated a wide range of constitutional questions presented by the Act.

The statute aimed to restructure the institution of marriage so as to equalize responsibilities and maintain women's financial independence in the face of parenthood. The case originated in California, the first state to adopt the new legislation, although others, spurred by the program of federal grants to states under the Act, were quick to follow.

The cornerstone of the law was its limitation of the working hours of married employees with pre-school-age children to no more then twenty-five hours per week. Pre-school children were eligible for free federally-funded enriched child-care centers, but only up to a maximum of twenty-five hours per week. Accordingly, the school week was changed to twenty-five hours per week over a twelve-month period.

The thrust of the restriction was to encourage both parents to remain in the labor force on a limited basis during their child-rearing years, since in the usual case, a family would require the pay check of more than one spouse working twenty-five hours. Proponents contended that it would eradicate the sex roles which had consigned women to lowest-paying, least-prestigious jobs—if indeed they secured outside employment after marriage. Since this meant that a woman would remain in the work force on a part-time basis after childbirth, she would be compelled to prepare for a career with no less concern than a man. With neither spouse a potential drop-out from the labor force upon parenthood, reentry problems as the children left the home would, advocates urged, cease to exist.

It was additionally argued that this provision would lead to the direct involvement of both parents in the care of their children and to equal division of domestic responsibilities.

Employment discrimination against parents subject to the twenty-five-hour limitation is, of course, illegal. A guaranteed minimum income available under legislation passed back in the Eighties eliminated financial hardship to those in low-paying occupations whose income would have been inadequate when curtailed by the twenty-five-hour weekly restriction.

The class action complainants contended that the various limitations violated the equal protection and due process clauses of the Fourteenth Amendment (apart from claims that they were "downright socialistic"). A majority of the court, however, with, I must say, two of my sisters dissenting, found a rational basis for the classifications in question, as well as for the general maximum hours scheme.

Our society now reaps the profound social consequences of this reform—population growth has dropped significantly; school buildings are in use all year round to accommodate the reduced school day and the consolidation with child-care centers; unemployment has decreased; a reduction in taxes is under study by the Congress in light of the lessened expenditures for public welfare.

As women have become self-sufficient, the need for alimony, or maintenance—as it is called under the Act—is now virtually nonexistent, (the exceptions being cases of physical or mental disability). There is also the hope that juvenile delinquency will decrease as parents' work hours correspond to children's school hours and parents spend more time with their families.

The divorce rate has already dropped; the sexes are less polarized. The effect of dividing sex roles between wife and husband has been to equalize women and men in a social as well as a legal sense. For the first time, marriage as an economic partnership exists in fact, not merely in potential.

The social transformation that has followed adoption of the Parental Responsibility Act can be more fully appreciated when viewed from a historical perspective—one which reveals only too clearly how it was that anatomy became destiny. The fact of women's inequality imitated their status in law, as nature all too often imitates art.

Long before talk of an Equal Rights Amendment, the judiciary defined the rights of women. Women's inequality in society was reinforced by courts constituted so as to be unrepresentative of women and unresponsive to their needs.

The premise upon which most of the judicial decisions in this country concerning women's rights have been built was refined to perfection in *Bradwell v. Illinois*. Decided in 1873, it was one of the first cases by the United States Supreme Court to uphold the constitutionality of state discrimination against women.

By more than coincidence, the case involved the application of a woman for a license to practice law. Only a woman of courage, prepared to accept the slings and arrows of the outrageous fortune besetting unconventional women, would have made so bold a challenge in that day and age. Myra Bradwell, however, was such a woman, and she wanted to be a lawyer. The Supreme Court sustained the denial of Bradwell's application by an Illinois court, and Mr. Justice Bradley's memorable concurring opinion epitomized the thinking of our highest court. This was how he dismissed the contention that the Fourteenth Amendment conferred upon women the right to pursue any legitimate employment, including the practice of law:

> It certainly cannot be affirmed, as an historical fact, that this [the right to pursue any lawful occupation] has ever been established as one of the fundamental privileges and immunities of the sex. On the contrary, the civil law, as well as nature herself, has always recognized a wide difference in the respective spheres and destinies of man and woman. Man is, or should be, woman's protector and defender. The natural and proper timidity and delicacy which belongs to the female sex evidently unfits it for many of the occupations of civil life. . . . The paramount destiny and mission of woman are to fulfill the noble and benign offices of wife and mother. This is the law of the Creator.

And so, judicial fiat, purportedly resting on divine intent, denied women the constitutional rights which our democracy granted all "persons." This led to the less than divine conclusion that, in fact, women were not persons under our Constitution. The principle of women as legal inferiors eventually became so deeply embedded in our case law as to defy elimination without amending the Constitution itself. A year after *Bradwell*, the Supreme Court in *Minor v. Happersett* denied women the right to vote under the Fourteenth Amendment. The struggle that ultimately led to passage of the Nineteenth Amendment was necessary to overturn that decision.

Although women were finally permitted to practice law (an event which, it turned out, did not provoke the wrath of the Almighty), and won their fight for the vote early in the Twentieth Century, echoes of *Bradwell* continued to reverberate in the judicial decisions of our land. Women were still subject to statutory disability and regulation in areas which touched almost every field of civil and criminal law. Much of this discrimination was sanctioned by established case law.

The so-called protective labor laws constituted one area in which courts had upheld legislated inequality. Ostensibly designed to protect women from exploitation by employers through adverse working conditions, these laws were used to protect women out of jobs, advancement and overtime pay.

The Supreme Court, in a number of cases starting with *Muller v. Oregon* in 1908, sustained the constitutionality of state laws regulating the employment of women (but not men) as to maximum hours and weights to be carried, minimum wages, prohibition of night work, and in 1948, in the case of *Goesaert v. Cleary*, the prohibition of licensing of women (with certain exceptions) as bartenders. Apparently, the Supreme Court did not favor the idea of women at the bar—in more ways than one.

Nor, as *Hoyt v. Florida* made clear in 1961, did the court view any more kindly the thought of women in the jury box. Their participation in these vital bodies was severely limited by statute in a number of states.

These laws and the judicial decisions upholding them did more than treat women separately as a class. They treated women as second class in both their rights and their responsibilities as citizens.

It was no easy task to alter ingrained cultural patterns of discrimination. By the early Seventies, however, there were signs that judicial attitudes were changing and that legislation drawn along sex lines might no longer survive constitutional challenge. Most significant was the Supreme Court landmark decision in *Roe v. Wade* and *Doe v. Bolton* on the controversial abortion issue, which at long last gave women the right of control not only of their bodies but of their lives. The Court in *Griswald v. Connecticut* had earlier held that the state could not impede the use of contraceptive devices by married persons without infringing upon a newly created constitutional right of marital privacy.

Two other decisions, *Reed v. Reed* and *Frontiero v. Richardson*, were encouraging, but neither provided the long awaited clear-cut precedent to make distinctions resting on sex, like race, "suspect" classifications. In *Reed*, the Court unanimously invalidated an Iadaho statute which gave automatic preference to males when equally related females sought to administer an intestate estate. The effect of the decision, however, was limited to prohibiting arbitrary discrimination against women, without holding that all discrimination against women was presumptively arbitrary. In *Frontiero*, four of our justices moved beyond *Reed* to state that "classifications based upon sex, like classifications based upon race, alienage, or national origin are inherently suspect, and must therefore be subjected to strict judicial scrutiny." The eight-one ruling in that case held unconstitutional a federal law requiring a female member of the armed services to prove dependency of her spouse in order for him to qualify for various military fringe benefits. Wives of servicemen were automatically entitled to such benefits, irrespective of whether they were, in fact, dependent.

Unfortunately, the views of the four justices were not a majority opinion; four other justices concurred in the decision, but solely on the basis of the due process clause of the Fifth Amendment. Three of these members of the court explicitly refused to address themselves to the suspect-classification argument prior to conclusion of all state ratification procedures concerning the Equal Rights Amendment. Women were thus advised that they might have to wait for a majority decision for as long as six years—the remaining time allowed for ratification. The auspicious trend suggested by *Reed* and *Frontiero* suffered a setback in 1974 with two cases which had been seen as vehicles to bring women within the equal protection clause. *Kahn v. Shevin* sustained a property tax exemption for widows, but not for widowers. *Geduldig v. Aiello* upheld a state disability statute denying women benefits for disabilities of normal pregnancy.

These legal disappointments led human rights advocates to redouble their efforts for ratification of the Equal Rights Amendment in those states which had not yet adopted it.

In recalling this era, I am asking those gathered here to realize that twenty long years after the Supreme Court had proclaimed in the 1954 case of *Brown v. Board of Education* that "separate" was inherently unequal—speaking of racially segregated public schools—there was still no comparable decision by the court concerning sex-segregated public educational institutions. Even integrated schools retained traces of discrimination—separate sports programs and home economics/shop classes and stricter curfew and parietal rules for women. Secondary schools expelled pregnant girls, wedded or not, and denied them readmission even while the high school impregnator went undisciplined. The service academies did little more than enroll a few token women, failing to provide them with facilities comparable to those for male students.

The criminal justice system remained infected with sex-based, differentiated crime and punishment. Private consensual sexual activity was still regulated by statute, the impact of which was more heavily borne by women. Decriminalization of prostitution was yet to come.

Just as the Nineteenth Amendment was needed to remove barriers to women's right to vote, so the Equal Rights Amendment remained an imperative in order to establish equality on a constitutional basis and put an end to the discriminatory practices and judicial interpretations which had perpetuated women's subordinate role.

Women could no longer wait for an enlightened judiciary to recognize their rights. In the area of sex discrimination, the performance of American judges was characterized by a law review commentary of that period as "ranging from poor to abominable." There was an obvious, immediate need for a substantial increase in the number of women lawyers and judges.

In 1969, it was reported to the National Conference of Bar Presidents that at last count there were not many more than 8,000 women lawyers, and that out of roughly 10,000 judges in the United States, fewer than 200 were women, of whom the majority were concentrated in the lower courts.

Despite the fact that women outnumbered blacks in the legal profession more than two to one, and more had been in it longer, by 1970 black judges already exceeded female judges, both in absolute numbers and relative to their proportion in the population, and had already achieved that which was still denied women: a seat on the U.S. Supreme Court.

Fortunately, said the Chief Justice with a smile, that chronic condition was remedied less than a decade later. One might conclude that sexism was more deeply rooted than racism. However, women's lack of comparable achievement of judicial positions also reflected their slower-starting feminist movement.

In 1971, President Nixon had an unprecedented four opportunities to make the first appointment of a woman to the Court, but failed to do so. Forty years after the first woman judge, Florence Allen, was appointed to a circuit court, there was still no increase in the number of women on that bench. Up to the beginning of the last quarter-century, Judge Shirley Hufstedler was the only woman sitting on a federal circuit court. Women appointees to the district court barely qualified as tokens. No wonder the talent pool of women candidates for the Supreme Court could be characterized as "small." The difficulty lay in getting federal and state executives to recognize that the dearth of "qualified" candidates for appellate positions resulted from their failure to make significant appointments of women to the lower courts.

The habit of passing over women for judgeships was longstanding. In New York, when 125 new judicial vacancies for the city and state were created by the legislature in 1968, it was not seen as scandalous that women should fill only two of these posts. In 1972, vacancies occurred on the Court of Appeals, the state's highest court, which had not had a woman judge since its inception in 1848. A major effort to correct this gross omission met with failure—even with the Governor's backing.

Obviously, one way women could solve the problems of inadequate representation was to become politicized. By sheer force of numbers, they could—when they put their votes to it—secure control of the judiciary, as well as the other branches of government, for in most states, as in New York, judges were popularly elected. This was the path taken by women mobilized into groups such as the National Women's Political Caucus and local political caucuses of women in each state.

The acceleration of women in government grew also out of a recognition that the rationale behind programs of affirmative action, developed in private industry to correct discriminatory hiring and promotion, were no less appropriate to the public sector.

Litigation challenged the exemption of elective employment from the Equal Employment Opportunity Act of 1972, leading Congress to extend that law by the end of that decade. The percentage formulae developed in such cases as the A.T.&T. back-pay litigation specifying goals and timetables for fixed proportions of women at various management levels then became analogous.

With this impetus, women moved rapidly into the political arena. Steadily increasing numbers of women captured elective office, until by 1990 the proportion of women in federal and state government representative positions was almost in balance with their percentage in the population. The predominance of these women were lawyers—women who did not face the man-made barriers that had confronted Myra Bradwell.

Women in law, as in other professions, such as medicine, dentistry, or engineering, until the Eighties, had been a pitifully small percentage. A major cause of this situation was the prejudice that legislatively and judicially denied women their free choice of a career at the bar. This prejudice was evident in the unmasked hostility of law schools which refused women admission or subjected them to arbitrary quotas; law firms which refused to hire them or degraded women with inferior, lower-paying positions; brethren who refused to admit those who had overcome the initial hurdles into the organized associations of the bar, and humiliated even those women who had attained the pinnacle of the profession. Florence Allen, the only woman ever to attain a chief judgeship of a United States circuit court, recounted in her autobiography, *To Do Justly,* that because of her sex she was unable to gain acceptance even from her junior colleagues on the bench. Their attitude mirrored the prevailing chauvinism which blocked any chance of her ascending to the Supreme Court.

In the early Seventies, there were more women law students than women lawyers. From that point on, the number of women lawyers rose steadily each year. Feminist law firms, many formed by women specifically to undertake sex discrimination cases, gave women a kind of representation they sorely lacked in the past.

Old attitudes, unlike old soldiers, were slow to die or fade away. Judges, law deans and bar presidents, all too often, were prone to speak of "A man who . . ." in describing one needed for a particular job. Similarly anachronistic bar associations continued to address new members as "Dear Sir."

Because of such subtle, often unconscious, vestigial bias, women lawyers brought suits against discriminatory employers, as they did in New York City, in the case of ten major law firms whose hiring and recruitment practices contravened fair employment laws; against a State Board of Examiners for discriminatory administration of the state bar examination; against a metropolitan bar association for discriminatory membership rules which clearly excluded members of the female sex.

Because of such blatant discrimination the Professional Women's Caucus, in 1971, filed charges under Federal Executive Order No. 11375, against all law schools in the country within the purview thereof for discriminatory practices and policies in hiring, student admissions and financial aid. Emphasizing that the discrimination against women was as real as the more readily acknowledged discrimination against blacks and ethnic minorities, a class action was instituted against a New York law school challenging the denial of similar preferential treatment to women.

Gradually, the profession began to respond. The major organizations of the bar formed special committees to deal with the problems of women's inequality. In 1972, the House of Delegates of the American Bar Association permitted a woman non-delegate to speak (a privilege so accorded only once before in the ninety-six-year history of the Association) on behalf of a resolution calling for affirmative action by law schools and law firms to end discrimination against women law-students and lawyers, and that resolution (which had previously been voted down by the A.B.A. board of governors) was adopted as official A.B.A. policy. Similar action had already been taken by the Association of American Law Schools, which threatened deaccreditation for discriminatory recruitment at member law schools.

The Higher Education Act which became effective in 1973 explicitly authorized termination of federal aid to federally-funded graduate and professional schools, including law schools, in the event of discriminatory admissions. The Equal Employment Opportunity Act of 1972 permitted federal suits to compel compliance with statutory prohibitions against sex discrimination.

The most profound change, however, came about after the long struggle for ratification of the Equal Rights Amendment was crowned with success. By 1980, our law, at least, reflected a sex-neutral constitutional mandate. Regulations imposing burdens upon women were repealed. Where statutory benefits were conferred upon women, the same advantages were extended to men or the statutes were redrawn so that functional classifications replaced gender-based ones. Thus, alimony was awarded to a "dependent spouse," female or male, rather than to a "wife," and was predicated solely on need and ability to pay.

Increasingly there was the recognition that even the strictest judicial interpretation of the E.R.A. and the most zealous enforcement of nondiscrimination laws in employment, education, housing and credit could not alone effectuate change in conventional social attitudes.

And that recognition has brought us to the Parental Responsibility Act!

In sum, our country's history has shown not only that the law is the key to social change, but that there is no law for all time—that law, like technology, may become obsolete as new needs emerge. Old ideas, like old machinery, require replacement. Each advance demands, first, the willingness of pioneers to press for legislative innovation; second, continued vigilance so that judicial interpretation does not erode the intent of the legislature; and, third, that society be prepared to adjust itself to changing perceptions. Only in that way, I conclude, can we guarantee the permanence of the guiding principle of equality for all and the continued progress of human rights in the coming century.

The newspaper reports the next day summarized the Chief Justice's remarks in some detail. None of the papers felt it necessary to call attention to the fact that the audience of American Bar Association members consisted equally of women and men. Nor did any of them make a special point of the sex of the principal speaker. However, *The New York Times* account did note that the Chief Justice wore a red dress with a gold pin on her left shoulder.

BIBLIOGRAPHY
"What's Wrong With Women Lawyers?", *Trial Magazine*, 10-11/68. Speech Before National Conference of Bar Presidents, *Cong. Rec.*, Vol. 115, No. 24 E815-6, 2/5/69. "The Legal Profession and Women's Rights," *Rutgers Law Review*, Fall 70. "Women in the Professions"; *Women's Role in Contemporary Society*, report of the N. Y. C. Human Rights Commission, 72. "Women and the Legal Profession"; *Student Lawyer Journal*, 11/70, *Contemporary Education*, 2/72. "The Role of Lawyers in Women's Liberation"; *New York Law Journal*, 12/30/70, reprinted *Case & Comment*, 3-4/71. "Women in the Law: The Second Hundred Years"; *A.B.A. Journal*, 4/71. "Matrimonial Law Reform: Equal Property Rights for Women"; *New York State Bar Journal*, 10/72. "Women and the Law," *Human Rights*, fall 72. "Women's Rights in Higher Education," *Current*, 11/72. "Marital Bliss: Till Divorce Do Us Part"; *Juris Doctor*, 4/73. " 'No-Fault' Divorce and Women's Property Rights"; *New York State Bar Journal*, 11/73. "Women and the Judiciary—Undoing the Law of the Creator"; *Judicature*, 2/74. "Prostitution Review"; *Juris Doctor*, February 1974. Speech upon installation as President of New York Women's Bar Association, *Cong. Rec.*, Vol. 114 No. E5267-8, 6/11-68.

3

On Using Her Mind and Body

12 THE END OF THE MEDICINE MAN

by Rona Cherry

MY FIRST CONTACT WITH the medical mystique came when I was growing up in the Fifties in New York. Every September, in a kind of seasonal ritual of prevention, my parents, my brother and I arrived at our family doctor's office, just slightly off a still semi-fashionable arm of the Bronx's Grand Concourse. As we sat in his waiting room, voices were lowered and conversation became stilted—out of respect, I thought, for the plump little man in white who wielded the hypodermic and spoke with paternal authority. In a sense, all of us were his children, and meekly took the pills and injections he prescribed without much question or comprehension. "The doctor knows best," his secretary insisted to us, and reassured by her faith we believed. But belief soured into skepticism the day when my mother, whose constant complaints of nausea had long been shrugged off by him as mere nerves ("foolishness," his tone implied) was diagnosed by a second doctor whom we finally consulted as suffering from incurable cancer. There was nothing he could do, he regretfully told us—the disease had spread too far. I was struck by the meaning of his diagnosis: my mother was going to die because our doctor was not the all-powerful healer we had thought.

Uncritical acceptance of the physician's infallibility is only beginning to change—largely through the efforts of women and women's groups. Females have always been more closely tied to medical services than males; a man could conceivably go through his life with only minimal medical attention, but pregnancy and childbirth make it almost inevitable

155

that most women, sometime in their lives, will be patients. And yet probably in no other area that so closely affects them must women submit to such a constant barrage of insult and condescension. Small wonder, then, that self-help programs, greater health education and a campaign for extended rights over one's own body were the almost immediate results of the women's movement of the late 1960's. The opening stages of a medical revolution are just beginning to take place—an upheaval in health care and health attitudes that will profoundly affect every woman alive in the year 2000.

The most striking change in medicine will be a startlingly different sex ratio among doctors. In 1974, women made up nineteen percent of entering medical school classes; by the year 2000 that will have soared to about fifty percent. Before then, however, the attitudes of pre-medical vocational counselors will have changed radically. "Girls today are still presented with a stereotype of medicine as a twenty-four hour a day profession that wipes out all other areas in one's life," a New York physician says. "As a result, many qualified women never apply." Undergraduate instructors still try to convince female students that as women doctors, they will never really be accepted or respected by their colleagues or patients. "They told me I'd be far more *comfortable* as a nurse," a young woman student at Dartmouth Medical School told me. "After all, I'd have the other girls to coffee-klatch with and much better chances to get an eligible young doctor—I wouldn't be competing with him." But by 2000, due to an analagous increase in the number of women college teachers, females interested in medicine will get far more encouragement from professors and counselors.

Once in medical school, women students will no doubt continue to encounter prejudice, but to a much diminished extent. More women will be medical school instructors and more male professors will have female relatives in medicine; feminists will actively monitor and combat disparaging actions towards women. Hostile and belittling remarks are still common in medical schools—some professors still intersperse girlie pictures among lecture slides for a laugh. When women make up half the student body, that kind of humor will disappear.

While there will be more women in all areas of medicine by 2000, the greatest gains will be in specialties formerly monopolized by men: obstetrics-gynecology, internal medicine and surgery. One all-important question, of course, is whether women physicians will behave differently from their male colleagues—they haven't always done so in the past. "In the years when there was little support between and among women medical students, women faculty members and women practicing medicine in the community, the easiest route to self-preservation was to agree with the predominant view of women as expressed in the 'men's club' atmosphere of medical school," says Dr. Mary Howell, an associate dean at Harvard University Medical School. "Many women physicians maintained their own self-esteem by believing themselves to be 'exceptional,' unlike other women. Most of them adopted the male-oriented view of women patients." Still, the consciousness of women doctors is being raised as much as that of any professional group. The influx of sensitive and aware females into medical school will thus bring a number of changes in health care for women by 2000.

"I think there is a strong machismo factor in medicine today that the introduction of more women will do something about," says one New Jersey feminist. "Male doctors tend to conform to the typical male stereotype in our culture—only more so. I think women doctors can help medicine become more compassionate and more humane."

Women physicians will obviously have a better understanding of the problems of women patients. Until now, many doctors have often been incredibly insensitive to women patients as people. A student reports in Dr. Margaret Campbell's book, *Why Would A Girl Go Into Medicine,* that a lecturer taught "the only significant difference between a woman and a cow is that a cow has more spigots." In the future, women patients will likely be routinely treated with more compassion and respect. A gynecological examination will probably be very different from that of today. A woman will no longer undress, lie back on a table with her feet in stirrups and quietly stare at the ceiling as the physician pokes around in her vagina. Instead, the doctor will tell her what is being done and why, explain how she can diagnose vaginal disorders and will openly discuss various methods of birth control. Women physicians will be more sensitive to a woman's needs and will be less eager to impose their own prejudices. As it is right now, some gynecologists refuse to provide women with certain contraceptive devices because of their own personal tastes. Author Barbara Seaman tells of one Southern gynecologist who refuses to fit diaphragms. "There is no sight so beautiful as a woman makin' love," he explains, "and nothin' so ugly as a woman insertin' a diaphragm."

There will also be a sharp reduction in the amount of surgery gynecologists now prescribe. Women with breast tumors, for example, have little say in their treatment—the doctors order them into the hospital at the first sign of any lump or sore that does not heal. As in the case of the First Lady, Betty Ford, breast cancer victims are forced to undergo extensive operations: simple surgery (removal of the breast, generally followed by radiation treatments) or radical surgery (removal of the breast, the lymph glands extending back under the armpit and the underlying muscles of the chest). Many women undergo the more radical surgery which frequently results in lifelong pain and weakness often without even knowing about less mutilating techniques, and yet many reports indicate that the more extensive procedure does not necessarily mean better chances of survival. In one study, cited in *Vaginal Politics,* 432 women were followed for at least five years after breast surgery—of these women, 324 had radical mastectomies and fifty-three percent were alive; of the 108 who had simple mastectomies, fifty-four percent were alive. Another more recent study also indicates that the radical surgery does not offer any advantage over the less involved procedure. And yet many surgeons continue to radically cut with hardly any consideration of the trauma experienced by women who undergo the surgery. In the future, however, a woman will be given more information about the options available to her. And it's likely that the radical mastectomy will be performed only as a last resort—if laboratory tests made at the time of surgery indicate that the cancer has spread to the lymph nodes. In the years ahead, doctors will also perform fewer hysterectomies, the removal of the womb. Once removed, the organ cannot be replaced, and a woman without a uterus is unable to bear a child. Yet in a recent study, a stunning thirty-three percent of all hysterectomies in a large union health group were found to be unnecessary since the conditions which led to the surgery could have been treated with drugs.

Paralleling a drop in unnecessary surgery, fewer drugs—barbiturates, tranquilizers, amphetamines and the whole host of anti-depressants—will be prescribed for women. At present, these "mood" drugs are often doled out whenever a woman goes to her doctor complaining of depression or anxiety. Men with similar problems are usually advised to "bear up" or consult a psychotherapist. In a recent issues of *Psychosomatics,* C.M. Brodsky reports that physicians often prescribe drugs to women feeling that housewives need not be mentally alert, since "they can sleep

anytime." A standard cliché taught at medical schools is that women have
a basic tendency towards hypochondria; pharmaceutical companies pro-
moting drugs in journals portray women in their advertisements as miserable and neurotic. In the future, however, anti-depressant drugs won't
be handed out so readily for long-term use. Instead, there will be more
private, group or family therapy, as well as vocational, educational and
marital therapy.

Advances in biology will certainly change women's lives. In the field
of aging, gerontologists predict they will be able to keep time at bay for
decades longer than at present and prolong youthful vigor into old age.
Women may be able to stay younger thanks to estrogen replacement
therapy, the administration of female sex hormones to compensate for
their loss after menopause. After estrogen production falls off in middle
age, women are more prone to heart disease and their bones begin to
become more porous and brittle (a condition called osteoporosis). Some
women even "shrink" in size and develop "dowager's hump," a stooped
posture characteristic of many older people. In her book, *Ageless Aging,*
Ruth Winter writes that she has seen some women in their forties age
twenty-three years in a ten-year span.

But when estrogens are given routinely, women will have firmer
muscle tone, tauter skin and osteoporosis will be almost completely
arrested. "At fifty," says Dr. Robert Wilson, a gynecologist who advocates estrogen replacement, "such women still look attractive in tennis
shorts or sleeveless dresses." Of course, estrogen treatment cannot keep
women young forever, but it does appear to retard the aging process.
This will have a profound effect on all women, since their bodies will
retain their relative youthfulness; and the prospect of the middle years
will not seem quite as frightening. The popular caricature of a woman,
hunched over with dry, wrinkled skin may prove to be an unnecessary
predicament. No longer will women feel threatened that they have lost
their femininity; the mental depression typical of many menopausal
women will be avoided.

Some physicians are even suggesting hormone treatment before the
onset of menopause. Dr. Wilson, for one, says that if hormones are given
in the middle thirties this will forestall most of the usual physical symp-
toms of aging. There are, of course, physicians who are reluctant to do
this because the administration of estrogen, which is a component of the

birth control pill, can possibly cause blood clots or even cancer of the breast or uterus. But physicians are testing to see whether the right doses of hormones can one day make it safe to administer. "This will, of course, offer a tremendous possibility for a greater length of vitality to women in their 60's, 70's and 80's," explains Dr. Caleb Finch, of the University of Southern California.

Reproduction as we know it will also have changed by the year 2000. Already, with new techniques of storing male sperm, a child can be conceived years after the death of the father. Recent reports suggest that by 2000 it may be possible to take an egg cell from the ovaries, fertilize it in a laboratory dish and then reimplant it in the uterus. Dr. Douglas Bevis, a professor of gynecology and obstetrics at the University of Leeds, told a generally skeptical medical conference in Britain this year that three children had been born normally after such a procedure was performed. Five years ago, Drs. Patrick Steptoe, Robert Edwards and Barry Bavister became the first to succeed in fertilizing a human egg in the laboratory. Since then, doctors have tried to reintroduce such eggs in a woman to overcome fertility problems. Many women have blockages in the Fallopian tubes that prevent the egg from being fertilized and proceeding on to the uterus.

The test-tube fertilization will mean that women who are classified as "sterile" and who would normally have to adopt children, will be able to give birth. Some physicians say that with artificial inovulation (as the procedure is called), they will be able to observe the developing embryo for any serious genetic defects. If there were any, they could then decide whether or not to reimplant the embryo. If the embryo is normal, it could even be replaced in the womb of a donor mother, thus allowing women who cannot go through pregnancy to have children.

In addition, it seems almost certain that by 2000 parents will be able to scientifically select the sex of their offspring. Since ancient times, couples have used a variety of methods to influence the sex of a child. Medieval women, for instance, drank a mixture of wine and lion's blood when they wanted a male heir. Even today, men in the Spessart Mountains of Germany take an axe to bed when they want a male child; they leave the axe in the woodshed if they want a girl. Recently, however, researchers in Berlin were able to isolate male-producing human sperm and are now testing whether it can produce normal children. So far, according to a report published in the British publication, *Nature,* rabbit sperm that was so collected has proved to be fertile.

The demographic implications of this new kind of choice are immense. Slightly more male babies are born than female ones, but the female's greater sturdiness means that by adulthood there are more women in the world than men. Thus, for generations a "spinster" was somehow pitied; a bachelor, admired. The assumption was that an unwed male could find a wife easily enough if he really wanted one (since there was always surplus of marriageable women). And yet were many more parents to select sons rather than daughters, within a generation or two the situation would be reversed. The numerically scarce female might then have her "pick" of husbands. Polyandry might become as widespread as polygamy is throughout the world today. Or if there were a sudden overabundance of females, a male might find himself in the kind of situation of which adolescent sex fantasies are made. What will probably happen, of course, is nothing of the kind; even when parents have the choice to determine the sex of their offspring most families will probably ape Nature—and elect roughly equal numbers of sons and daughters.

As scientists continue to investigate human reproduction, they are simultaneously studying new forms of birth control. The Pill, taken by eight million American women, has long been known to increase the risk of strokes and the formation of blood clots. By 2000, researchers hope to have perfected a more sophisticated pill for women which will interfere with the reproductive cycle without affecting other body systems as is the case with the present Pill. If this is not possible, many women see a return to more traditional forms of contraception, such as the diaphragm, foam and condoms, because of their fears about the Pill. In the years ahead, however, the best solution of all may be the male pill. After years of talk about pill-type contraceptives for men, it appears likely in the not too distant future that there will be a marketable pill which men will take either once a month or every other month.

For years, it has been known that male hormones such as testosterone and other androgens suppress sperm. But increased amounts of androgens in the bloodstream caused unfortunate side effects for many men including proneness to heart attacks. Investigators hope to find minidoses which can kill sperm without complications—but research has been slow, since drug companies have given almost no support to male contraceptive research. Nevertheless, with increasing pressure from the scientific community and various feminist groups, it is only a matter of time before a safe, simple male contraceptive is perfected. "Thirty years from now the big deal in locker rooms will be which of the various birth control pills the men are taking," predicts Dr. Elizabeth Tidball, of Georgetown University Medical Center in Washington D.C. Even so, contraception may in the end remain a woman's responsibility. It will be difficult for a woman to prove whether a man she has met only recently actually has taken his pill. "Women take their pills because they are scared they'll get pregnant," says Aileen Jacobson, a Washington D.C. feminist. "But it will be hard to check out whether a man has taken his." In many cases, a woman will probably still use some method of contraception. But in relationships where there is more trust, the man and woman will probably alternate taking their pills to minimize potential side-effects.

For those women who do decide to have children, childbirth will be a very different experience than it is today. More women will give birth at home, with nurse midwives performing many of the functions that doctors now do. While midwives disappeared years ago in almost all sections of the United States, except those without doctors, they continue to practice throughout the world as paraprofessionals who stay with a woman from the time labor begins until after her child is born. "In fact I've heard that in Japan, the physician stays until he sees the baby's head. He walks out, gets the fee and someone else delivers the rest of the baby," says Dr. Howell of Harvard Medical School. Women will be awake during delivery and the child's father will be there. A woman who chooses to go to a hospital will also have more control over her baby's delivery. She will enter the hospital, have the baby and go home almost immediately.

New surgical techniques will make it easier to have the child. One procedure recently developed in Sweden cuts delivery time in half by applying an electrical vibrating device that relaxes the cervix of a mother's uterus. The vibrator is used by midwives who perform most deliveries in Sweden. By reducing the delivery time, the childbirth procedure becomes less painful and often eliminates the need for anesthesia.

By 2000, I believe, the health care system will concentrate more of its energies in prevention rather than cure, and focus much of its attention on the rural and urban poor. But the poor (and poor women in particular) have always been justifiably wary of traditional medicine: too often it used them as convenient subjects for experiment or novice doctors' experience. One way to eliminate that monstrous face from medicine will be to move it directly and unpretentiously into the community—to sacrifice gleaming hospital complexes for genuine rapport with the residents of the ghettos, barrios and Appalachias. By 2000, there will be a widespread network of neighborhood health clinics whose main responsibility will be preventive medicine. Young women will come to the clinics to learn and understand their bodies, to recognize the right conditions for carrying a child and what to do if they decide on abortions. The clinics will be staffed in large part by women—some of them doctors, many more of them public health nurses trained as community specialists to perform basic medical skills. To these women, often residents of the communities where they work, their patients will be their equals and, not uncommonly, their friends.

Along with the spread of this type of health care there will be a corresponding demystification of medicine in society at large. That means no more doctor as Great White Father, whether kindly or stern—and no more patient as reluctant or willing child. The dashing Dr. Kildares, with their air of secret knowledge and special favor, will have gone for good. Women will have learned to appreciate their bodies in knowledge rather than ignorance, and the medical men and women of the year 2000 will regard their task of caring for the healthy and ailing human body as the ancient Greeks saw it—as both a privilege and a duty.

13 SOCIAL SEX: THE NEW SINGLE STANDARD

by Robert and Anna Francoeur

In the Passover seder the youngest male asks "Why is this night different from all other nights?" In the same context we would like to ask you "Why is genital intercourse different from all other forms of social intercourse?" Why do we Americans insist on segregating sex and setting up a distinct set of moral values for sexual relations which we do not apply to other interpersonal relations? A chapter entitled "The immorality of having lunch with your neighbor," would be slightly absurd. But the title "The immorality of having sex with your neighbor," would likely be a perfectly natural subject for interesting, perhaps titillating reading.

The concept of "social sex" suggests that we should eliminate the distinction between genital and other forms of interpersonal relations. It means that we should not have one set of values to govern erotic and genital relations and a distinct set of values for all other relationships. The relationships of men and women can run the gamut from a silent smile, nod or handshake to genital union. This spectrum should be integrated within the *total* context of everyday human life, not isolated from it. When sex is integrated, it needs no special ethic to guide it. Basically it requires only a careful application of the much abused Golden Rule: Do unto others as you would have them do to you. Or, as Alex Comfort, author of *The Joy of Sex*, writes: "Thou shalt not exploit another person's feelings and wantonly expose them to an experience of rejection [and] Thou shalt not under any circumstances negligently risk producing an unwanted child."

Emotions, Property and Babies

The isolation of our human sexuality from the overall context of our lives can be traced in our Christian traditions to a fear of the human body, a fear of sex and women, and a fear of the emotions unleashed in erotic relations. Somehow we have gotten the message that our intellect is something apart from and far superior to our bodies with their emotions. Somehow our emotions are not exactly human. True man, the male, should be a rational, controlled creature, with strong ego and self-identity. (Real men don't cry, especially in public.) Women, on the other hand, have been pictured by men as somewhat less human because of their presumed weaker emotional control. Women are still put down for their supposed changeableness, unpredictability, and illogic. Our minds must always remain in total control over our erotic emotions, our irrational passions and our sensual enjoyments. "Nothing," Thomas Aquinas wrote in the Thirteenth Century, "so casts down the manly mind from its heights as the fondling of women and those bodily contacts which belong to the married state." Our bodies with their "private parts" and everything about them that hints of emotions, sensuality and passion are somehow tainted, dirty, animalistic in this traditional view.

The realities of everyday life, however, made it impossible for Christianity to completely reject erotic love, despite the pleas from theologians and religious leaders that total abstinence and virginity were the ideal Christian life. In the Third Century, Augustine found a way to redeem concupisence—the loss of self and rationality in erotic passion—by sanctifying its end result. Sex could be tolerated if restricted to marriage because there it could produce new members for the kingdom of God. Centuries later Thomas Aquinas spelled out the "Three R's" of sex segregated from everyday life: sex only with the right person, your spouse; sex only for the right reason, procreation; and sex only in the right position, male on top.

If the fear of our bodies with their "uncontrolled, irrational" emotions has been a dominant theme in Christianity's persistent efforts to segregate sex, two other concerns reach back to the very roots of our Judaeo-Christian traditions, the male's concern over the integrity of his property and the male's concern over the inheritance of his property by legitimate heirs.

For centuries, in our legal and social codes, women have been relative creatures, subject to the economically independent male. In the Old Testament, women were the property of either their fathers or their husbands. A man who spoiled the female property of another male was bound to compensate him for the damage, while the female who allowed herself to be polluted or adulterated by the seed of a male without property rights over her womb could be stoned to death.

This concern over female property is still very much with us. Consider, for example, its expression in our marriage ceremony. "I now pronounce you man and wife;" and with the addition of the letter "s" to his title she drops her family and given names, and thus becomes some male's wife. The bridegroom becomes a man because another adult male has just given him a piece of property—his daughter, the bride. It is annoyingly clear that our society and religious traditions view the marriage of a man and woman as the legal transfer of female property from one male to another, as well as the recognition of the groom as an adult as a result of this transfer. Another good example is our belief that love is a finite commodity, like property, and cannot be shared without being diluted or lost. Jealousy then becomes an indicator of true love and exclusive possession.

Children were used by theologians like Augustine to justify genital union in marriage, but they have also been a third and crucial reason for segregating sex from everyday life. Men gathered valuable property which they naturally wanted their legitimate male heirs to enjoy when they passed from this world. Fathers thus jealously guarded their daughter's virginity because prospective husbands wanted unhandled merchandise. Husbands, in their turn, jealously guarded their wives lest another male sow his seed and raise a question about their heirs' legitimacy.

Transitions

In the three decades between the end of the Depression era in the 1930s and the early 1960s, we Americans came about as close as any culture to totally separating human sexuality and genital relations from the continuum of everyday life. We denied and hid sex in a way that only carried to its logical extreme the common tendency we inherited from our European ancestors. With the emergencies of World War II over, the mass media, magazines, novels and television all focused on restoring harmony by putting women back in their place, in the kitchen and nursery. In creating the "feminine mystique," we succeeded in segregating sex by isolating women from everyday life in the world.

But at the same time other currents in these decades were setting the stage for the present sexual revolution. Both world wars gave women a taste of economic independence and accomplishment, to the point where now over half of all American wives are gainfully employed outside the home. Psychologically women began to break out of their relative existence as property—"his wife" and "their mother"—when in 1963 Betty Friedan labelled and diagnosed the "unnamed disease" of these decades as "the feminine mystique." Effective contraceptives which came in the 1950s, and the recently liberalized abortion laws have had a devastating effect on our traditional fears of the unwanted pregnancy. In the late 1960s, our younger generation suddenly awoke to the joy of nature's sensuousness and the beauty of the human body. Finally, a major change occurred within organized religion: the Roman Catholics' Second Vatican Council and a parallel variety of Protestant conferences officially recognized sex as a natural and acceptable part of the total social picture. The public awareness of population problems and the open advocacy of contraceptives by religious leaders helped shift the meaning of genital intercourse from reproduction to communications.

Today we are caught in a major transition, a stage where our old values and guidelines no longer function as efficiently as they once did. We are still very uncomfortable with our sexuality, but we are learning to accept and integrate it in our lives. Our work ethic still enables us to feel guilty about relaxing and enjoying sensual pleasure—and yet we dream. We are uncertain about the impact of contraceptives and the extent to which we really want psychologically, economically and sexually liberated women. As we slowly reject the old values and guidelines—fear, suppression, property and reproduction—we are caught between the known past and the unknown future—sexuality is totally integrated in everyday life.

"Caught" is a good description of the situation, because all of us are more or less puzzled and upset by the turmoil of the sexual revolution.

The freedom young adults enjoy in their relationships, the confusion of unisex fashions and hairstyles, the seeming promiscuity of coed college dormitories and premarital co-habitation threaten many people who were raised in a very different pattern. As parents we are concerned about the risk our children run of being hurt emotionally, or even destroyed as they explore new lifestyles. We envy their freedom. We also become morally indignant at their "promiscuity" and confused about parental roles when our children confront us with new lifestyles. We are disturbed by what we see happening among our married friends: tensions, affairs, divorces. Children marry or leave the nest and often the parents decide that fifteen or twenty years together has been enough. Contented housewives suddenly wake with restless questions about their self-fulfillment. Their husbands become increasingly nervous and threatened. Books like *Open Marriage* and *The Joy of Sex* become bestsellers. Men and women who are not interested in being liberated suddenly feel like a new minority with the pressure of "not being with it" and are very confused.

Part of this confusion stems from the conflicting interpretations given to the sexual revolution. Obviously this revolution is forcing some profound changes on our middle-class American views of marriage and the family. But are these changes a prelude to and sign of western civilization's decay and corruption, or are they the painful birth pangs of a more humane and fulfilling way of life?

We favor the more optimistic view and would like to explore it here by focusing on some of the unexpressed and little appreciated values we find in the new lifestyles.

Integration

Most people who view the sexual revolution as the corruption and end of our civilization see only a complete hedonistic license in the new lifestyles and freedom. This license violates everything they have held true and dear in terms of male/female relationships, commitment, fidelity, love and continency. Our reason for not accepting this negative image is simply that we think there are some very important moral values evident in the sexual revolution which can make for a better world. Foremost among these is the refusal to segregate human sexuality with its broad range of erotic and genital expressions, and the refusal to accept a traditional special ethic for sex distinct from other human communications.

A hundred years ago, John Humphrey Noyes, the founder of the Oneida Community, foresaw some of the consequences of shifting the main function of genital intercourse from reproduction to social communications.

> Separate the amative from the propagative [in genital intercourse]—let the act of fellowship stand by itself—and sexual intercourse becomes a purely social affair, the same in kind with other modes of kindly communion, differing only by its superior intensity and beauty . . .
>
> In a society trained to these principles, as propagation will become a science [through effective contraceptives and our growing knowledge of human heredity], so amative intercourse will have a place among the "fine arts." Indeed, it will take rank above music, painting, sculpture, etc.; for it combines the charms and benefits of them all. There is as much room for cultivation of taste and skill in this department as in any.
>
> The practice which we propose will give new speed to the advance of civilization and refinement. The self-control, retention of life, and ascent out of sensualism, which must result from making freedom of love a bounty on the chastening of physical indulgence, will raise the race to new vigor and beauty, moral and physical. And the refining effects of sexual love will be increased a thousand-fold, when sexual intercourse becomes an honored method of innocent and useful communion, and each is married to all.

The Oneida Community's practice of "complex marriage," in which each member of the community was married to all other members, had some interesting Biblical arguments. The Oneida members believed that monogamy, the exclusive and idolatrous bonds which bind the average American married couple in cast-iron roles and selfish modes of behavior, was "the grand apostasy of Christiandom." " 'The new commandment is that we love one another,' " Noyes wrote, "and that not by pairs . . . The abolishment of sexual exclusiveness is involved in the love-relation required between all believers by the express injunction of Christ and the Apostles and by the whole tenor of the New Testament." Decades before the 1880s, when middle-class Americans suddenly became enraptured with a romantic and jealously exclusive concept of married love—which has turned married couples into caged twin-packs with no personal identity apart from their existence as couples—the Oneida Community was concerned about the alienating effects that overly-possessive love can have in destroying a community. Their distinction between propagative and amative intercourse finds some interesting echoes in the distinction Roman Catholic theologians make today in stressing the primacy of unitive intercourse over procreative intercourse.

With women no longer incubators owned by men, but on a par with men, and with the procreative function of genital intercourse reduced to once or twice in several thousand acts of genital union, the whole range of erotic relations and expressions, from the passing smile through all sorts of verbal and physical intercourse, becomes "a purely social affair." Its prime morality is the Golden Rule, "For the whole law is fulfilled in one word, 'You shall love your neighbor as yourself' [Gal. 5:14]." In this broad framework we might consider the function and morality of what some have called "recreational sex." "Swingers," who engage in the exchange of sexual partners because they enjoy intercourse with a variety of people other than their spouses; the man or woman who finds an occasional "one-night stand" rewarding; the person who unexpectedly gets turned-on and decides to joyfully bounce the bed springs with someone he or she may never see again—these relations may not be immoral as we would traditionally label them, provided they observe the basic moral guide of not wantonly exposing another person to hurt in any way. The same would apply to casual and uninvolved erotic (non-coital) expressions which have as their sole purpose the joyful sharing of a given moment. This idea deserves some thought by all who expect to function realistically in the future.

Loving Concern and Knowing

Within the frame of the Golden Rule, two traditional values are worth highlighting as guides for those relationships which we value highly and decide to invest time and energy in.

The first is "loving concern," or *hesed* in biblical Hebrew. Loving concern is the prime characteristic of fidelity. God's loving concern for His chosen people is the eternal basis for His covenant with mankind. Loving concern was and, ideally, still is the basis for family life—the father's loving concern for his wife, children and household and the children's devotion and loyalty to their parents. Loving concern also bound the servants to their master and his household. It bound blood relatives together and gave security and unity to the twelve tribes of Israel. In the New Testament loving concern became the Christian agape.

The concept of loving concern can be applied as an ideal in all human relationships. Good human relationships should enhance, rather than limit, the spiritual freedom and growth of the persons involved. They should be a way of expressing a compassionate and consistent concern for the well-being of another human. Human relations should nourish the fuller development of each person's creative potential.

The expression of loving concern in the Judaeo-Christian tradition gives us a good basis for examining the application of the Golden Rule in relationships which involve a variety of erotic and genital expressions in bonds of some depth. As the United Presbyterian statement on *Sexuality and the Human Community* suggests, "those sexual [erotic and genital] expressions which build up communion between persons, establish a hopeful outlook on the future, minister in a healing way to the fears, hurts and anxieties of persons and confirm to them the fact that they are truly loved, [these] are actions which can confirm the covenant Jesus announced."

The opposite of loving concern is self-centered exploitation—the care-less use of another person as a mere object. The Presbyterian statement concludes: "We regard as contrary to the covenant all those actions which destroy community and cause persons to lose hope, to erode their practical confidence in the providence of God, and to lose respect for their own integrity as persons."

We now find some interesting inversions in traditional conclusions. Though law and religion approve genital intercourse between husband and wife, a spouse can use the sexual relationship to exploit the partner, to destroy their sense of community, to cause guilt or shame in the partner, or to weaken, even destroy, the partner's sense of hope and self-respect—wife or husband can become a mere object around the house. If this happens in a marriage, the whole relationship is perverted. The same conclusion applies to non-marital relationships. But when the relationship and its various expressions, erotic and genital, become the "vehicle of celebrating joyous and creative communion between persons," then we have a good relationship. And this conclusion applies whether the two persons are married to each other or to third parties, and also when they lack both civil and religious licenses to engage in genital intercourse. (In some relationships, exploitation and the use of another person as a sex object can be mutually accepted and meet the real needs of the two persons, in what ordinarily would be judged a destructive and immoral relationship.)

Our reference to sexual and genital expressions as a "vehicle of celebrating joyous and creative communion between persons" leads us to the other basic ideal we would like to see stressed in relationships. In the ancient Hebrew world, genital intercourse and human sexuality were integrated in everyday life. The genital union was *yahdah*—"knowing" another person in the joyful defenseless communion of being naked together both physically and spiritually. This suggests an ideal to be sought in those relationships we really value. If, however, the two ideals of loving concern and knowing become obsessions, they can interfere with natural physiological functions, producing impotence or anorgasm. When this happens the remedy often used in sex therapy is to ignor completely the ideals and stress the individual's self-enjoyment.

These moral values cut across the traditional moral taboos against any erotic or genital communion among single persons and persons not married to each other. Even while the values create new responsibilities, they also open the possibilities of new levels of communications beyond the superficial amenities of friendship for married and single persons in all combinations. Human sexual expression then, in the words of the Oneida Community, "becomes an honored method of innocent and useful communion."

A New Function

Applying the ancient biblical values of "loving concern" and "knowing" to non-marital relationships and integrating both erotic and genital expression in these relations suggests an important new function for human sexuality in our society. Alex Comfort argues that if our society ever gets rid of its fear of sex, its property ethic and its romantic myth that you can only love one person intimately at a time, then we might find that the relationships expressed in purely recreational sex, swinging and in non-marital sex can become "a uniquely effective tool in

breaking down personal separateness" in our alienated society. Comfort
believes that social sex will then express and cement the equivalent of
blood kinships, just as it does in some tribal cultures. This bonding
function may also be reinforced by the strong reward social sex offers in
meeting our suppressed needs for variety and acceptance.

In a society whose population size is stable, where families have only
one or two children, and where our few blood kinsfolk are scattered, we
still need the psychological and emotional support once provided by the
intimacy of the extended family. In the family where bonding is by blood
relations and marriage, the incest taboo usually controls any erotic or
genital implication of the physical closeness and intimacy this pattern
accepts. Today many couples are creating their own intimate networks
or "intentional families." Going beyond the traditional boundaries of
friendship, these couples are including unrelated adults in their lives in a
way once reserved only for closest blood relatives. This means a new
physical closeness as well as an emotional involvement in a common
present and future. In this "intentional family" there is no incest taboo,
only the adultery taboo and the myth of jealous exclusive love—both
weakened by contraceptives, new values and the understanding of our
needs for support and intimacy.

In our culture we assume that any physical contact between a man
and woman must and will end up in genital union. To prevent this we
have a taboo against most physical contact—a taboo which creates a lot of
very isolated and frustrated people who need the emotional support and
intimacy that touching in itself can bring. As children we were hugged,
embraced and carressed by our parents. We sensed and shared a closeness and security in touching. Then, as we approached puberty, these
avenues for satisfying the human need for security and support vanished.
Years later the door opens again for us, but then only with our mate,
where sensual touching is a prelude to marital intercourse.

In the eroticized society we foresee, most of us will develop a
long-term primary relationship with one person. At first this relationship
will be intense, romantic, and jealously exclusive. Then as our relationship becomes secure, we will gradually develop a constellation of supporting, reinforcing satellite relationships, varying in their intensity,
duration and levels of intimacy. In this eroticized society touching and
even erotic intimacy will no longer automatically imply genital intercourse. With sex no longer segmented from life, a wide range of erotic

non-genital expressions will become quite natural and common in our lives. Sexuality will become polymorphic, similar in some ways to the diffused sensuality children experience but with the added dimension of sexual communion possible on a variety of levels. No longer will we be obsessed with our anxiety-ridden compulsion to perform genitally at every opportunity. Genital intercourse, both marital and comarital, may be less frequent than now but, integrated in a diffused sensuality, it might well be more valued and enjoyed.

Fidelity

Today, marital fidelity still means only one thing: sexual exclusivity. In the ethic of integrated social sex, fidelity means a loving concern, not for property that can be lost, but rather for another person in whose growth and future we share as they also share in ours and is a commitment to one's own potential, as well as an embracing response to that of the other person. Fidelity is an openness to the challenges of tomorrow, a flexibility and commitment to the future.

In these two systems of thought adultery also has quite different meanings.

When sexuality is isolated and restricted to marriage, you can engage in sex with your spouse for a variety of reasons, from making babies to having fun because you have a license. But the license only partially redeems sex; it does not make it something good and wholesome by integrating it in the total framework of life. As a result sex outside the marital bond, while it may be exciting and tempting fun, only adds the minor negative of being illegal and immoral to the licensed indulgence of sex in marriage. Adultery, in the classic view, can be either biological or psychological—a dilution of a couple's emotional exclusivity.

One real problem with this classic view of adultery is an unanswerable question: Where do you draw the line? If a wife has sexual intercourse with a man who is not her husband, she has committed classic immoral and illegal adultery. Even if she daydreams about this experience, she has already commited adultery in her heart. But what if she just lies in bed naked with him? What if they have mutual orgasm but not vaginal penetration? Embrace and kiss? Hold hands tenderly and meaningfully? Where would you get uncomfortable about adultery, for yourself or for your spouse? The logical consequence of viewing marital fidelity as genital exclusivity is that we have to place very strict boundaries on the relationships men and women not married to each other can enjoy. Any intimacy or physical contact beyond the most innocent and superficial has the potential for adultery. Married couples then become caged, isolated and inseparable, struggling to weather all the dangerous relations that tempt them on every side.

When sex is no longer motivated or guided by the reproductive ethic, the question of adultery transcends the issue of genital interlocking and focuses on violations of the Golden Rule with the ideals of loving concern and knowing. "I would not call an act adultery, if it's an act done with loving concern," states Jesuit theologian Thomas Wassmer.

The positive image of integrated sex creates an interesting logic. When sexual relations provide joyous communications between husband and wife, there is a natural desire to include others in their joyous sharing. Opening up their intimacy to embrace others becomes something positive, and definitely not something dirty, immoral or illegal. In *Honest Sex*, the Roys put this logic in an unusual biblical context: "It is utterly ridiculous to say on one hand, 'Greater love hath no man than this, that he lay down his life for his friends,' and to assert immediately that it is impossible and unnatural for a man (or a woman) to agree to share his (or her) spouse with another."

Jealousy though is a reality we cannot avoid, or escape. We've been brainwashed to believe that jealousy is a sure sign of true love, the conviction that you can only love one person intimately at a time, the belief that human relationships must be competitive. However we define jealousy, the important thing is whether we view it as something positive and desirable, or as sickness and insecurity. If we view jealousy as a negative and destructive emotion, we will learn to cope with it and keep it under control with open honest communications. We will try to find out why we are jealous. Is it because we are afraid of losing the loved one? Afraid the intruder might be better in bed? Envious of the time, money, and/or energy our spouse is putting into the other relationship? Or are we upset because instinctively we feel the other person is predatory? Once we better understand the causes behind the feelings we lump together and call jealousy, we often find that we are not dealing with jealousy at all, or that our jealous feelings have receded.

Our Reeducation

These rapid changes in values, the anxiety they produce, the confusion that comes from the different options and lifestyles suddenly open to us, the arguments about what might best help us cope with radical change in society, all combine to make it impossible to offer a clear, neat guide for our own reeducation. If we then ask what we as parents can do to help our children cope better with these changes, it is even more impossible to say for sure what we can or should do. A few decades ago parents seriously thought they were doing their children a service by protecting them from problem-solving. Many of the so-called "flower children," who reacted to this upbringing, now find they cannot cope with the problems of everyday life, let alone the problems of raising their own families. For most of us in our middle years the problems of our own reeducation are inseparable from our challenges as parents.

Parents must create an environment in which children can develop their self-identity to the fullest. Somehow we should provide our young people at home and school with an environment that promotes problem-solving. We can nourish their curiosity for analyzing human relations, for foreseeing possible results, pros and cons, possible benefits and likely risks—and then encourage them to make decisions. One practical way we can help ourselves and our children with problem solving in human relations is to study the patterns of sex and family life in other cultures. The history of sexual behavior is fascinating, and it also contains rich insights into the benefits and costs of various patterns of sexual freedom, marriage, and parenthood. In *Man's World, Woman's Place,* Elizabeth Janeway warns that "Those who are hit hardest by change are those who imagine that it has never happened before." Knowing about other cultures, other patterns of marriage, and our own changing American sexual behavior is a good way to prepare ourselves and our children for the inevitable changes we already see coming.

A good self-identity and awareness of other patterns of sex, marriage and the family will help us and our children stand against the pressure from peer groups to conform. It will make all of us tolerant of other behavioral patterns and other value systems. It will make us sensitive to the needs of others who perhaps cannot handle being disturbed by all the changes they want to ignore. A knowledge of other cultures and of our own social and sexual history will give all of us a better understanding of our values, and will help us make decisions with more self-assurance.

A second obvious goal for us as individuals and as parents is to integrate sexuality into our everyday lives instead of continuing to isolate and hide it. In practical terms this means that we have to become comfortable and at ease with our own sexuality, our own bodies and our own sexual behavior, as well as that of our children.

At a recent educational conference Dr. John Money, an internationally known specialist in gender identity, suggested that children should be accustomed from their earliest years to nudity in the home. When the naked human body is hidden in the closet, or behind closed bedroom doors, children naturally make certain assumptions about their own sexuality without a word from their parents. In most societies children casually observe their parents' sexual behavior in the course of everyday affairs. Our European and American isolation of adult sexual behavior and our denial of our children's sexuality is a recent and unusual innovation. We deny our children's sexuality until they enter puberty and isolate their education as sexual persons to a special course in school and a few lectures at home. What message do we communicate with this pattern? Are we telling our young people that sex is so dangerous and uncontrollable we want them to be as innocent of it as possible for as long as possible? John Money argues that this double segregation creates unnecessary confusion for our children about their sexuality and gender identity. Ideally the integration of nudity and sexual behavior should begin in earliest childhood in the home, but shifting the way we live at home with a seven- or eight-year-old can cause confusion—unless we shift gradually. In the long run, however, children instinctively learn to handle with ease, the conflict between our efforts to integrate sexuality in our home life and society's pervasive segregation of sex.

We should become more at ease with touching and caressing our children at all ages. We can also become more flexible in the roles we share as men and women.

A society that is changing as rapidly as ours must provide its members with some real psychological support. In practical terms this means that our schools have to start educating parents and other adults to the changing roles and functions of the family and sex. Where to find qualified teachers for this is a serious problem. Courses should be available in our schools for those who want to find out about the history of the family, and learn about the history of human sexual customs.

Our churches also should be involved in this education, offering programs dealing with old and new values. These courses will naturally present and defend the particular value system of that church, but they can and should also present the views of others without distortion and with a real tolerance for pluralism. Many churches have already recognized the important support people are finding in the sensitivity and encounter movement. Realizing that the methods of this movement might help their married couples, many churches have developed weekend "marriage encounters." On the surface this seems good, and it probably is—but only if the leaders of such groups recognize that new values must be discussed at the point when they are opening up new ways for their people to relate. Recently a television documentary showed the very emotional closing of a marriage encounter in a Catholic church. The couples were obviously thrilled at the new openness, intimacy and sensitivity they had achieved in three days intensive work. Like children with a new toy, they hugged and embraced each other. As we watched we wondered whether any of them had candidly faced the tensions, emotions and problems that would surface with their new sensitivity toward relating. Did they ever discuss what they would or should do when they became sexually aroused while hugging someone else's spouse? If these sessions isolate or ignore the erotic and sexual potential of a new sensitivity and openness, then the encounter can be more damaging than helpful in the long term.

Wherever the support comes from—our schools, our churches, or informal spontaneous discussion groups—men and women today need a variety of open, non-threatening forums where fears and concerns can be shared while learning to deal effectively with the future. This new open attitude toward sexuality and genital intercourse may be one of the best hopes for bringing people into communication with one another as whole persons in a society increasingly frightened by isolation and alienation.

14 A DEGREE IN ENLIGHTENMENT

by Carole Rosenthal

MY GRANDFATHER, who was smuggled to this country in a potato sack and who arrived with only three words of English and forty-two cents, knew the value of a dollar. When my mother wanted to go to college, even though by that time he could afford it, he refused to send her. "Why bother?" he said. "It's not worth it." It was taken for granted that she would work only if she couldn't find a husband, and my mother was a pretty woman. The only person in the family to champion my mother in this controversy was Aunt Chasha. "You're being short-sighted, David," she told him. "In college she could meet a doctor or a lawyer!"

A four-year college education in 1939, the year that my mother graduated, cost $1,050. In the mid-sixties, when my sister and I graduated, it cost from $9,500 to $12,000 for a Bachelor's degree.

But there was never any question that we would go to college. Our parents were more liberal—and more affluent—than those of many other girls we'd gone to high school with in Virginia. My mother had fought hard for her rights and she wasn't about to let ours slide away. Besides, she told us, times had changed.

Perhaps not that much. There have been more changes for women on the nation's campuses in the past five years than in the entire quarter-century preceding. In fact, so many new possibilities are opening quickly, that trying to analyze the future of women and higher education is a little like a post-medieval mapmaker trying to chart outer space after reports of Magellan's travels.

Looking backward, I remember ducking social jokes from paunchy uncles about going to snare a "Mrs." degree. I remember ignoring slightly crasser innuendoes about what kind of antics I was apt to get "highly educated" in. But most of all I remember my shock when, three weeks before my graduation, the Dean of English, who had applauded my plays at the campus theater, and who had read my poetry and knew my grades, took me aside and asked me casually what I planned on doing after graduation.

"Do you know shorthand? You ought to be thinking of your future now—"

He meant it kindly, but a filigree of panic prickled on my brow. *He was the Dean!* College was supposed to be my calling card to the future. And suddenly it clicked: ah, *this* was the reason they herded girls into the auditorium on Career Day at high school and tried to talk us into taking education courses. . . .

The year I graduated from college about eighty percent of the women in my class had majored in education. They were the only group of female graduates assured of professional-level employment. (Even that "safe" profession backfired in the 1970's with the teacher glut.) And the rest of us? . . . We knew there were interesting jobs out there somewhere, but we'd never really mapped plans, as many of our boyfriends had, because the probability of marriage had blurred the fine lines of our mental cartography. Ambivalence and anxiety paralyzed our planning. ("You'll end up just a housewife, anyway!" "Do you want to be a ball-busting career woman? . . .") We crowded into overflow courses in Marriage and Family Relations where Dr. Clifford Addams, who also wrote for the *Ladies' Home Journal* showed *statistically* that female college graduates' marriage chances decreased for each year after graduation. . . .

"Well, it's not as if we're uneducated. Of course we'll find jobs!" we said.

A sudden rash of pinnings and engagements swept the class just before graduation day. The history major next door accepted work as a fashion co-ordinator in her hometown department store. "Bell is hiring me as a telephone representative," my roommate happily announced. The girl across the hall, who had no prospects, O.D.'d on aspirin and her weepy parents came and took her off to a hospital in Pottstown, Pennsylvania. The rest of us crossed our fingers and tried to look confident

("I'm going into publishing," I told everyone brashly), while campus recruiters from I.B.M. and Dow Chemical ran over pension plans and advancement opportunities with male seniors, who were suddenly scurrying seriously across the Mall in new haircuts and narrow ties. What now?

Dr. Shirley Weitz, a social psychologist who teaches a graduate course on sex differences at a New York school, states that young women have not until now given much realistic thought to their future. "The problem is that if you don't think you have to do anything, you don't prepare for it. A lot of women see themselves as having a short life with only a big abyss looming after graduation." This despite the fact that over one-half of American women between eighteen and sixty-four are now working; that more than two-thirds of all women with five or more years of college are active in the labor force.

Before the year 2000 we will see the effect of more realistic job counseling for women—a shift of attitudes, opportunities, and an astounding variety of career choices.

When I applied for a job at a well-known publishing house after graduation, I relearned an old cliché: a picture is worth a thousand words. Or even more for women. The position was "editorial-trainee"; only women with college diplomas need apply. It turned out to be mostly secretarial. The first thing, of course, was to administer a typing test, the second to try me out for spelling. I felt confident. I'd been a Virginia state champion. The third test involved—literally—illuminated flashbulbs. Their personnel interviewer took my picture with a giant Polaroid. "What's that for?" "We're going to send it upstairs with your files," she said. "They want to know what you look like."

And after sixty seconds, frowning, she added, "I wish you didn't look so sour!"

Photographs and college diplomas: both were social filters for screening out applicants who wouldn't "fit in." That was the market value of four years of classrooms and tests and all those dollars. To be fair, the male "trainees" didn't have it easy either; the work was boring. But if *they* ever had to pose for photographs, no women on our floor heard about it, and they got paid more, they were promoted a lot faster. Did they have to call down for coffee in the morning, to type or sew buttons? To be a woman was to be irrevocably "low-status," regardless of your background or abilities. It was to have your Phi Beta Kappa key re-marked on as if it was a novel bracelet charm.

Status is defined sociologically as any sort of social value. If a parti-cular trait is held highly, that trait is "high-status." Sociologists distin-guish between status of two kinds: ascribed status—characteristics you are born with, which has mostly to do with lineage and sex; and achieved status, which is based on accomplishments and effort. Women have automatically had lower ascribed status, regardless of their education or achievement.

A person's *achieved* status may change, but *ascribed* status remains relatively constant, only shifting as the values and attitudes of the entire society change.

One of the most painful personal situations occurs for women when they achieve recognition for accomplishments that are highly valued by the society, but are still treated as inferior because of ascribed status. A woman physicist may be a "dumb bonde" when she's behind the wheel of a car, or be treated with condescension at her bank, or in any number of social encounters.

"It's hard for an educated or accomplished woman to know how she's going to be reacted to in any social or job situation," social researcher Lana Smart explains. "Will she be responded to for her abilities, or according to some social stereotype of women?"

When there is a discrepancy between women's achievements and aspirations and how they are treated in society, as well as what oppor-tunities are available to them, this gap may become filled with confusion and uncertainty, causing tremendous psychological stress. Women may drop out of competition. Matina Horner's "fear of success" studies, in which women predict bleak futures and punishments for competing successfully with men, are by now well known. Women have been psychologically "put in their place." But will they be staying in that place for long?

I went back to graduate school after some time in the "editorial-trainee" typing pool because I was tired of being treated like a promising child who was allowed to help around the house by doing menial tasks.

And I thought that if I took more courses, got more training, had more credentials, I would eventually catch up.

In college, although much of the curriculum is male-dominated and male-oriented (I had only one female professor as an undergraduate), women were allowed to compete more equally on the basis of their abilities. Ironically, extra schooling qualified me to teach in college myself; but in the traditionally male schools I seemed always to be in competition with other women, rather than men, for the few available posts.

Do you remember the part in *Alice in Wonderland* where Alice complains about having to run as fast as she can just to keep standing in the same place? Well, several years ago, before an especially grueling graduate school exam, I was fantasizing about how much easier my life would be, if only my mother had named me "Doctor" instead of "Carole." I could stop running, I wouldn't have to prove myself, to prove my abilities, again and again. No more maddening credential chase in order to be treated as an equal, able and intelligent human being. Acceptance, even in a patriarchal world, should flow so sweetly and automatically with such a title.

In 1975, I wish to revise that fantasy. A four-year college education in our inflationary economy, now costs between $10,000 and $20,000. Better, at least for the purposes of my resumé, that my mother should have called me "Ralph.". . .

Does that mean I'm cynical about the future of women and higher education? Not at all. In the next twenty-five years we are going to see the social values go topsy-turvy. The entire concept of higher education is changing.

For us in the Sixties, trudging reluctantly back to the dorm for our 10 P.M. curfews, it was impossible to imagine that coed dormitories, pass/fail grading systems, student representatives on the Board of Trustees and open classrooms could happen and be accepted as normal. The accelerated rate of social change will continue to fan out—we're in a transitional moment of history, a period of instant archaeology. Will established fixtures of the educational system be cultural artifacts by the year 2000?

Basic school configurations are changing. Experiments at lower levels of schooling are now affecting people who will be entering college and creating new educational systems. To predict educational change accurately we would have to foresee underlying structural change. The passage of the Equal Employment Opportunity Act, the Comprehensive Health Manpower Training Act, and the Education Amendments are only the tip of the iceberg.

So what can we expect by the year 2000? A movement away from attendance at schools and universities? The spread of multiversities rivaling the megalopolises? The collapse of an antiquated education system outpricing itself? Women opting to leave the home completely? Or reproducing themselves through parthenogenesis or cloning and becoming the only students and teachers in the university, the only professionals on the job market? How far out can we go? Maybe by the year 2000 the society will tire of abrupt social change. Will we then technologically control the rate?

Women are pioneering new educational terrain by seeing beyond the blackboard horizon and pushing in the direction of a new vision. It is a humanistic vision.

In the year 2000 the cry that the classroom has nothing to do with life—the most frequent complaint of all students—will no longer be heard. A livelier, more relevant approach to classroom learning is stressing the synthesis of feelings with facts. Life experience will be integrated with schooling, and students will want to learn because they will feel more personally affected. Today there are more than one-hundred womens' studies programs, and over the past few years there have been more than 5,000 courses given on women.

A course begun by the state system of California in 1971 was called Self-Actualization. Offered for college credit, it emphasized the exploration of life goals and was led by a psychotherapist. A course now current at a Midwest school is team-taught by people in history, psychology and economics. Each instructor attends all classes, regards herself as a student, and freely asks questions and offers personal experiences. Activist projects—such as working in the community, interviewing elderly women in nursing homes, and videotaping ethnic celebrations—are alternatives to writing traditional term papers or taking exams in a New York women's history program.

Imaginative approaches to teaching mark the women's studies programs. These teaching techniques will act as important models for future educational reform. Because they strive for integration of the formal with the personal, and because they are interdisciplinary, the women's studies movement is actually setting the pattern for the kind of curriculum men will be demanding in the next twenty-five years. In the early Seventies, many traditionally minded male educators name-called women's studies "trivial," or "merely eye-catching." They shook warning fingers that it was a fad, a fleeting dust-storm on the academic landscape. However, those professors may find themselves like politicians without a constituency as students—male and female—demand more attention to their changing needs. There is a reaction against the depersonalization and moral cynicism bred by fact-giving and analysis split off from human values.

In the past, universities have been run by men who saw the world as a place segmented into different formal disciplines: history, botany, engineering, English. But women's studies at their best abolish artificial lines; the programs cross disciplines. They may call upon students to make use of knowledge in psychology, sociology, political science, the humanities, and mathematics all in the same course.

"One person can do a lot of different things," states Kathleen Earley, a twenty-nine-year-old mother of two, who is both a science writer and a fiction author. This year she added college teaching to her activities. "Why cut someone up into artificial pieces? Why not integrate knowledge and skills in the classroom? We want our kids to grow up whole and balanced, why not set examples for them at all levels of education?"

A nineteen-year-old coed at an Ohio college pondering the impact a course in women's studies had on her feelings about education, says, "When classes are more like life, I don't end up forgetting what I learned as soon as I pass my exams."

Like many women, she found that women's studies strengthened the tie between academic interests and human relationships. "Ideally, women's studies courses are excellent vehicles to teach problem-solving and critical analysis," states Dr. K. Patricia Cross, a Research Educator. Students learn how to document and organize material and how to seek out alternative solutions.

Prodded by the high success rate of women's studies, some faculty members are opening their classes to dialogues between men and women, in which both sexes can examine mutual problems, antagonisms and destinies together. The result has sometimes been astonishing to everyone concerned. One college instructor, whose students surprised him at the end of the semester by spontaneously organizing a farewell breakfast celebration, recalls his terror that the class would get out of hand during the first few weeks of class. "We were sitting in a circle and I suddenly realized I didn't have a desk to hide my personal feelings behind. It was humbling, but it made me realize how much I had relied on my teacher role for a crutch."

Nevertheless, the freer give-and-take in the classroom, and the valuing of personal experience, will naturally erode the arbitrary roles of both student and teacher. The stereotype of one group who sits passively in a classroom taking notes, while a professor paces the front and expounds authoritatively, will hopefully disappear. No one person will hold the monopoly on class time. Everyone will teach everyone else according to his/her experience and knowledge. Scientific experiments, for instance, will be group projects that may extend far beyond the classroom. The style of the future will be that of a collective.

There may be flexible live-in learning units. People will live together for intense absorption of information and lifestyles, then move on to other different learning units, passing along the attitudes and information. (Sound familiar? Like a primitive intertribal network? In the year 2000 we may look back to the methods of our forebears.)

During the years when we still have student and teacher categories, "students" will take more active responsibility in running classes according to their needs and interests. An engineering student can lead a class on contemporary theater if she or he knows a lot about the subject. Or a person can structure questions for the group as a whole to explore. However, as Dr. Tobin Simon, a New York instructor of English who has been experimenting with innovative teaching techniques, asserts: "Involving a student on the level of his or her interest or ability has been a subversive idea up until recently. Teaching open and interdisciplinary courses requires immense amounts of preparation and a willingness to admit that you can learn from your students."

Around the university, however, women will benefit most immediately from this "subversion." The compartmentalization of time and information into semesters and class periods has always worked against the fragmented time-schedule of women, and against their social training as well. The male-structured curricula have tended to downgrade areas in which women excel. But suddenly these talents—women's interest in interpersonal relations, a concern with emotional realities—take on new importance. For example, a so-called feminine virtue—the ability to cooperate freely with others—was often a disadvantage within the old competitive classroom. If collectivism predominates, the values will reverse. And in 1975, it seems sensible for all to start appreciating cooperation between people for the very survival of our planet.

Women's social training takes on added importance when new job trends appear. Overnight, new courses are springing up to train people for work in the burgeoning social professions: counseling, working with the underprivileged, the physically handicapped, the mentally ill. People are living longer and a new kind of teaching will be required to reconcile conflicting values that must now be incorporated during a lifetime. There's already a lot to learn. The social services are our fastest-growing career area, and they require patience and sensitivity to another's needs—skills that women have been trained in since infancy. The educational institutions need to utilize their "feminine" resources. One sociologist, Jeanne Binstock from the University of Massachusetts, predicts that women will soon be the "policy-makers of all those industries that deal with issues of human motivation and internal needs." When women head programs in the arts, in advertising, in entertainment, we will see the emergence of "still-unimagined forms of education."

Women, then, are molding the shape of colleges both from within and without. They are doing this by talking, by demanding to be heard. Colleges—nudged by certain economic realities—are listening. It is a fact that there are over half a million empty classroom seats. Women are consumers; they have learned the importance of wielding economic clout in the educational marketplace. Women and part-time students are the most rapidly increasing segment of the college population.

What do women have to say? What do they want from institutions of higher education? The point women are making over and over again is that they refuse to settle for a meager half-loaf of life. They want jobs, they want mobility, they want important human relationships. Education should affect their daily lives. Learning, they say, is for life!

"We also want to move beyond the classroom," women have been telling educators. The hallowed halls of the institutions are pushing outward, the walls of the campus are being stretched into surrounding neighborhoods and larger communities. Before the year 2000, the practical application of classroom material beyond the lecture hall will free individuals to be with their families at the same time they attend college. The learning space will extend into the individual homes. Television already provides a home education resource.

Although every home will have self-programmed and computerized teaching machines, dialogue between human beings will become even more important. Advanced technology will offer more free time. We may see a resurgence of the close family unit (rather than the demise so often predicted), when more time is spent learning together by families engaged in common activities. Vacations will be part of the education experience: The Museum of Natural History in San Diego, for instance, offers tours to Baja California where children and adults can watch the grey whales spawn in Scammon's Lagoon. All ages, young and old, will have to pool their valuable information in order to keep up with what is happening.

Not only will universities sponsor home training and offer consulting advice to families and larger groups, but the community will become consultant to the university. Some college city-planning programs, for example, already work directly with the residents of neighborhoods. Historical researcher Robert Sink suggests that university libraries will become more alive with the filmed and taped ideas, memories and experiences of neighboring community residents. The cooperative project of recording this information truly takes the classroom "into the streets."

"Classrooms located on the campus are only one alternative for education," contends Ena Dubnoff. She is a California architect and college instructor. As a former Columbia University graduate student who received a scholarship grant for doing design work in India, she emphasizes the importance of "getting beyond the four walls to see how people are going to live with your ideas."

Students in the Integrative Studies Program, an approach to nontraditional education offered by Brooklyn's Pratt Institute, have gone far beyond the four walls. They include a sixty-year-old woman artist who did archaeological and cultural field work in Africa, a twenty-year-old woman who produced radio programs about political topics while living in Washington, D.C., and a photography major who returned to his native Puerto Rico and recorded his cultural observations with a camera. This program, according to Lenore Drumheller, a coordinator, "allows each student to create a unique course design based upon a learning objective agreed upon in advance with a faculty advisor." Like the older University Without Walls approach, now in location at over twenty colleges across the country, this system offers equality of access no matter how much time a student has for study. A person can stay on the campus, work at home, or travel—according to the individual design. And how "old" or "young" a student is never becomes a question.

In the year 2000 most students on campuses will be over twenty-five. "College-age" will no longer be sixteen to twenty-one, as people return to school at many different points in their lives. For refresher courses, to start or finish their degree work, for career training, to find out about new ideas, or just to seek the stimulation of old ones. Men and women will be able to study at their own pace.

In the CBS television play, "Tell Me Where It Hurts," a husband is overheard complaining about an over-forty wife who is returning to college. "I told her she'd be fifty by the time she got her degree. 'I'll be fifty anyhow,' she told me!"

Older women are in the vanguard of this movement. "It is not continuing education we want," one woman states. "It is continual education." According to David Elsner, writing in an article "Mrs. Suzy Coed," there were close to 500,000 women over thirty on the nation's campuses in 1972, double the attendance ten years earlier. Schools all across the country are starting to offer special courses, and even in some cases special scholarship funds, for returning adults. The University of Michigan, Spalding College in Louisville, the University of Arizona, Fordham University: all recognize the difficulties of the older student.

"I'm on the waiting list for a day-care center," says Patsy Jorgenson, a New Jersey mother of three who describes herself as the only freshman pre-med student whose zoology exam was interrupted for someone else's sniffles. "But then it's touch-and-go to find time for studying. Lately I've been asking administrators if something can't be done for people like me."

As women speak up, colleges are taking their problems seriously. A recent survey by the Women's Bureau found four hundred twenty-five campus prekindergartens around the country. A nursery school for infants as young as three months was introduced experimentally at the Old

Westbury campus of the State University of New York. Course hours are being juggled at many schools to accommodate unorthodox time schedules.

What about life experience? How much will that be taken into consideration? At Brooklyn College up to half the credits necessary for graduation may be awarded on the basis of an adult's previous accomplishments in life or on past jobs, and a series of local television announcements attempted to publicize this innovation. Such imaginative programs are beginning to proliferate. They anticipate the erasure of artificial dividing lines between "education" and "learning." Author-lecturer Robert Disch explains the difference between the two concepts—"education you do because the bureaucracy demands it; learning never ends."

Mr. Disch teaches at the unique Institute of Study for Older Adults, which is sponsored by the New York Community College and which offers free college courses to people over sixty-five. Its classrooms travel directly into places where the elderly live and congregate—hospitals, nursing homes, churches—and it deals with issues and ideas instead of usual "busy-work" and "crafts" programs for the aged. Many *students* are in their eighties and nineties.

For these very old as well as for the young, "relevance" is a key word. Just as younger women are demanding to be heard in four-year colleges, so their grandmothers are requesting courses like the Sociology of Aging, and Current History—both presently offered by the Institute for Older Adults. "I'm not going to play bridge or learn how to polish stones just to give myself something to do," one seventy-six-year-old asserts. "I've got a lot to learn and a lot to share."

Robert Disch observes that at the present time over eighty percent of the classes held by the Institute are filled by women, "who seem more willing to take intellectual risks." He believes that as cultural patterns in general change, and as new social attitudes are incorporated, more men will follow. "The biggest hurdle is getting older people past their own feelings of inadequacy about what they don't know, and after that . . . they're alive!"

By the year 2000, old people may once again be venerated—not for "wisdom of age," but because they are representatives of the growth possibilities inherent in humans. "Why not venerate them?" one gerontologist asks. *Their* continual growth and learning assures that they will have a greater store of knowledge and experience than other members of the society. They will serve as excellent role-models, giving us all something to look forward to.

All people, all ages, at all levels of society will be teaching each other. There will be no more "Teacher sez!" when the new learning style fans out.

Children might well be teaching adults when the year 2000 draws near, since they are among the first to learn many new facts, to spot new trends. And how about the possibility of courses in which the unique perceptions of childhood are relearned by adults? *And* taken seriously as an alternative world-view?

Marathon problem-solving seminars? Already commonplace.

"Future counseling" will be available, and free information centers, like Women's Exchanges, will spring up everywhere.

Diverse groups gathering together for educational encounters that result in a collectively produced project? A recent weekend retreat in Rye, New York, brought author-diarist Anaïs Nin together with people who felt their lives had been influenced by her work. The result: an independently published book, *Celebrations with Anaïs Nin.*

In the next twenty-five years there will be a greater proportion of female professors and female administrators on campuses. Women will be strongly represented in the sciences, in mathematics, in chemistry and engineering, in medicine and in law. In physical education programs coaching facilities will be male and female.

Much has been made of the importance of this visibility for young women, but what about the impact of this phenomenon on men? Will men suffer from this?

In the year 2000 we will look back on this as a silly, antiquated and culture-bound question.

"Not at all! That we even wonder shows how undeveloped our concept of sexual equality is," English instructor and novelist Marilyn Coffey argues. I interviewed Marilyn in the conference room of the Humanities building in the private college where we both teach. "Why should one group be deprived if the talents of another are recognized? Especially when women want to share those talents, not to take anything away. Actually, men should be complaining because they've been cheated of access to the experience and accomplishments of more than half the population."

She laughs and opens the table of contents to the two freshman anthologies—collections of short stories and articles—that our predominantly male faculty has chosen to use for this coming year. In one, eighty-three out of ninety of the works are by men; in the other twenty-eight out of thirty-six. Terrible, we both agree. Our voices grow a bit louder and some other teachers, and a few students, hear us talking and wander in to join the discussion.

"Women have much more experience with men than the other way around. Men grow up afraid of women because they don't understand them. Even Freud was exasperated and asked, 'What do women want?' He didn't know because he had too many preconceptions. Becoming familiar with what women think and do besides bearing and caring for children would actually make men more comfortable."

Toby, a male instructor, is sitting on the table and pushes abruptly at his wire-rimmed glasses. "But do you think job discrimination can be eliminated if men are more comfortable with women?"

"Sure. It's not the whole battle, but it's part of it. Contempt is the other side of fear. Everyone wants to believe the people they're frightened of are inferior."

"Battle?" Toby smiles. "That doesn't sound like very cooperative language."

Marilyn doesn't answer for a minute, swinging her hair back on her shoulders. "Women are the lowest-ranking members of the department, and have been since I started here in 1966," she says slowly. "I guess our 'battle' is more than a figure of speech. Does anybody know the percentages offhand?"

An older professor who ducked in, then out again, has been listening at the door without saying anything. He sits down, his arms crossed tightly. Finally he shakes his head. "The part I can't believe, Marilyn, is that you're actually counting. What difference does it make how many stories are by men and how many by women? I've been teaching here for twenty-six years and to tell you the truth, I never noticed." His jowls are quivering. He's upset. "I can't believe you actually counted. It seems so petty."

Meanwhile, without the technological aid of a pocket computer, it's taken me a full five minutes to figure out the percentages Marilyn was asking about. About one-third of the department is made up of women, but they are all massed at the bottom. Women make up one hundred percent of the part-timers, seventy-five percent of the instructors, and fifty percent of the assistant professors. Above that they are not represented at all. No full professors, and no associates . . .

We're a small department, although a very good one, and shrinking because an inflationary economy in 1975 is cutting down on enrollment figures across the country. Overall, since 1966 women in colleges and universities in America have made a slow crawl toward higher ranks— last year our department voted its first woman into a tenured position. The Carnegie Commission on Higher Education has reported that colleges have underpaid women faculty by $150-$200 million. If four-year colleges survive (pessimists point to soaring costs, optimists claim new innovations will lessen operating expenses), then women stand a good chance of catching up by the year 2000.

"Who knows?" Toby is saying. "You can't really predict the future. Maybe nobody will need a degree in the year 2000. Maybe we're talking ourselves out of a job. What if the lines really break down between students and teachers. Who's going to pay us then?"

Everybody laughs nervously. It might be true. A lot of questions go unanswered. The older professor keeps shaking his head.

"We want more than job security," Marilyn tells Toby. "And I'm talking not as a woman, but as a human being. We're more than what we do to make money."

I'm thinking back on those male college seniors in the Sixties running to meet job recruiters with their button-down shirts and sober self-importance. There was a tremendous social pressure on them to get those jobs; to compare those pension plans. To split off inner needs for the sake of occupational efficiency. For women there was an equivalent pressure to ignore our vocational future. Our anxiety over having to choose between our "femininity" and accomplishments kept us from looking ahead. The gap between our achieved status as an educated person, and our ascribed status as a woman cleaved us in two.

Both sexes suffered equally, if separately.

And now what? Do women want to be corporate templates of the male business world? Or of the male-dominated academic world? After all the clichés about women as paper-dolls are said and done (I hope it was yesterday), are women really looking forward to being society's cut-outs?

Women want job security, but they don't want to live artificially patterned lives. Pointing to an integrative vision of higher education, women are saying, *learning is for life!* That life should be full of rich human experience. Sure, we're still counting what we're not getting, because those gaps need to be visible. We don't enjoy keeping those kinds of counts. Hopefully, the numbers game is almost over.

By the year 2000 a higher education may well provide a degree of enlightenment beyond the value of a mere diploma.

15 WHEN THE VEILS COME TUMBLING DOWN

by Sheila Collins

Now women the world over were shut up from within and without, because of the veils which patriarchal religious systems had devised for them to wear. None of the values, wisdom, insights or talents which were locked up inside these women could come out, and no new ideas, experiences or opportunities could come in. And the Lord said to some women, "See, I have given into your hands the women of this earth with all their rich gifts and manifold wisdom. You shall march through the banks and office buildings, the factories, the kitchens, the fields and religious houses, all the women who desire to see women free and strong going through at least once. Thus you shall do for seven years. And seven women shall bear signs which read: "Equal Pay for Equal Work," "No More War!" "Our Children Need Day Care!" "Women Bear Up Half the Sky," "Sisterhood is Powerful," "Women of the World Unite!" "Mountain Moving Day is Coming." And in the seventh year you shall march around, arm in arm, now a great army. And when the call is sounded, as soon as you hear the phrase, "Liberation means wholeness," then all the people shall shout it with a great shout. And the veils will come tumbling down from their eyes. And women and men together, hand in hand, shall walk proudly into the future.

—after Joshua 6:1—5

EVERYWHERE TODAY WOMEN are casting off the veils of compliance, complicity and comfort which have kept them in tow to a male-dominated system of values and objectives—in religious areas as elsewhere. Sometimes the veils which women are shedding are palpable: the heavy, dark veils that Moslem women wear as a sign of being possessions of their husbands; or the veils of Roman Catholic nuns, which signify possession by the Church. At other times the veils are symbolic—veils of ignorance, apathy, fear, complacency, self-dislike, the internalized taboos with which religious systems have surrounded women to keep them in their "place."

What shape will religion take when the last veils come tumbling down? Are women likely to become more or less religious than in the past? Are women contributing to a reform of the old religious traditions? If so, what effect will the increased participation be likely to have on their theology, rituals, organizational management and religious architecture? What different ways of envisioning God, what new images and symbols might be likely to be expressed in such a religious reformation? Are women in the process of creating a new religious vision unforeseen by anything that has yet appeared, or will their final freedom signal the end of organized religion altogether? These are a few of the many questions which the demise of the veil suggests; but first, let us consider what we mean by "religion."

Over the last few years religion has received a rather scant press in the secular world, except in the strange and exotic forms such as the Maharaj Ji and his followers or in the spectacular events surrounding the Children of God sect. Most people regard religion as somewhat tangential to the issues that concern them most: the state of the economy and their own pocketbooks, vocational concerns, personal relationships, and perhaps politics. At best, religion takes up two hours of a Saturday or Sunday, its former grandeur as legitimator of kings and arbiter of moral values having long since been supplanted by the political, economic and psychiatric professions.

But let's consider the question of women's influence on religion in a much broader context than religion is popularly thought of these days—religion seen as the glue which has held civilizations together, while serving to define the boundaries of reality, making sense of the greatest mysteries of human existence—birth and death—and setting limits within which human conduct must operate. The Industrial Revolution fostered the idea that science had taken over the functions formerly served by religion; but the more modern science has discovered about the nature of reality, the more we are confronted with the ultimate mystery at the heart of the universe—that mystery which religious people have always referred to as "God."

In the last few years, the worlds of science and religion have begun to converge—as physicians admit the efficacy of such "non-scientific" processes as faith-healing and acupuncture, as physicists converse with psychics and experiment with altered states of consciousness, as biologists wire plants for affective response and study Eastern Holy Men to learn the mechanics of bio feedback. Far from being ancillary to other fields, religion—which organizes our responses to the unknown—may be fundamental to all. Religion has been, and may continue to be the most powerful and pervasive force with which women will have to contend in their efforts to achieve equality and self-actualization.

Organized religion—whether Judaism, Christianity, Hinduism, or Maoism—is first of all myth and only secondly doctrine and practice. Myths, which are stories told to explain the "why" of certain universal phenomena (for example, why the world was made, why there is evil and disease, why women can't do the same things as men), are composed of powerful images, symbols and archetypes which find deep psychic resonances in those they affect. For this reason they are perhaps the most difficult societal constructs to change.

Over the centuries it was religious myths which provided the bases for most of the great systems of law. Mary Beard who, in 1946, wrote one of the first comprehensive assessments of women's place in history, pointed out that the Common Law as it developed in England (which contained laws restricting the rights of women and children) was based chiefly on the Bible, as well as certain principles derived from Roman law. The English Common Law, in turn, formed the basis for much of American jurisprudence. In Moslem countries laws concerning property and the family come directly from the Koran, the Holy Book of Islam.

Even long after laws and governmental systems have been reformed or superseded, religious myths will continue to operate on a subliminal level preventing a complete transformation in social mores from occurring and causing painful feelings of dissociation in those persons for whom the myths no longer "work." I have seen these feelings of dissociation emerge in consciousness-raising groups, as women struggle to overcome the internalized myths of "virgin," "super-mom," and "siren," the only female images bequeathed to them by the Judeo-Christian tradition. We know that the myth of Eve—the inferior yet seductively powerful woman—has lasted well beyond the Civil War and women's suffrage amendments which were the legal remedies designed to do away with that myth in the United States. Yet similar myths may continue to operate in societies less professedly "religious" than ours.

Joseph Campbell, one of the foremost scholars of comparative religion, links the rise and fall of civilizations with the "integrity and cogency of their supporting canons of myth." Myths, he states, "evoke and gather toward a focus the aspirations of a people." When the prevailing myths no longer work in this way for a major segment of a civilization, it dies.

In speculating upon the future of women and religion, we must look not only to their role within religious institutions, but to the far more subtle effects which women are likely to have on the prevailing mythology and at the way these myths are likely to be transformed as women begin to create a different social reality. One of the properties of myths is that they never entirely disappear. Human beings have always been creators of meaning—hence, myth-makers. Myths may be reversed, key elements in them may be transvaluated, or they may otherwise be altered, but they are likely to be with us as long as we are human. If Joseph Campbell is correct about the function of myths, then women's attempts to shed the veil of religious limitation and superstition—that is, to change the dominant myths—may be one of the most significant indices of the future course of human civilization.

In any attempt to foresee women and religion twenty-five years from now, it may be useful to reflect for a moment on the changes which have already occurred. In 1853, Antoinette L. Brown was ordained in the Unitarian Church as the first woman cleric in the United States. In the summer of 1973, while rummaging through the British Museum Reading Room, a modern church woman came across the long forgotten sermon which had been given at Ms. Brown's ordination by a very brave gentleman for his time, the Reverend Luther Lee, who declared with simple eloquence: "If males may belong to a Christian Church, so may females; if male members may vote in church, so may females; if males may preach the Gospel, so may females; and if males may receive ordination by the imposition of hands, or otherwise, so may females. . . ." On July 29, 1974, on the Feast Day of Sts. Mary and Martha, eleven Episcopalian women, assisted by three retired bishops and in defiance of their church's laws and traditions, made the same argument for ordination as the good Reverend Lee had done a century before.

The old gothic church in Philadelphia in which the extraordinary ordination service took place was described as "jubilant" and "festive," for it had taken women well over a century from the time of the first woman's ordination to challenge openly the age-old myths and laws which have relegated women to an inferior position in the Christian church. Except for women like Antoinette Brown, who moved into a position that was open, and others like Mary Baker Eddy, Mother Ann

Lee, Aimee Semple McPherson, or Dorothy Day, who either formed their own religious sects or carved a niche outside the established religious institutions, few women have challenged the church head-on. In spite of an unsuccessful bid by Anna Oliver, in 1880, to become the first ordained Methodist woman, it was not until 1956 that the Methodist Church granted full clergy rights to women and not until 1971 that two of the three Lutheran bodies in the U.S. opened the ministry to females.

After centuries of inaction, events in the last three or four years have telescoped rapidly. Catholic nuns have shed their confining habits for more informal and expressive dress, and along with the habits have gone many of those internalized inhibitions. Catholic sisters have begun quietly to assume some priestly functions in spite of the official Papal prohibition against it and many are reexamining and questioning the whole notion of celibacy. Some orders have even become lay communities rather than give in to what they regard as high-handed and arbitrary policies by male celibate superiors. The joke of the season is that you can no longer tell a nun by her cover!

In 1970, the Episcopal Church agreed to permit women to serve as members of the formerly all-male House of Deputies and in addition opened up the diaconate, a lower order of clergy, to women. 1972 witnessed the first ordination of a woman to the rabbinate in Reform Judaism, the appointment of the first two women to the teaching faculty of the prestigious Harvard Divinity School, and the election by two of the major Protestant bodies—the United Presbyterian Church and the American Baptist Churches—of female presidents.

In the same year that women were winning seats in formerly all-male bastions, they were also beginning to initiate the kind of "guerrilla" activities, which would lead to a deeper challenge of the male authority systems of the churches and would provide the kind of precedent eventually needed by the Episcopalian women who were to defy their church in 1974. On Reformation Sunday, for example, four Pasadena, California ministers' wives, in a variation on the Wittenberg theme, nailed 9.5 "Feminist Theses" to the door of the offices of the Southern California Conference of the United Church of Christ. On the other side of the country, a group of women, all members of St. Clement's Episcopal Church in New York City, held a series of women's worship services in which they ritually burned 3,000 year's worth of sexist quotations about women frox both religious and secular sources on the altar and celebrated the lives of famous and infamous women as saints, many of whom had never associated themselves with Christianity. About the same time, a small group of women from the Orthodox and Conservative branches of Judaism, calling themselves *Ezrat Nashim* (Aid to Women), issued a "Call for Change" to more than 500 Conservative rabbis who were attending a meeting. The "Call" declared that a "separate but equal" apologetic for the role of Jewish women was untenable.

The Year of Our Lord 1972 was also the year in which the first of a series of highly significant conferences on "women exploring theology" was held at Grailville, a Christian women's community in Ohio. There, seventy women—theological students, seminary and college professors, lay women, ministers and other women concerned about the influence of the church and Christian theology on women—gathered for a week to theologize together out of their own experience as women. The influence of these events and the "permission" they have given women to *do* their own theology has subsequently infected a wide range of people and institutions across the country.

Within the last two years, women have made even more significant breakthroughs in the religious field. The Board of Global Ministries of the United Methodist Church—the body that oversees all of the domestic and overseas mission work of the 10.5 million member denomination—suggested an affirmative action plan calling for women to occupy forty percent of its executive positions and fifty percent of the non-episcopal positions on its Board. In a startling move, officials of the Conservative movement, the largest branch of Judaism in the United States, announced in 1973 that women could be counted along with men in the *minyan,* or quorum of ten persons required to hold religious services. The action came after women students at New York City's Jewish Theological Seminary argued vigorously for recognition of their rights as "complete persons." One suspects, however, that the first National Conference of Jewish Women, which had brought over 450 women from every branch of Judaism to New York to discuss liberation in Jewish terms and to call for reforms in the *Halacha,* or Jewish code of laws, had a lot to do with the Jewish elders' decision to flow with the rising tide!

Perhaps the most significant symbolic breakthrough for Christian women in 1973 was the appointment of Claire Randall as General Secretary (Executive Director) of the National Council of Churches, a body representing thirty-two Protestant and Orthodox churches. Ms.

Randall's appointment was important not only because she was the first woman ever elected to head that august body of churchmen, but because she is also a committed and outspoken feminist, a woman who has dedicated the last few years to the development of new forms of theologizing among women and to more open, collegial styles of organizational management. Her appointment is analogous to that of electing Gloria Steinem to head General Motors!

Naturally, as women press for greater participation in clergy roles and other positions of leadership, they are entering the theological and professional schools in greater numbers to prepare for the careers which they hope will be opened to them. In some schools their numbers have doubled and tripled within the last three years. These leaps in enrollment have all occurred only within the last three or four years, so that as yet the professional ministry doesn't reflect the changes. In the United Presbyterian Church (one of the most liberal churches in terms of official policy positions regarding women) the number of ordained women has doubled in the last five years; yet, in spite of this, women still constitute less than one percent of the total number of clergy. With such a minute support base to work from, it is no wonder that women clergy still find it difficult to win the kinds of rights which their sisters in many secular occupations have already achieved. According to a recent study of eight Protestant denominations conducted for the National Council of Churches, women ministers serve smaller churches with smaller budgets (about half the size served by men), and earn salaries which are, on an average, nearly four thousand dollars less than those earned by men. Nevertheless, women *are* affecting the religious sphere and in more profound ways than many imagine.

Since crystal ball gazing by any one person is likely to be a risky adventure, I have put the question of the effect of women's increased participation in the churches to several women who are aware of the action which is taking place.

Ann DuBois Conrad, who is currently Coordinator of Employment Opportunities for the United Presbyterian Church and formerly a community mental health worker who has done research on the effects of religion on mental health, commutes from her home and husband in Philadelphia to her job in New York City. Ann represents the changing lifestyles to which the church is having to adjust! I asked Ann what effect she thought the increased participation of women in the church was likely to have on the polity (that is, church government), theology, rituals and architecture of the churches. She replied:

> I predict that there *are* going to be some changes. You can already see them in the way women organize worship—very different from the way men do it. Women's worship is much more free-form, much less, "the hymn goes in this place and the prayer has to go in that." In women's worship there is more of an attempt to be inclusive, to let the entire congregation participate, and much less division between clergy and laity. Traditionally, we have seen that women have been more involved in the mystical side of religion (at least those who were visible) much less concerned with dogmatics. I would think that because of this basic style, some of these other areas are going to be affected, for example, the polity of the church. Churches will have to become much more participatory in style, rather than hierarchically oriented as they now are.

I asked Ann why she thought women's style of operating was different from that of men and whether it wasn't simply a function of women's lack of power that they tend to operate in a more participatory manner.

> I think it's more profound than that. I don't think that women would operate in the same way that men do if they had the power, although we don't have enough women in power yet to prove that thesis. I believe, however, that there are physiological/personality differences between men and women. I think that women are more in touch with the *yin* and *yang,* the creative life force. It may be a function of their being more in touch with children, although I find the same thing in women who are single or who have never had children. Part of the difference may lie in the fact that women are more open to their feelings than men and thus more open to other kinds of data—psychic data, perhaps, intuitions and nonverbal messages.
>
> This basic difference in style will radically affect church architecture. There will be much less of the chancel separation between clergy and laity; there will be more opportunities for "house churches" and smaller groups of people who get together in clusters for dialogue and mutual sharing; there will be much less of the presentation/lecture format that we now have on Sunday mornings.
>
> My experience also leads me to believe that women tend to combine life and religion, rather than making religion into a Sunday morning affair. If women begin to have a voice in the planning of churches, we may see the end of those big old churches with their empty pews. For example,

Broadway Presbyterian Church in New York is considering knocking down the sanctuary and constructing an office building on the site. The church would then rent a couple of rooms and have much more money for programming and more viable, creative space to use.

Ann's comments about the differences between the worship and organizational styles of men and women are confirmed in the experience and ministry of Lois Rose, who works as a minister with the United Church of Christ in Massachusetts. Recently, I visited Lois to find out how her ministry is progressing and what she thinks about the future of women in the ministry. Over coffee in her farmhouse kitchen, with her children and their friends dashing in and out, we enthusiastically shared our ideas and visions concerning women and religion.

Lois' style and pattern of ministry are a divining rod for the kinds of changes that we can expect to see in the profession. This vivacious woman had attended seminary years ago, but had had to drop out when the first of her three children was born. She never returned. Last year, at the age of thirty-five, she fought for and won ordination from her church on the basis of her life's experience and on certain equivalent accomplishments—such as the co-authoring of a book with her husband on theology and science fiction. She now works one-third time as assistant pastor of a small United Church of Christ, assisting with the pastoral calling, doing some counseling, and leading worship every other Sunday. Another third of her time is spent as chaplain to a Christian community for persons who are troubled either mentally or physically—those recently released from mental hospitals, the elderly senile, or young persons drying out from drugs. The rest of her time is spent with her family, garden, and other numerous intellectual and aesthetic interests (she has recently taken up playing the harp).

I asked Lois how she feels about her own ministry and if she ever experiences difficulty or frustration in being in a man's profession. Her response is typical of more and more women who are entering the profession:

> I like my job and all the things I'm doing. In fact, I really enjoy the variety that the parish minister has, the change of rhythm that it involves, the variety of ages and kinds of people that one deals with. I even enjoy working on sermons, as I feel they are a good discipline for me. But when it comes to worship, and breaking through that whole rigid liturgy thing, I

feel as if I am banging my head against a wall. I'm fine if there is a group of women who ask me to come in and do a women's liturgy with them, but I don't know what to do with the regular services. I suppose I could demand that we order a new set of hymn books, but what hymn books do you order! They're all just as bad. I suppose I am handicapped in one way because I have to work with an older man who has been in the ministry for a number of years. While he is open on one level, and gives me a good deal of freedom, he is at the same time loaded with unconscious blind spots. What good does it do to change all the pronouns one Sunday [from male pronouns to more generic forms] and then find that they are all back in the next!

What I have decided is that I would like to work on worship and celebration without having to confront all those old stereotypes and images. I may try to get together a parallel group, perhaps of young people in the area who don't ordinarily go to church, and get an experimental service going at an entirely different time. We could use jazz and dance and all those things that are "in" right now; and then, in that context, I would like to try some really radical things in the liturgy that would reflect the changes I have come to in my theological thinking.

I asked Lois what those changes in her thinking were, and she began describing her favorite sermon "The Web of Life," based on the Old Testament Book of Job, a story which has traditionally been interpreted as God's testing of man's faithfullness in Him. But the insights Lois had come to as a result of wrestling with the meaning of that ancient story had not been derived from any of the traditional biblical commentaries because, she explained, "none of those commentators ever understood the Book of Job. They understood it in the context of patriarchal religion!" Lois then explained that the meaning of God's words to Job were not about his faithfulness or lack of it, but about his inability to comprehend an entirely different and much more complex reality—a reality which the modern science of ecology, Zen Buddhism, American Indian theology, artists, poets and mystics of all ages have pointed to. In order to present this sermon in church, Lois had had to use a blackboard, as well as words, to draw diagrams and symbols of the reality she was describing. "What I was trying to do," she explained, "was to rip apart the normal way in which people think."

Thinking of Lois in the chancel with a blackboard gave me an idea: the original meaning of "rabbi" was "teacher." Jesus himself was a teacher. Whoever decided that ministers were supposed to be "preachers"! I asked Lois how the congregation had responded to this rather unusual sermon. "Oh, they loved it. Some of them are poets and others are elderly Quaker women; they know all about such things."

"You know," she added, "I never once mentioned women's theology; but that's what it's all about."

Lois Rose's unorthodox approach to giving sermons, her casual, off-beat style coupled with her genuine warmth and interest in people, and her intuitive sense of the varied rhythm of her life and work has undoubtedly begun to change the traditional image of the minister or priest. The entrance of greater numbers of women into positions of leadership in the churches and synagogues is bound to break the conceptual connection between "leadership" and "authority." Not all will be as different from the norm as Lois Rose, but simply that they are women will inevitably bring some changes.

I asked several women who are working to broaden the concept of "ministry" and to open the field to women why they thought the entrance of women into this field would make such a profound difference in the style and functuoning of that profession. Their answers reflect both the excitement and fear which women experience as they begin to challenge deeply held cultural assumptions.

Here is Susan Savell, a young woman who is finishing her Master of Divinity degree at Union Theological Seminary in New York and who is also working as a consultant to a newly established Commission on Women in Ministry under the National Council of Churches:

> What fascinates me about the recent ordination of the Episcopal women is that all but two of those women who went ahead and took radical action are women who did not want to buy into the traditional definition of the priesthood. In other words, they were the ones who were the most willing to challenge the hierarchy—the structure as well as the theology—as they went into that institution. I think they are being punished by being expelled because they dared to challenge it at all. Even if they had been "good girls" according to the hierarchy, I think they would have met with the same resistance.

Beverly Harrison, Professor of Ethics at Union Theological Seminary replied:

> There were one or two women in that service who were the most traditional in terms of their understanding of the priesthood. Thus, it is possible

to take even a very traditional image of commitment and, at the point at which you get radicalized on the "woman question," to use the tradition in a very radical way.

The exchange which followed between Beverly Harrison and Susan Savell provided further clarification on the way in which the participation of women could have radical—and perhaps even threatening—results for the future:

> *Susan:* I talked to several "middle Americans" recently about the Episcopalian ordination and they asked me, "What will these new priests be called?" "You can't very well call them 'Father'." I told them that they might try the term, "Mother," but that doesn't really do the same thing. I wonder if people don't really need someone to look up to—a Father-figure. I feel that the expectation of that dependency need by people in the churches has got to be challenged, but I am also afraid of what will happen when we do challenge it.

> *Beverly:* I think Susan is tapping the basic threat level of women in religion, which is the authority problem. Women just cannot culturally carry the ambiance of projection which has traditionally been involved in religious experience. When that breaks down, the possibility for a kind of religious experience which projects authority outside of oneself has to give way.

Sally Bentley, a senior divinity student at Union Theological Seminary and the editor of the first book to deal with the impact of feminism on the church *(Women's Liberation and the Church,* 1970) replied:

> Women are making the most progress in those churches which historically and theologically are the least hierarchically ordered, so that the authority of religious experience is centered in the person, rather than in the priest as mediator or in the sacraments. I see escapist religion (which we see in the current rise of fundamentalism) as a regression backward into the old authoritarian model. If authoritarianism in religion is on the rise, then I don't see any place in it for women—at least in terms of leadership. We simply won't be accepted in that kind of role.

Susan's personal response to Sally's gloomy speculations was interesting because it reflects a direction which more and more women are taking as they get in touch with their own religious experience and yearnings, quite apart from what they may have been taught.

> I see my own struggle with religiosity in two ways: first there is the repulsion of moving into those authoritarian structures and actually choosing that as a style of ministry. I *do not* want to choose that! The other part is looking at my own religious experience and history and discovering that I'm getting more in touch with my own person as a source of religious authority. This is one of the reasons I'm becoming more and more attracted to the Eastern traditions, although, they have that guru-disciple tradition which tends to set up authority figures again. But the newer spirituality—the eclectic forms which are emerging at places like Esalen [in California]—focuses very much on the responsibility of the individual and on developing a theology out of one's own personal experience. I think that way has more room for women than any of the institutionalized religions. If we're talking about the future and what options are open to women, then I see that as a potential space that women can move into; and because it is still a new area, we can begin to create new definitions of religious experience—although what's missing there for me is a real community and a sense of the ethical dimensions of religion.

Susan's conclusions, based on her own experience as a Protestant, are echoed almost uncannily by Maralee Gordon in a statement made at the first Midwest Jewish Women's Conference in November 1973:

> We are living in a time when we are breaking up that male domination and taking control of our own lives. To me and to many of you, it is inconceivable and senseless to go to a rabbi or other male authority to determine what is right for me, a woman, to do, what role I will play in my community, what guidelines I should follow. For more and more of us it is untenable to accept the authority of males over the life of females. And so it is that we must begin to be scholars and authorities ourselves.

Women are moving into the religious institutions in increasing numbers partly because of a desire to see simple justice done, but more importantly because they hope to make some basic changes in the mythology which undergirds these institutions and inevitably affects our unconscious desires and motivations, our relationships with people and to the world. The more liberal, less authoritarian and dogmatic religious institutions have naturally been those that have been receiving the brunt of the women's efforts, for the path of least resistance is generally the first to be pursued. We are now beginning to see challenges made to more conservative religious traditions. The challenge to the Episcopal Church is likely to have far-reaching implications for the Roman Catholic tradition, especially since the resignation of two men from influential positions in the Episcopal Church in sympathy with the position of the women. There is increasing evidence that Jewish women will no longer take a back seat to their husbands and sons in the matter of religion. Jewish women are also beginning to examine their heritage and are discovering that, at least in terms of history, they have much in common with their Christian sisters.

As women move into institutions which were formerly off-limits, they will bring with them new expectations and orientation. Whether because of cultural conditioning or some innate differences (the old argument between heredity and environment has never been successfully resolved), women tend to be less oriented toward rational, linear, hierarchical modes of thinking and acting, and more interested in relational, affective and intuitive modes. Studies made of women's speech qatterns, as well as the work being done by Dr. Nelle Morton, professor emeritus of Drew Theological Seminary, bear out this thesis. After studying hundreds of taped discussions among women and observing the differences in male and female patterns of interaction, Dr. Morton finds that, in general, women have a much surer grasp on the organic, interconnectedness of all things—that which Ann Conrad describes as the mystical side of religion—or what Lois Rose was getting at in her sermon. These observations have also been confirmed by feminist psychologist Ann Schaef, who developed a schema of what she terms "male" and "female" systems.

In making such generalizations about the influence of women on institutions, we must also take into account the reactions of men. Because of their own conditioning, men tend not to see women as authority figures, and if women are not perceived that way, they simply cannot carry that weight. There will also be differences generated in the image of the "priest" or "rabbi," as pregnant women stand in the pulpits, bring their children along on pastoral calls, or ask for assignments in which both husband and wife can share the ministry on an equal basis.

But beyond the inevitable changes which women are going to bring about simply by being female, there are other changes that will occur as women with a distinctly feminist background and philosophy enter the holy sanctuaries. Because they recognize the ways in which human cultures have tended to institutionalize inequality and injustice, religious feminists are extremely concerned that they not perpetuate those same inequalities as they struggle to win places in the organization. Most of these feminists also seek to preserve the best that was learned in a feminine culture. They realize, that although women may have been back in the church kitchens while the men were out front making the decisions, there was something important being learned in those kitchens. Perhaps it was a healthy sense of one's limits, perhaps a kind of support system which the men in their jockeying for power had never developed.

Feminists who are seeking greater roles in religious institutions thus hope to humanize and democratize those institutions. Such women believe that they are engaged in a movement to recall their particular religious traditions back to their roots—which, through the course of history, were covered over with cultural accretions. If such women are seen as "radicals," then they proudly bear that label, for the etymology of the word, "radical," is "root." A woman who attended the first Midwest Jewish Women's Conference stated the purpose of that meeting this way: "We came together to try to understand our role in Judaism, and differences between what Jewish law says it is, what custom says it is, and what we believe it is and should be." Many Christian feminists believe that the intention of Jesus was not to establish a new church with a priestly order and all of the trapqings which Christianity eventually adopted, but to demonstrate with his own life that men and women of all races and stations could live together as equals.

It is interesting to observe the kinds of changes religious feminists are making in the institutions with which they are involved. The Women's Division of the Board of Global Ministries of the United Methodist Church—with its strong feminist contingent—has begun to try to break down the barriers between "professional" and "non-professional" staff by encouraging clerical staff to make more of their own decisions and by including them in meetings to which formerly only "executive" staff were invited. The Commission on Women of the United Methodist Church has taken a critical look at the way church money is wasted on meetings held in expensive hotels and on excessive air fares and has decided to break this pattern. This Commission has also shown considerable concern for the rights of ethnic minorities in the church and society—whether they be male or female—and has sought to eradicate racial and class barriers wherever they are found.

Women in the United Presbyterian Church, troubled about the inequities which exist in the employment patterns of women in the church, have begun a union for women employed at every level—from local church secretary to national church executive. Church-related feminist meetings have been notable for their openness to new ways of conducting business. Most of them prefer rotating leadership and consensual decision-making as a way of avoiding the establishment of hierarchies. Many such meetings have become the occasion for the resolution of personal problems as well as political solutions, and there has been a genuine desire to try to network people together, so that no one is excluded from the decision-making.

But changing deep-seated institutional patterns is not easy. Sally Bentley, who has organized a network of women in theological seminaries across the country discusses the frustrations inherent in such a struggle:

> It seems that no sooner do women begin zo enter seminaries in any numbers, than they quickly find themselves embroiled in the exhausting work of changing the very institution which they initially felt would be the vehicle by which they could enter the vocation. In order to be fully and usefully prepared for this vocation, they must engage in curriculum reform, agitation to hire women faculty and administration, recruitment of more women, both as support for them in seminary and as sisters in future vocational endeavors. Seminaries are not stupid; they know that women will work hard in these areas, and they often are slow enough to pick up in such areas as recruitment or placement work for graduates, so that by the time they do, the initial groundwork has been admirably laid—by the students!

Beyond these changes of leadership, women's most exciting contribution to the religious field will come in the area of mythology; for as the centuries-old veiws come down, women are beginning to perceive a new reality.

In some ways this reality is not new at all—its seeds have been present, though dormant, in every age. Part of the excitement among women who become interested in exploring their own religious history is in finding those lost seeds—just as Lois Rose discovered what she believes to be the key to Job, unforeseen by any other biblical scholar. Included in the recovery of religious heritage is the discovery of the hidden religious "herstory" of women. Protestants, Catholics and Jews alike are taking a second look and are redefining the meaning which had been attached to women by male interpreters over the centuries. Catholics, for example, are reevaluating the role played by the Virgin Mary and are finding it, at best, to have been an ambivalent one. At times Mary was the only symbol of human graciousness in an otherwise frigid and fearful world, while at other times she was used by the church hierarchy to keep women in a subordinate role. But Catholic women are also discovering other women in their herstory who can act as inspiring and significant role models— women who can provide us with a sense of the continuity of women throughout history. St. Teresa of Avila and Catherine of Siena are two such figures.

Jewish women are reevaluating the role played by women like Sarah, Rebecca, Leah and Rachel in their history. Though in the biblical account, Sarah is accorded status through her husband Abraham, Jewish women have discovered an alternative explanation of those events. In the *Legends of the Jews* (old Jewish traditions and myths that survived in people's heads rather than in the Torah) it is Abraham who owes his importance and status to Sarah, who may have been in actuality a Chaldean princess.

Christian and Jewish women (and many who consider themselves neither) have discovered a common ancestor in Lilith who, according to Jewish myth, was Adam's first wife and claimed equal status with him but flew away when she discovered that equality was not in the cards for her. At a 1972 conference on Women Exploring Theology, a group of Protestant, Catholic and Jewish women updated the Lilith myth to apply to their own experience, doing what Joseph Campbell calls creative mythologizing. "Mythological symbols," he has stated, "touch and exhilarate centers of life beyond the reach of vocabularies of reason and coercion."

In addition to the recovery of their own religious heroines, women are looking seriously at the anti-heroines portrayed by their religious traditions and are trying to come to a less biased assessment of these figures. Eve, the source of every Western woman's shame, has come in for a more positive reassessment as a female who took some initiative and who was reaching for knowledge. Is it so wrong to want to reach for knowledge? Other figures like Jezebel, Joan of Arc and the nearly nine million people whom the Christian church persecuted as witches are also being reconsidered.

In addition to transforming the mythological figures, women are also seeking the hidden herstory of the women who played a part in the religious life of their traditions over the centuries: women who were hidden scholars, like Paula de Mansi, who wrote commentaries to the Bible in Thirteenth-century Rome, or women who listened to and followed their own inner religious voice, like Ann Hutchinson of the Massachusetts Bay Colony. There were the women who, during the middle ages, held as much ecclesiastical and political power as many male bishops, and there were women who, in the Nineteenth century, without any power at all raised their own money and administered their own domestic and foreign mission boards until they were at last absorbed into the male-dominated superstructures.

The search for a recoverable past which women are pursuing is much more than mere intellectual curiosity. It is the beginning of the reconstruction of an overarching mythos, or view of reality, which is likely to have vast personal, social and political implications. Here is one woman's expression of what the exploration into her religious past has meant for her personally. Deanne Ruth Shapiro is white, middle class, and female. She is also Jewish, a fact she had previously found hard to reconcile with her growing feminism.

> To celebrate my identity as a woman immediately brought into question celebration of my reappropriated historical Jewishness. Never an observant Jew, I had found meaning in affirming my ethnicity and historicity as part of a five thousand year continuum of Jewish people. How then to celebrate this identity without celebrating the patriarchq which sustains (and continues to sustain) Judaism throughout its history? . . . Understanding my identity as the process of interpreting and integrating my participation in various human communities, I am enabled as a Jewish woman to feel continuity between my experience and the experiences of generatiocssof Jewish women who have preceded me. Until now they have been my mothers and grandmothers and I their rebellious child; now they have become my sisters, and in our sisterhood as Jewish women the historical tradition has a spiritual meaning never before available to me. My unity with them and my unity within myself are one. I am one; it is a gift of

self, of life, for which I am indebted to my sisters in ways no words or pictures can ever express.

In the heady atmosphere which accompanies the intellectual questioning of traditions, women are also stepping beyond their own religious boundaries to look seriously at the ways in which other religious traditions have mythologized reality. Zen Buddhism and other Eastern traditions, Druidism, African religious forms, mysticism, astrology, gestalt therapy, and the religions of the Great Mother Goddess which preceded the rise of Judaism are all being scrutinized for the light they shed on women's search for meaning. In this quest, religious feminists not surprisingly find themselves meeting up with women who consider themselves non-religious (in the traditional sense) but who now find religious questions exciting as a result of their evejgent feminism.

What are likely to be the social ramifications of this search for a new mythology? The old mythos—the one constructed by male priests and theologians over the centuries—was used to limit woman's power so she could be effectively subordinated to the economic and political interests of men. Its effect was to isolate women from each other and from their own past, to create in them a fear of male religious and political authority, to deny their own religious experience, and to create a false sepajation between mind and body, inner and outer experience, male and female, sacred and secular, intellect and emotion. As women recover their past and use their own female experience to reinterpret reality, we are likely to see those cultural dichotomies begin to break down.

We can already see this happening in the ministry of Lois Rose and in the comments of Susan Savell. Women are indeed learning to trust their own perceptions and to challenge religious and other authorities of "expertise" where such authority is inimical to their own experience. The separation between religious authority and "believer" is also being broken in the way in which women are now *doing* theology. As an academic discipline, theology used to be thought of as the preserve of men who had at least three titles after their names and a chair in some prestigious theological school. Now, women with or without academic theological training are getting together in groups to do theology collectively using their own experience as a starting point. Many see the women's consciousness-raising group as the model for the new forms in which theology must be done.

The difference between the way women do theology and the way it is handled in theological seminaries is striking. Women almost always deal on several levels at once. For them, theology is often intensely personal and therapeutic as well as intellectually stimulating; it is spiritual and political, physical as well as mental. The whole person is used to explore questions related to the meaning of life. When I attended theological school in the early 1960's, the discipline was almost totally intellectual, with almost no relevance or relationship to my daily life. I left seminary disappointed, thinking that religious studies were only for those who delighted in intellectual argumentation.

Perhaps as women begin to dissolve the notion that religious authority is always located in someone or something "out there," we may see the end of the priestly caste as a group of people who mediate the ways of God to men. But if the priest or clergyman disappears, then who will minister? The people? That, religious feminists point out, is what this whole religious business was about in the first place! Ann Conrad foresees the ordination of women to the ministry, priesthood or rabbinate as an interim measure, or as just one of the many forms which "ministry" will take in the future. "We've got to begin thinking about the ministry of the lawwoman, the ministry of the secretary, the ministry of everybody," she says.

As a result of women's participation in the reconstruction of a religious mythos, we are also likely to see a breaking down of the divisions which have separated one religious or ethnic group from another. By focusing on the "woman question" and on the search for a meaningful herstory, women of various faiths and races have been brought together, and in that exchange they have discovered that the barriers, which had seemed so insurmountable before, were false. While recognizing the divergence of their heritages, Catholic and Protestant feminists nevertheless find that they have more in common religiously than they do with the men in their own faiths. There are many areas in which Catholic, Protestant and Jewish women are working together in the religious field, each recognizing that she has something to learn from the other's heritage. Perhaps the most significant coming-together of women thus far was a World Council of Churches' sponsored meeting held in Berlin in 1974 to explore the issue of sexism in church and culture. There, 154 women from forty-nine countries struggled with race, class and language barriers to affirm their solidarity as women and their desire to work for the emergence of a more just and peaceful world.

It goes without saying that the participation of women in the creation of a new mythology is likely to have radical consequences for the future course of religion itself. Until now, the dominant myth in most Western religious systems had to do with a Father-God, a masculine, anthropomorphic figure who was generally conceived of as located outside of the person and of nature. Women have levelled a salvo at that image from which there is no recovery. Not only have they pointed to places in the Bible where God is conceived of in feminine terms, but they have demonstrated that much of the "given" religious doctrine and ritual was really an attempt by males to reappropriate the naturally occurring functions of the female. What if the ritual of circumcision were simply a primitive attempt to emulate the menstrual flow of women, which early man associated with the ability to give birth? What if the sacrament of baptism is a return to the amniotic waters of the womb, and rebirth through Christ represents a reversal of birth from the female? In other words, the loftiest religious rituals might have arisen as a result of sexual jealousy!

Does this mean that women are debunking the entire religious dimension? Far from it! they reply. What women are beginning to tell us is that our religious traditions and mythologies have been far too narrow. A white, male God cannot any longer represent the aspirations of a pluralistic world. Perhaps we need a multidimensional concept of God—a God that is both *in here* and *out there,* a God that is both changing and constant, a God that encompasses both male and female, that is white, but also black and brown and red and yellow and all the shades in-between.

But women are beginning to realize that even that God is too narrow. I asked Ann Conrad what she thought the image of God would likely be in the future. "I think there will continue to be the concept of a personal God," she replied, "for women have always gravitated to the personal dimension of religion; but I think we are also going to see more cosmic images of God appear. After all, living in the space age must be having some influence on our psyches!" Lois Rose's God is certainly much more cosmic than the Sunday School image she grew up with. Indeed, her God is the very web of life itself, the interconnectedness of the whole creation. Lois' understanding of God came very close to a description given to me by a young woman who comes from a long line of Irish Druids. As women perceive the idolatry of the old forms in which God has been housed, they are stretching their own minds, and ours, in startling new directions.

Women are also likely to reshape that branch of theology which deals with moral or ethical decision-making, with definitions of right and wrong. Before now, religious systems have tended to separate ethical decision-making from "spiritual" or purely personal religious experience and private morality from decisions which are made in the public sphere. In modern America these dichotomies have resulted in people who attend church on Sunday to "get religion" and then go out on Monday and practice bigotry—or in the assumption that the "Church" is not the place where politics or economics or the ethical consequences of capitalism or socialism are discussed, because these topics have nothing to do with "religion." But Christianity, and to some extent Judaism, is not the only culprit. The dichotomy between personal experience and corporate responsibility is also found in some of the now popular Eastern religious movements, such as that espoused by the Guru Maharaj Ji or the Transcendental Meditation movement in which personal religious "experience" or "knowledge" is emphasized to the exclusion of concern for systemic evil.

Because of their understanding that the personal is political, religious feminists are going to be insisting that their religious traditions learn to integrate the personal religious experience with corporate concern for social justice, ecological sanity and an end to war. Such women are becoming increasingly intolerant of the either/or approach to life. "What we are experiencing," explained Sally Bentley, "is the break between exercising our own authority and wanting to empower people to *their own* authority. How do you do both within the framework of institutions which are already authoritarian?" Susan Savell replied:

> The two options that I see are either to move into those authoritarian structures and take our own sense of authority with us, and therefore either work for the demise or the renewal of those institutions, or to begin to explore new options that take the nurturance and the creation of personal authority very seriously and begin from that point to create new communities that are ethical and that take an ethical stance in relationship to the world. I guess what I'm feeling now is that no institutional religion is sufficient in this respect.

What women like Sally and Susan are saying to us is that the prevailing mythology has separated the caring, nurturing concern for humans and the quality of life from the realm of power. This happened when care and nurturing were given over to women who had no power, and power was given over to men whose lives were increasingly isolated from the areas in which care and nurturing take place—power, unchecked by the ethics involved in caring, becomes unbridled and often tyrannical; and care, with no access to power is reduced to servitude. Both are distorted in our religious and political life.

We are probably going to see women reshape that branch of ethics which deals with interpersonal relationships and sexual behavior. The ethics of the old traditions have simply been unable to cope with the changes created in this area by the so-called "sexual revolution," the women's movement, gay activism, and the development of new technologies in the bio-medical field. It is not surprising that traditional religions are unable to deal with these changes when we consider that they are based on a mythology which considers women inferior and any sexual relationship outside of marriage "unnatural," if not evil. Right now too many people are wandering aimlessly in the maze of confusion created by new sexual freedoms. They realize that the old shibboleths no longer work, but there are no new guidelines, no ethical perspective to replace the old guidelines. As more women take over the leadership of our religious institutions, we will begin to see a way of bringing all of those new and rather frightening freedoms into an ethical perspective—a perspective which will enable people to get handles on their own desires, fears, obligations, compulsions and inhibitions and to act in a responsible yet liberating way. Concerned female religious leaders will lend strength in the movement to develop a strong, inner self-authority.

The changes I have been describing thus far are still trends rather than realized objectives. Whether they will be partially or fully achieved by the year 2000 depends upon a number of variables, the first of which is the ability of the secular women's movement to succeed. The initial impulse to radically transform the religious arena came not from religious traditions, but from involvement by women in religious professions in the secular women's movement. This bears out Dr. Beverly Harrison's (Professor of Ethics at Union Theological Seminary) thesis that the authentic religious impulse—that impulse which enables one to stand outside one's culture and to look at it critically—is generated not in the formal religious institutions of our society, but in political movements, so that if one focuses exclusively on the religious institutions as the source of religious energy and innovation, one is looking in the wrong place.

If, as a result of the secular women's movement, more and more women are turned on to the possibility of becoming whole, self-actualized persons—if more women desire to share *both* the home and the world with men—then we will see the changes occurring in religion that are described in these pages. But if for some unforeseen reason the pace is slowed, then the movement for religion's revitalization will falter also, because it is women who make up the majority in the churches across this land. The Father God of Judaism and Christianity has served men well. The majority of men have no compelling need to commit patricide, and so it is the women from whom the fresh religious impulse in our time will come. And if women are fearful of removing the veil, we will have more of the same inconsequential religiosity, with religious institutions becoming increasingly marginal to the mainstream of the culture.

I doubt that the pace of change will diminish. If the last three years are any indication, we are likely to see the changes accelerating.

Very shortly, the major Protestant denominations will have to make some major adjustments, as women who are now in seminaries begin to move out into the job market (where there are currently too few openings). Ann Conrad thinks this just might push the churches toward a redefinition of "ministry," so that the function of ministry could be applied to many other types of work than it now is. Right now, there are ordained women running community women's centers or working as professional counselors whose work is officially a form of "ministry" even though they are not attached to a "church." Churches have not yet been able to provide enough financial backing for these alternate ministries, but have provided "in-kind" support, such as building space and mimeograph facilities, in some cases. Essentially what such women are engaged in is a tent-making ministry—the form which ministry took in the early Christian church before the emergent of a paid and highly powerful priestly caste. Again, women are calling their religious traditions back to their roots!

Perhaps by 2000 we'll see the simultaneous existence of two antithetical religious streams. As more and more women become involved in the creative critique of their own traditions and as they search for new forms of "ministry" and "church," they will begin to pick up allies. If those allies—whether they be women or liberated men—are found inside the churches and synagogues, then they will work from within religious institutions to reform and rejuvenate them.

However, to rejuvenate religion may mean the eventual dissolution of religion as an "institution," so that religious activity, like an amoeba, will regenerate itself and begin to permeate the whole culture. We may then see all of life—the birth of a child, the death of friends, sexual love, political struggles, disappointments and triumphs—as the "stuff" of religious experience from which we draw our images and symbols and which we celebrate either singly or corporately. When that time comes we may celebrate the depths of life spontaneously in whatever communities those depths are touched, whether they be the depths of anger, fear, sorrow, pain, despair, or joy and thankfulness. And to celebrate life (which is the basic function of religion) we may use tears and laughter, rage and exhuberance, dance and song, poetry and prose, old traditions and innovations.

But there are those who are threatened by such a vision; and thus the second variable which will affect the pace is the threat/liberation quotient which any radical challenge to the status quo must take into account. To work for the dissolution of institutionalized religion poses a threat to those men who have staked their identity, indeed their entire economic well-being, on those institutions. But the movement of women into the religious arena implies an even greater threat than that. When significant challenges are made to the mythology which has upheld a civilization for centuries, people react in one of two ways: either they find that challenge liberating and become a part of it, or they retreat head-long into the old securities. Those who retreat have some awareness that the old mythologies are dysfunctional, but their fear of change and the unknown is even greater. Large numbers of women, as well as men, can be threatened at this point. If people continue to opt for security over experimentation and renewal, then we will see the simultaneous existence of a highly institutionalized religious conservatism based on the "saving" of individual souls, along with a non-institutionalized form of religious experimentation which begins to permeate the political and economic sectors of our cultural life.

Religious feminists are well aware of the dangers their challenge to the reigning mythology implies and are not apt to be quite so optimistic about the future as their sisters in the secular world. They know that their religious quest touches the very wellsprings of the human enterprise—the way we perceive and organize reality. Until now, the Western world has operated quite efficiently on the old dualistic model which created barriers between male and female, mind and body, humans and the natural world, sacred and secular, personal morality and political decision-making. Economic and political as well as religious institutions hinged on these divisions. Thus, to change the dominant mythology implies a change in our secular institutions as well—a change away from *both* the United States and Soviet versions of the techno-totalitarian state toward a polymorphous, participatory, democratic socialism.

The third variable which will affect the course of religious renewal is the rising voices of the Third World and the changes which are likely to be made on the national and international scene as the balance of power begins to shift away from the developed to the developing world. Both in the United States and overseas, black, brown, red and yellow peoples are beginning to develop or to reassert mythologies based on their own history and cultural experience. As these mythologies gain ascendence, they come into direct conflict with the prevailing mythos developed in the white, Western, affluent male world.

Thus far, the movement among women to revitalize the religious enterprise has been generated by white, middle class women, simply because these women have not been engaged in a struggle for simple physical survival and thus have had the time and space necessary to think about the meaning of life. There are many points of contact and agreement, however, between the mythology being developed by white women and the visions which are arising among Asians, Africans and Latin Americans—although these mythologies are still largely the product of males in those cultures. As Third World women achieve economic and political emancipation within their cultures, they will add their rich store of images, symbols and experiences to the myth-making enterprise. This is already happening in parts of Africa, Latin America and among black and Hispanic women in the United States.

Women who are laboring to give birth to a new religious vision may eventually find their allies among those women and men of other races and cultures who, against much greater odds, are nurturing the seeds of their own liberation. The bishops who ordained the eleven Episcopalian women in defiance of their church's orders recognized the connections which their act was making with others. In an "Open Letter" to their church they stated that they were taking this extraordinary action as "an act of solidarity with those in whatever stratum of society, who in their search for freedom, for liberation, for dignity, are moved by the same spirit to struggle against sin, to proclaim that victory, to attempt to walk in newness of life." It is significant that the most outspoken advocate of the stand taken by these women was Dr. Charles Willie, an Episcopal layman and a black man, who saw clearly the connections between sexism and racism.

When the veils of women the world over come tumbling down, we may *see* at last the vision of that kingdom described by the Old Testament prophet Isaiah, in which the wolf dwells with the lamb, the swords have been broken into ploughshares, the eyes of the blind are opened and the ears of the deaf unstopped, and in which the tongues of the dumb sing for joy. My own vision of that kingdom has Moses and Christ, Buddha and Mohammed, the Great Goddess Ishtar and the Virgin Mary all dancing in a ring, first one and then the other stepping into the center. It is the dormant seed which has been the generating impulse in every genuine religious revival.

16 WOMEN IN MOTION

by Lucinda Franks

TURN YOUR THOUGHTS back about twenty-five years. When the Total Human had not yet been born and the average body was just a neglected dormitory for the mind. Try to remember those sedentary days when the finely-tuned work of art called the human anatomy was pounding and screaming to get out from under dimpled scallopped layers of fat, sagging muscles, and aching bones entering the final and fatal stages of benign neglect. Who would have thought then that society would rediscover a secret as old as civilization, a secret that would intensify a human's joy in life, that would cleanse the brain, and turn agitation and unrest into peace of mind.

There is a quaint and amusing quality to our memories of the late Sixties and Seventies. The picture of the Halls of Academia, encrusted with myths, where the professor sniffed at the thought of wasting precious brain cells in the pursuit of brawn; the housewife driving the car a mere half-mile for cigarettes; the middle-aged man huffing and puffing to chase the dog; the teenage girl "getting out of gym" by pleading it was that-time-of-month; the low esteem with which any form of physical exertion, save sex, was regarded; the inability of the general populus to extract pleasure from participating in sports.

Now that we are in the Year of Our Lord 2000, with modern technology and a rebirth of the age of reason having joined forces to put a world hurtling toward catastrophe back on course, it is hard to move back in time—to recall a period when there were no integrated golf and baseball teams, when women athletes were not vying for football scholarships, when indeed it was not known that women are capable of being as strong pound-for-pound as men and, with equally strenuous training, can match or surpass them in many sports.

Lest we forget, however, there *was* a time when Little League and high-school ball teams were all-male, with coaches swearing they'd dynamite the field before letting girls in, and actively defying court orders for integration. There *was* a time when women were regarded, in the words of one sports philosopher of the Seventies, as "truncated males, which should be permitted to engage in such sports as men do—but in foreshortened versions." There even was a time when acrobatics, diving and equestrian sports, where women had proven themselves uniquely superior, were not popular spectator events in this country; the same people who now thrill at watching fine performances of balance, quickness of manipulation and rapid reflexes in these events were the ones back in the Seventies saying that those singularly female skills would never draw sports crowds, which counted on sheer male rough-and-tumble, blood-and-guts spectacles for their enjoyment.

It was somewhere around the mid-Eighties when sports finally became an "in" thing. It took years and years to arrive, having begun in the early Sixties with President John F. Kennedy's physical fitness campaign. Yet it was almost as if the door opened overnight. Suddenly the concept of sports had changed, and the very word shifted in its connotations. Just as in the Seventies, good nutrition suddenly became faddish with "natural and health foods," so did exercise and games skyrocket in status. They no longer evoked images of smelly locker rooms, tile floors, exhaustion and former ninety-nine-pound weaklings with muscles the size of watermelons. And female athletes all at once were transformed from "Amazon Lesbos" to "goddesses," thanks to the appearance of Billie Jean King and other coolly feminine tennis pros, who started Americans down the road to female sports-star worship. The emergence of these female superstars signaled an era of enlightened spectatorship. They liberated the world of sports by shifting the emphasis from the love of size and brute power to a broader appreciation of beauty, virtuosity and intricate skill. Sports began to be a multifarious experience for both spectators and participants—a physical and spiritual reaching out, transporting the individual to realms undreamed of by the "acid-eaters" of past decades; or simply a rediscovery of the historic and delightful activity in which our primal ancestor indulged: playing with his fellow.

At the heart of this change was a realization of what coordinated bodily movements, as expressed in a sport, could do for a sense of well-being. The idea was as old as man. The Greeks had known that a sound mind is inside a sound body. Kierkegäard had used the word kinesis—Greek for "motion"—to signify a deep existential change in the mode of being. It was a truth well-known, but somehow buried beneath the surface of man's consciousness—like the cat that looks all around the room for the bell that is tied around its neck.

People began to examine the generally well-balanced state of mind that many athletes seem to have. Statistics were taken, polls and studies were made, and the reasons were sought. Athletes came forth with personal descriptions of the almost religious feeling that came upon them after they had stretched their bodies to the limit; runners spoke of the trees merging with the ground as they raced, swimmers told of the moment when the water seemed to propel them forward, persons who exercised regularly professed to be in harmony with nature and themselves—a quality they feared would disappear if they stopped their regimen.

Remember the famous experiments at Pennsylvania State's Health, Physical Education and Recreation College, when finally someone decided to put the old maxim "a sound mind in a sound body" to the test of science? Two groups of high-school seniors were chosen and given Scholastic Aptitude Tests. One group then went through a six-month program in which members trained two hours a day doing a variety of physical exercises; the second group, the control group, simply continued its normal study and play schedule. At the end of the experiment, the two groups again took the SATs, and, while the control group's results remained generally the same, the exercise group members' scores rose dramatically. Some youngsters who had not previously qualified for college—save an occasional "finishing school"—now achieved scores which met the admission standards for some of the toughest Ivy League universities. The experiment made headlines everywhere.

It was that experiment—there had been similar less dramatic tests of the relationship between exercise and mental functioning which had been largely ignored by the public—that put exercise on the top priority list for Americans. Pop phrases and catchwords were coined: "Body in motion," "Let's play" and "Jog awhile." It could not be denied that exercise improved clarity of thinking, alertness, ability to absorb complex ideas; it increased blood flow to the brain, strengthened the cells, and without a doubt acted on the regions of the brain to decrease anxiety and induce confidence and inner harmony.

And then "gamesmanship" was redefined. One must remember that in the Seventies, the need to win, and the need to have one's favorite team win, was crucial—so crucial, in fact, that the means used, the art of the game itself, was secondary. It's hard to imagine when winning was so important that it could make or break a man's self-esteem. Now, the conquering of one's opponent is not the prime mover in games; it is conquering *one's self*. Dr. Seymour Kleinman of Ohio State University, one of the first to stress this new dimension to sports, this inner contest with the self, used to cite the words of Michael Marine, who wrote about boating in an American Youth Hostel newsletter:

> When I first started boating, I thought my satisfaction and elation came from competing with the river and winning. I would attack it again and again, trying evermore difficult maneuvers . . . occasionally, I would even have delusions of winning the war over this inanimate river. Finally, however, I came to the realization that it is not a struggle between me and the river. The river, with all its dynamic action, is only a catalyst. Boating is a means of self-expression and my competition with the river is me overcoming myself, affirming myself, and realizing myself in my struggle toward victory, toward the absolute, toward self-control.

Both spectators and participants have now come to place less emphasis on winning or losing than on the way the game is played. In elementary schools, young children now devote half the school day to playing outdoors. Although supplied with balls, nets and other equipment, they are left to make up their own games with their own rules. Older children's games are structured in a way that lets everybody win. The Harris Games, named after Dr. Dorothy V. Harris of Penn State, are designed to reverse two traditional but still disquieting facts about sports: there are many more losers than winners, and the ones who need to win most generally lose. The Harris Games are intricately structured so they do not discriminate against the weak, the fat, the clumsy or the slow. Instead, the complicated series of games favors each player and brings out the one particular thing each can do better than anyone else: the fat child wins the game where weight is important; the small boy, where smallness is crucial. This early conditioning has been proven to have dramatic effects on ego and body image, teaching young people to feel comfortable with their bodies, to be proud of themselves and to move with greater ease.

It is well-known that more high-school students than ever are qualifying for athletic teams, that more are passing physical fitness exams with high scores. Psychologists say this is not only because of the intense national popularity of sports, but also because children who used to shy away from physical output—because it was a source of pain and humiliation—are now allowed to enjoy it without the threat of being harshly judged.

The People's Republic of China was decades ahead of us in learning about the mysteries and gifts of the body in motion. Peking and Shanghai thirty years ago looked like our big cities look today—free of polluting cars, full of bicycles and joggers. In the old days, people used to pass the time having parties, drinking liquor and watching television. If they did venture outdoors, it was to rest on park benches and on beaches. Only the kids, sometimes with their fathers, played games. Now, of course, people celebrate their bodies. School gymnasiums, neighborhood baseball diamonds and playing fields have replaced the corner cafés and "singles bars" as adult hang-outs. And just as years ago, the Chinese started the practice of rigorous exercise each morning, so now has a dawn jog for every family member—from toddler to grandmother—become as essential as brushing the teeth.

Much of the credit for all these changes belongs to women. Their full and equal entry into the sports arena, after years of chipping away at this narrow and selective male-dominated field, expanded it into a healthful and consciousness-raising pastime for everyone. It is ironic that women should be at the forefront of the "Body Movement," having launched their modern liberation campaign in the Sixties and Seventies with a demand for men to stop ogling the female body and start paying attention to the female mind. Once it was generally accepted that the female mind was as sound as the male mind, the battle turned back to the body—to prove that it was more than just a pleasure trove for man.

The array of myths about women and sports fell like dominos. It was proven that, up until menopause, a woman's bones, though smaller, were no more fragile than a man's, that a woman was *not* more likely to be injured while playing than a man, and that in fact the injury rate per participant was generally lower for girls than boys—in both contact and non-contact sports—because of the girls' extra padding of fat. Breast pads were soon devised for women athletes, similar to men's jock straps. Coaches were convinced by medical testimony that the well-guarded uterus was one of the most shock-resistant internal organs in the body and that strenuous activity actually increased muscular support around the pelvis. Similarly, it was accepted that vigorous exercise helped both menstruation and pregnancy (the U.S. Olympic Committee stopped advising its swimmers and other athletes to use the pill to prevent menstruation from coming during their contests). The scientific discovery that men also enjoy monthly cycles, with attending emotional highs and lows, also helped to dash the legend of the "female curse." The widely-held belief that women athletes developed bulging muscles turned out to be scientifically unprovable—a woman's physique is genetically determined at birth, and no amount of exercise and training can radically change it. When women began to train strenuously for serious athletics in the Eighties, it turned out that with the same amount of training they developed less musculature than men, and instead used a higher percentage of already-existing fiber. Those shotputters with bowling-ball shoulders turned out to have had the basic bulges in the first place.

Centuries of ignorance about and lack of research on the female physiology were overcome. Women, exhilarated with this new sense of physical power, began the slow process through the Seventies and Eighties of throwing over the "femininity game"—luring, baiting and netting a husband—for the far simpler and honest games that men had enjoyed for years.

After long research into the female physiology, there now appear to be only a few sex-linked differences between the male and female performance in the sports arena. The average female is still born smaller than the average male, and thus is at a disadvantage when at a random sample women are pitted against a random sample of men. Moreover, she is at a disadvantage when performing in a climate where heat and humidity are high, since the body temperature of a woman must rise two to three degrees higher than that of a man before she begins to perspire and cool off. It was this discovery that led to the successful movement to have lacrosse and field hockey meets postponed from the traditional spring and summer season to late fall and winter.

Women athletes who have undergone steady and rigorous training also have overcome the historic heat dissipation handicap of the average female—that is, that the female has fewer functional sweat glands than the male. It was definitively established that women in fact had, in earlier times, not exercised as much as men had, and had thus lost the use of a high percentage of her sweat glands; these needed to be reactivated, and were, by rigorous exercise. The change in conditioning has not altered a basic difference in the female frame, however, and her wider hips and lower center of gravity still place her at a disadvantage in some sports.

Nevertheless, women keep closing the gap between men's and women's world records, and it now appears as if a woman may well become the fastest long-distance runner in the world. Blossom Larrieu broke a new world record for the mile run for women last month—2.45.1 minutes, just 20 seconds behind the men's record; women, who were more than fifteen percent slower than men when women's participation in this event began back in the Sixties have enjoyed a much greater improvement level than men. The records for the one-hundred-meter dash have also come closer together (9.9 seconds for women against 9.6 for men) with women catapulting ahead while men have shaved much less of their time of twenty-five years ago.

Women have long equalled—although not beaten—men in swimming events (the record for the men's and women's four-hundred-meter freestyle is the same), with the sexes running neck-in-neck in improvement levels over the past ten years. The reason for this, of course, is that, although women over the years have reduced body-fat deposits to perform better, they have also proportionately lost the original advantage of buoyancy in the water that the extra fat provided them.

For years, women have been surpassing men in equestrian sports where their sensitivity in handling the reins gives them a distinct advantage. They have also excelled at diving, gymnastics, and acrobatics, recognizing and exploiting the special feminine qualities of grace, elasticity, and rapid motor adjustments which these sports demand. Of course, women have long shown themselves men's equals in riflery and archery and, more lately, in golf. For many years, the record for swimming the English Channel has been held by women, because of the insulation against cold that her extra fat (always slightly more than man's even after heavy lifelong exercise) supplies.

What are the reasons for women's fast-approaching equality with men in many sports? To understand them, we must return to the misconceptions of the Seventies and trace the process of enlightenment. Back in 1974, when the bulk of research on the female physiology could barely have filled one small library shelf, it was recognized that the trained woman athlete could always beat the untrained man. But given a man and a woman of the exact same build and training, it was believed that the man would always win because of his greater muscle mass, larger maximal oxygen uptake—or aerobic power—and proportionately bigger heart and lungs. Women were believed to have less stamina and less potential for reaching the heights of male athletes. It took a long time but eventually it was recognized and accepted by coaches—who had long been as moveable as the Pyramids on the issue—that women's physical inferiority was the result less of physiology than of a lifetime of deprivation. It had been so socially unacceptable for a woman to engage in strenuous activities, and she had been encouraged so often to depend on others to defend her—to act as her arms and legs—that she did not know she was capable, for instance, of even lifting a television set. Careful conditioning from a very early age taught her to use only a fraction of her strength, to draw back her hands at the last second when hitting out or throwing, to equate muscle power with scorn and rejection. This conditioning was intensified from the time of menstruation and was discovered to be the main reason why she sharply declined in performance ability after puberty, in comparison with her brother's continuing improvement.

At first it was thought that even if this conditioning were removed and woman given opportunities to develop in the same way as man, her innate biological inferiority would prevent her from ever being able to compete with the male athlete. It took research by physical education scientists at Penn State, the University of California and others to finally break the last ball and chain of opinion that was holding sportswomen down.

Until the late Seventies, an athlete's maximum aerobic power (the capacity to extract oxygen from the air and deliver it to the working muscles) had been measured relative to his total body weight and was considered the best indication of his endurance capabilities. According to tests, the aerobic power of the female was only seventy to seventy-five percent of that of the male.

A number of scientists decided that it would be fairer to measure aerobic power in relation to fat-free body weight—in other words, the working muscle. It was found that square-inch for square-inch of muscle, women are as efficient as men in the use of oxygen. The discovery that at least in the laboratory women had as great an aerobic work capacity as men led to other tests to see if women's muscle power pound-for-pound was also as great. Not only were women found to be as strong as men in relation to lean body weight (total weight minus the weight of fat), in many tests their muscles proved to be stronger.

The problem, of course, was how to reproduce these laboratory results in real life. The solution was to get rid of the fat deposits, the padding, the dead weight that slows up women's performance, and to utilize more of the already existing muscle fibre. That is exactly what women did. They trained as hard and as long as men—after years of being restricted to moderate practice, which insured they would be only half as good as men. The long distance runners were the first to lose the extra body fat because of the miles and miles they ran in training and the resulting caloric expenditures.

The fact that men have about twice the muscle mass of women was finally discovered to be meaningless. Just as men and women utilize only a small percentage of brain cells, so they use only about a quarter of their muscle fibre. This discovery put an end to the practice in the Sixties and Seventies of feeding female athletes, especially in the Eastern European countries, steroids. Women athletes who trained as strenuously as men were found to slowly increase use of muscle fibre, and reduce fat. Today, there is virtually no difference in strength between the average-trained male athlete and the average-trained female of the same body weight; the relative values for fat and lean weight are similar for both of them and although the woman generally retains slightly more fat padding than the man, she makes up for it by a greater use of her muscle fibre. It appears that the sedentary lifestyle of women has been largely responsible for the longstanding belief that nature meant her to be weaker.

Because men and women no longer have different training programs, U.S. women no longer are at a disadvantage in international meets—as were the U.S. Olympic team women back in the Seventies. Coaches found long ago that women could endure, and in fact needed, the kind of tough practice that men underwent. They have proved themselves able to do three hundred sit-ups; to run one hour straight; to lift seventy-five-pound weights. Such training has helped them develop endurance—a quality in which men always had the edge, until now.

An integral part of training for women had, since the mid-Eighties, been a reeducation course aimed at erasing societal conditioning and bringing out the natural competitive instinct and achievement motivation in them. Utilizing psychotherapy, psychodrama and hypnosis, the courses were mandatory for members of the Amateur Athletic Union and the Association for Intercollegiate Athletics and were used in physical education courses in most high schools and universities. They were aimed at wiping out the traditional female need to fail when competing with a man, as well as severing the link between success motivation and the voracious feminine need for praise and approval. Results were so good, with women shedding their fears and feelings of inadequacy and finally throwing themselves into the game for its own sake, that most courses have now been discontinued.

Little League teams now generally have a preponderance of girls, which is ironic considering it has been only twenty-six years since the Little League Baseball Organization was forced by court orders to allow girls on its teams. Medically, however, it was inevitable. It has long been known that girls aged nine to twelve are larger and stronger than boys, because they mature earlier.

At the high-school level, all sports are integrated and there are no longer "boys" and "girls" squads; such teams as golf, tennis and swimming generally consist of equal numbers of each sex. Because of the larger size of the average male, and thus the greater strength, only a few of the best women athletes make the football and wrestling teams, however. At first, desegregation had to be won through separate suits by individual athletes and in a few cases by an agency of a state like Pennsylvania, which challenged the school systems' right to sex-segregated sports. Finally, the passage of the Equal Rights Amendment forced every high-school physical education department in the nation to integrate teams and provide equal facilities and equipment to young women and young men.

On the college and university scene, the passage of the Education Amendments of 1972 forced educational institutions receiving Federal assistance—virtually every college in the nation—to give early equal treatment to men and women. Title IX of the Act prohibited colleges to exclude anyone on the basis of sex from participation in, or benefit from, any of its educational programs or activities, including sports. Although the regulations governing Title IX were slow in being issued and even then vague and open to many tests and challenges, they finally forced colleges to slice up athletic budgets evenly between men and women. Before that, most universities were allocating only a fraction of their budgets to women's sports, even though half their student bodies were female. The universities, after much rancor and protest, were forced to cut back their men's athletic budgets and skimp on the revenue-producing sports such as football and basketball to give the women a greater share. Women, freed from having to throw bake sales to raise funds for their travel, spent more time in rigorous training and eventually reached levels in which they could compete with men. Now, of course, since most sports have become integrated, the men have their money back. The Association for Intercollegiate Athletics for Women, which had traditionally forbade its member colleges to give athletic scholarships to women, changed its policy to fit the times, and now women are receiving scholarships for everything from lacrosse to football.

Title IX, as well as the ERA, totally reversed the college sports scene. No longer were women prevented from taking courses in wrestling or men from volleyball. No longer were squash or handball courts closed to women, and no longer were tables of "high protein foods" open only to male athletes. Sportswomen were allowed equal access to swimming pools and other training grounds, given equally good equipment (goodbye to the cast-off mits, "old gyms" and torn uniforms), and eventually given an equal number of athletic scholarships. After a number of experiments with integration and semi-integration of teams—rich colleges tried three teams for each sport; one female, one male, and one mixed, while others tried two "separate but equal" teams—women have finally gotten good enough to make mixed teams a reality. The most successful mixed teams are in swimming and track where relays can be played, but baseball, basketball, lacrosse, field hockey, soccer and some individual track events have also been successful, with the average woman not being far enough behind her male counterpart to be considered a liability. Although a very few women have "competed up" to join the male-dominated college football teams, most are satisfied to play on the women's teams. Football, as well as rugby, ice hockey and wrestling still have one team for each sex.

On the professional circuit, there used to be a vicious circle in the Seventies whereby tournaments of women's golf, tennis and bowling would not get television coverage unless there was a big purse offered, but sponsors wouldn't provide the big purse unless the tournament was televised. That Catch 22 of women's sports was soon ended, and by the Eighties men and women were earning equal prize money.

Women have come a long way in twenty-five years. Perhaps that is why all this uproar is happening now. Men are frightened by the sight of all these lean compact women—most young girls today do look like they stepped out of an Egyptian fresco. It is not that women no longer look like women—their muscles, though more outlined, are no bigger, and the sloping feminine lines are still there. It is the uniform absence of a traditional *thickness* in the female form that seems to be disquieting to the people making the most noise. "You can't pinch women any more, you can't even get hold of them," grumbled one of the leaders of the New Male Chauvinism Movement recently. And it is true that flesh seems to be the sole province of the over-forty these days. The NMC complains that women have usurped every last asset unique to males: "First, women have a stronger constitution and a longer life—their survivability is superior to ours. Then they equal us mentally, and moreover claim they have the secret of the universe stashed somewhere in their consciousness, They give birth to life, and now they're saying they're just as strong, if not stronger, than we are." One of the more legitimate concerns of the NMC Movement is the fear that with the decreasing fatty tissue in active, exercising young women today, a danger is being posed to the species. If the female fat layer is not there to protect sex tissue and the stomach during pregnancy, they ask, are we not raising a generation of female bodies that will be unable to protect their unborn babies? Are we gradually making female fat obsolete, and will the reproductive organs be the next to go? NMC sportswriters are calling sportswomen puppets, charging that they are mimicking males instead of being what they are best at. They are demanding that women quit competing with men. The hue and cry is great. You would sometimes think we were back in the Seventies.

4

*On Her
New Worlds*

17 MOTHER EARTH REVISITED: WHEN WOMEN IN POLITICS ARE OLD HAT

Bella Abzug
interviewed by Mim Kelber

RECENTLY, A SATELLITE NEWS SERVICE reporter visited Earth for a month-long series of interviews with leading personalities in the United States. He had the rare opportunity to spend an afternoon with American stateswoman Bella S. Abzug, now living in semi-retirement in an underground commune on Capitol Hill. Ms. Abzug, who is working on her memoirs, celebrated her eightieth birthday on July 24, 2000, and remains vigorous, outspoken and involved. Herewith, excerpts from the taped interview with the feminist octogenarian.

SNS: You have had a long and fascinating career in American politics and government. How does it feel to be on the sidelines?

BSA: What makes you ask that? I'm still very active. I lecture, teach, and write and I'm on the phone for several hours almost every night with the President.

SNS: What do you talk about?

BSA: Everything. As a matter of fact, just the other night she asked me if I would consider accepting an appointment as Ambassadress to one of the satellites—I forget which one, France or Britain. I know she meant it in a generous way, but I told her that after having spent so much time as Secretary of State negotiating the non-aggression pact with the Lunar White House, it would be like a demotion to a colony appointment.

SNS: The whole story of how you negotiated that pact has never been told. Are you ready to tell it now?

BSA: Well, Ms. Magazine has the serial rights to my memoirs, so I'm not at liberty to go into details. I can say that it was the most difficult assignment of my life and one I had hoped would not be necessary after the Great Liberation Agreement of 1984. We thought we had at last worked out a sensible compromise, but the instinct toward violence remains very strong.

SNS: It wasn't so much an instinctual drive, was it, as a policy of sexual and political reunification? At least, that's the way we learned it in political science courses at Lunar University.

BSA: Yes, the goal was to restore the Pentagon Party to power in U.S.A.-Earth, which presumably had been abdicated under the 1984 agreement. Fortunately, there was division within your ruling party on whether it was worth returning to Earth, and I was able to take advantage of that policy schism to negotiate the non-aggression pact. Also, U.S.A.-Lunar still depends on our raw materials.

SNS: That may not continue for very long. As you've probably heard, the most recent Mars expedition turned up some exciting discoveries of oil and mineral deposits.

BSA: Exactly. That was what we had hoped for and held out as a strong inducement when we negotiated the 1984 Liberation Agreement. You might say we agreed to divide up the Universe. We took Earth, the male great powers took Space, including the moon and all those man-made satellites. It was our hope that Space exploration would provide a peaceful outlet for their aggressive tendencies, and that the Lunar White House and Lunar Kremlin would see the mutual advantage of cooperative outer space expeditions. We're anxious to cooperate too. The sooner they can transfer their Lunar and satellite colonies to other planets, the sooner we will get back the moon.

SNS: Do you have any plans for the moon?

BSA: We have an Artemis Task Force doing a long-range study of peaceful uses. We may just let it alone. That's what I would do, but many of the younger people regard me as a hopeless reactionary on that subject. If it were up to me, I'd concentrate on clearing up the mess here on Earth.

SNS: It is quite a mess, isn't it? I hadn't seen it since I was a very young child. My family left in the midst of such chaos and terror that I've just blotted out most of those memories. I do remember how beautiful it was once. But it's probably too painful for you to talk about the Holocaust. Forgive me for bringing it up.

BSA: Nonsense. None of us can ever forget, those of us who were lucky or unlucky enough to survive. Our good green planet turned into a wasteland of horror. But we have to look to the future. As you say, you were too young to remember much about those days, but if you've done any traveling I think you'd have to admit that our Reconstruction effort has made remarkable progress, especially in the last few years.

We still have to live underground, of course, but some of our women scientists have developed very effective radiation-proof clothing for surface work. Our architects have designed extrusive geodesic domes that they believe are inpenetrable to fallout, and some Earth surface colonies are being built on an experimental basis. Our chemists at the Davis–Childs Institute are improving the taste and quality of synthetic foods, although they still have a long way to go. God, what I wouldn't give for the taste of a sour pickle now! But the main thing is that we've developed an equitable system of food distribution, and everyone gets a minimum subsistence diet and vitamin supplements. Priorities in food rations go to the children and to the sick and handicapped.

SNS: What about the elderly?

BSA: The horrible fact is that there just aren't too many of us left. The initial death toll was enormous. As far as we can estimate, some fifty-million people died in the first half hour of the nuclear exchange, even though the U.S.A. and Soviet Union were not directly hit. The fallout effects, of course, brought frightful casualties here in the U.S.A. and all over the world, and those are still continuing. Our mortality rate remains very high, and cancer has replaced heart disease as the leading cause of death. We're devoting at least twenty percent of our budget to medical research, health care and environmental studies.

SNS: You look remarkably healthy. How did you manage to escape the radiation effects?

BSA: Sheer luck. I was on a Congressional subcommittee investigating charges of discrimination against women coal miners in Kentucky. We had only recently made a break-through on those jobs, and the women complained that the miners weren't giving them enough wash-up time. We were in a fairly deep pit and we just stayed there until a rescue team came for us.

SNS: Ms. Abzug, living conditions on Earth remain so difficult and perilous that I must ask you a question that has bothered me for a long time. When the Great Liberation Agreement of 1984 was negotiated, why did the leaders of the American women's movement choose to remain on Earth rather than go to the moon with the White House-Pentagon expeditionary survival force? Weren't you getting the short end of the bargain?

BSA: Didn't we always? Maybe it had something to do with an image of Mother Earth that we didn't want to give up. Maybe we were bound to our ritual role of the compulsive housekeepers, the women who cleaned up the messes made by men, nursed the wounded in their endless wars, emptied the bedpans, wiped up the vomit, took care of the kids, changed the diapers, repaired the egos, put the families and houses back together. Well, we had finally inherited the biggest mess that men had ever made. Their obsession with violence had just about destroyed the livable surface of the world.

SNS: Now really, isn't that a simplistic interpretation of what happened? As I recall from the history books, it wasn't just men who were responsible. Weren't there a couple of women at the heads of governments when the nuclear war broke out?

BSA: I believe there were one or two, but it didn't matter. They were prisoners of the past, bound to their military dogmas, acceptable to men only because they didn't challenge their basic creeds. I remember arguing back in the 1970s that the women who would make a difference in government would be those who came out of an organized movement, who came with an ideology and a determination to reconstruct society for men as well as for women. I must have said it a thousand times. I'd be out on the streets campaigning for a woman candidate and some man or woman would grab me and say, "You don't expect me to vote for so-and-so just because she's a woman, do you?" and I'd say, "Not just because she's a woman, but a woman who..." and I'd go through a litany of the woman's accomplishments and beliefs. As it happened, we had some remarkable women running for office in the 1970s.

You know, in all those years I never came across a woman candidate who campaigned for a bigger military budget, or worried about a missile gap, or argued against gun control. Sure, a few of them voted for those things when they got to Congress, but they weren't leading the pack. Women in politics were interested in other issues. They talked about child care centers, reform, protecting the environment, the needs of the elderly and "reordering priorities"—a shorthand term which meant the government was spending its money on the wrong things.

After the Watergate scandal in the early '70s, when that neurotic creep Richard Nixon made a mess of the White House, we found greater acceptance of women in politics and government. They were perceived as a cleansing force, pure, healing—the traditional role, but on a different plane. It got to the point where in the '76 campaign the power brokers went through the motions of pretending that a woman might be picked for the Vice Presidency (of course, they had no intention of letting that happen), and they even put a few women into the Cabinet. The tokens were getting bigger and shinier, but they still weren't worth much. As it turned out, it was too little and too late.

SNS: Our Lunar history books don't tell us much about that Watergate episode. Nixon is treated as a great statesman who got into bad company and, through some kind of aberration, lost the Presidency.

BSA: Just the kind of nonsense one would expect from Pentagon historians. Nixon wasn't an aberration. He epitomized the soul of the militarists, if he or they had one. He worshipped the bomb and his little black box. He got a personal thrill in bombing the hell out of those poor, agonized people in Indochina. The last Christmas, when that particular war had just about ended as far as we were concerned, he boasted about how he was going to bomb the Vietnamese like they'd never been bombed before. And he did. He had to have one more thrill.

He talked about a generation of peace, but it was a public relations slogan for him rather than an attempt to deal with the forces leading us toward a nuclear catastrophe. Some women felt that Nixon's behavior reflected the sexual undercurrent in the military psyche, the identification of war with manliness, the obsession with longer and longer missiles, the desire to be Number one—on top, the thrust for the orgasmic big bang. Maybe they were right. Nixon was always the hollow little man, trying to be one of the boys, with his stag parties, his foul language and his craze for football. If anyone talked about cutting the military budget, it was like threatening to castrate him. What struck me was that he never seemed to be comfortable with women. Either he put them on a pedestal and described them as saints, as he did with his family, or he sneered at them as "dogs." He molded his wife and daughters into plastic dolls, though one of them showed some real passion and brains, and I always liked her. I thought she had guts.

SNS: Wasn't that a masculine quality?

BSA: My God, no. Women were never weak. It was just convenient for men to describe them that way to justify keeping them down and "protecting" them out of their rights. Actually, though some traits were described traditionally as masculine or feminine, in my experience the whole range of emotions and temperamental characteristics appears in both men and women. I still remember how amused I was during those last days of the Watergate crisis when so many men were appearing on television and breaking down in tears. Nixon cried. Congressmen and Senators cried. The commentators were choking up. If they had been women, everybody would have said it showed they were too unstable emotionally to govern.

SNS: Did you cry?

BSA: No. Not then.

SNS: Isn't there a contradiction in your thesis? First you're saying that men are more aggressive and violent than women, then you claim they're really the same.

BSA: It's much more complicated than that. Women and men alike experience hate, love, anger, greed, fear, compassion, generosity and courage, but as society has evolved, for a complex of economic and political reasons certain of these feelings became identified as manly and were mobilized for the purposes of the state and the maintenance of power. Women were assigned a more passive role. Division of labor, division of emotions. Certainly women were and are capable of violent behavior, but search through history and you'll find that the Amazons were the rare exception. Women didn't institutionalize violence. Men did that. Women didn't make war. Men did. And they used it for power, for profits. Until the Holocaust, men ruled the world, owned its wealth, led the armies, flew the planes, guided the missiles, dropped the bombs. Women were used just as accessories. It is one of the great ironies of history that the misuse of women touched off the nuclear exchange.

SNS: I never heard anything about that. What do you mean?

BSA: You know that in '76 there was a terrible food crisis. Millions of people were starving to death in Africa and India. The women's movement took the lead in organizing demands for massive airlifts of food. They picketed the White House and called for sending the famine countries wheat and protein instead of arms. Of course, the government had to do something. The Presidential campaign was in full swing then, and some publicity guy dreamed up the idea of sending the wives of the candidates on a bipartisan mercy mission in a plane called "The Spirit of Betty Crocker." The plane was hijacked at a NATO base in Spain by Arab terrorists who demanded nuclear weapons in exchange for release of the wives and the food. Of course, there was consternation everywhere. The U.S. government had no alternative but to say that it would not be blackmailed. One of the candidates addressed the nation on TV and said no sacrifice was too great for world peace. Nothing was heard from the wives. Before the deadline given by the terrorists expired, the plane was attacked by Spanish Army troops in a daring but unsuccessful rescue attempt. That was the beginning of the end. While the United Nations Security Council was passing its usual "regret and deplore" resolution, Syria bombed Madrid, Israel went on alert, the war between Turkey and Greece started up again, South Vietnam conducted its first nuclear bomb test, and then almost the entire Middle East and Southern Europe went up in a cloud of radioactive plutonium. We still don't know who triggered the nuclear exchange, but it could have been any one of a dozen nations. Our government had been handing out arms and nuclear material like popcorn for years and we had H-bombs stocked at bases all over the world. It was madness.

SNS: Wasn't it incredible that the U.S. and the Soviet Union didn't get bombed too?

BSA: Well, they had their hotline. Even more incredible was that after fifty-million people were melted or blown apart in thirty minutes, some Pentagon strategists argued that what had happened showed we could survive "limited" nuclear wars. That argument lasted until people began dying of radiation effects and most of our food supply and water was contaminated. Except for canned stuff. It was eerie. Everything looked normal at first. Buildings, homes, cars, highways were all intact. People kept on working. But within a week they were dying by the thousands, and the panic was on.

SNS: How did the women actually seize power?

BSA: It didn't happen right away. Let's just say the men finally abdicated. As soon as the Half-Hour War started, the President took off in his flying Fuhrerbunker. He had a standby fleet of seven superjets which were called the Advanced Airborne National Command Post. There were three at Andrews Air Force Base in Washington reserved for the President, high officials, advisers and a large military staff. The others were at the Air Force base near Omaha, headquarters of the Strategic Air Command. The idea was to get the White House crowd and the Pentagon brass safely above the mushroom clouds so they could keep on giving orders while the rest of us poor slobs died on the ground. It was the ultimate in status.

SNS: Well, I can see how they would feel that continuity in government was essential. How did they decide who would go?

BSA: That had all been worked out in advance. The President and most of his cabinet, the military command, technical and medical crew and other staff, the Chief Justice and the two chairmen of the Congressional armed services committees. The Vice President was left in Washington as a surrogate.

SNS: What about their wives and children?

BSA: They had to stay behind. Otherwise, the leaders would have been accused of nepotism. Instead, they took their secretaries.

SNS: Women?

BSA: Of course. There were a few dozen on the planes. When the news got out in the press, it created a lot of resentment. Inevitably, some of the headlines called the President's plane "Noah's Ark" and one columnist suggested the women had been taken along for breeding purposes. The result was a lot of women on Earth had their consciousness raised.

SNS: But eventually the Command Post planes had to come down.

BSA: They had to refuel, of course, and after a few weeks the President set up his White House operation at the Aerospace Center in Houston. By then, they had pretty well worked out their plan for the Lunar White House expeditionary force. The Kremlin had reached the same decision. Under pressure from the UN, the two powers agreed to set up satellite space stations for the governments of the lesser nuclear powers. Except for the Chinese. They weren't interested. Somehow they're surviving, though we still don't have much information on how or what they're doing.

SNS: I was in one of the first space capsules that colonized the moon. My father happened to be a geologist, and my mother and sister were allowed to go too. They belong now to something called the Daughters of the American Pussycats.

BSA: I'd expect as much. The Pussycats were women who accepted the caricature roles of femininity and boasted of their submissiveness. Our Black sisters used to compare them to the house "niggers" on the old slave plantations. After the Women's Liberation Movement seized the Aerospace Center in 1984—we used force for the first and last time—we included in the Agreement that wives would have the option of going with their husbands. We also had a quota for single women volunteers and I suppose it's no secret now that some women liberationists went too. We did have a split among the women leadership, and those who felt most strongly that we shouldn't just cede space to male power were allowed to infiltrate the expeditionary forces as secret agents.

SNS: Why did the women wait until 1984?

BSA: We were occupied with disaster work, epidemics and the staggering job of trying to reorganize a society underground. Of course, we're still doing that. And then we had to wait until the men got the technological facilities ready for the Lunar expeditionary forces. Meanwhile, we had to establish contact among the remaining women's organizations, set up a skeleton government, and work out our demands. By the time the White House and Pentagon were ready to start their shuttle service to the moon, we were ready to go on strike.

SNS: In our history books, they say a crackpot group called the Lysistrata League tried to seize power.

BSA: That was one of the classic techniques we used. It was only partially effective, and there was no way to enforce it. Still, our guess is that at least a third of the women in our country joined in the abstinence strike for varying periods of time, and it had its effect, especially among the military men, who were our main targets. They weren't in very good shape when we took over the Aerospace Center.

SNS: As you saw it, what were the major points in the Great Liberation Agreement?

BSA: The first point wasn't too hard to agree on. The male government leaders wanted to go, and we wanted them to go. But we made their departure conditional on their agreeing never to come back. We established priorities on who would leave. We had to allow them a certain number of scientists, doctors, nurses, technicians, and IBM types.

Some women and children. We had quite a dispute about the lesser male politicians. Nobody wanted them, but we finally gave them a quota that could be filled by volunteers. Our first concern was to get rid of the militarists, munitions makers and their hangers-on, especially the American Legionnaires, VFWs, and gun lobby crowd. At the same time, we dismantled all the nuclear installations and rounded up every gun we could find and destroyed them all. Anyone who had owned a gun automatically qualified for the moon trip. Recently we turned the Expeditionary Task Force over to the UN for supervision. They have space capsules taking off at the rate of several a week from different parts of the globe, and I think it's fair to say that the worst of the lot are gone now.

SNS: It's remarkable that you've retained the basic American governmental structure, with a President, a Congress and Supreme Court. The transition from male to female power seems to have been accomplished very smoothly.

BSA: Yes, on the whole everything we did was within the Constitution. When we seized the Aerospace Center, there was a vacancy in the Vice Presidency. We had the President appoint one of us before he handed in his resignation, and she automatically succeeded to the Presidency. It took a couple of years before we could hold national elections.

SNS: Did you have an outright ban on men running for government office?

BSA: No, that wasn't necessary. If men wanted to get on the waiting list to go to the Moon, they had to sign a nonintervention-in-domestic-affairs pledge. That still left a great many men who wanted to remain on Earth and they're slowly being accepted into our political life. In fact, more and more of them are trying to get into Congress.

SNS: Do you think you will ever again have a male President?

BSA: If a qualified man comes along, I suppose it could happen. But, in all frankness, I think it will take many years before the nation is ready for that.

SNS: I've had some opportunity to interview men in different underground capitals around the country. Aside from a natural concern with their health, they seem to be quite well adjusted and almost content. I was really surprised.

BSA: You shouldn't have been. You have been observing a phenomenon that bears out what the women liberation theoreticians predicted many years ago. The traditional male–female roles have disappeared, and men as well as women are liberated. Since all citizens are required to work at some useful task and receive equal pay, the man no longer has the burden of having to support a family alone, nor does he feel threatened if his wife or lover works. In a society still grappling with enormous problems of survival, all work is important and recognized as such. So it doesn't matter to the man whether he works in a child care center, as a cook or as an engineer. Women also work at every kind of job, though we've given priority to training them in scientific and technical skills. We can't take a chance of losing control of the aerospace centers. And, also, the men feel terribly relieved that they're no longer expected to be killers, aggressors or rapists. We still have an occasional case of rape but any form of sexual violence has become taboo as a result of early childhood training. We expect that particular crime to disappear eventually.

SNS: I've heard that this government engages in a program of brainwashing which starts almost in the cradle.

BSA: Call it what you will. All societies create behavior models, and they utilize all aspects of the culture—schools, newspapers, television, literature and the arts—to reinforce those models. Our emphasis is on teaching our children to abhor violence and to work together for the good of society as a whole. We haven't developed a Unisex race, but we have pretty much stripped away the burlesque trimmings that turned women into commercial and sexual objects in the old days. One of our most popular class trips is a visit to the Marilyn Monroe wing of the New Smithsonian Institution. It has a great collection of sexist artifacts from the Hollywood era—falsies, fake eyelashes, wax breasts, black lace panties, wigs, etcetera—and there's a continuous performance of the old "I Love Lucy" TV series, with subtitles to explain what's going on. The children find it very funny.

SNS: Before the Holocaust, the main trend in the women's movement, aside from the stress on equal rights, appeared to be to encourage the development of individuality and self-fulfillment, no matter where it led or what it did to the family. What has happened to individuality?

BSA: We can't afford the old concept of individual expression, which was a kind of rebellion against attempts to force women into specific patterns of behavior. Now that women are no longer predestined to limited roles, there is a more disciplined acceptance of service to society. Within the confines of our rigorous survival program, women can do anything. The family certainly has undergone revolutionary changes. The old nuclear family—even the description is anathema now—is disappearing, though I've noticed that within the communes there are subgroups made up of couples and their children. I wouldn't worry about human beings turning into dull, unisex robots. We're trying to build a new world in a dangerous and hostile environment. That brings out the utmost in human ingenuity, diversity and creativity.

SNS: I won't stay much longer, but just one last question. In spite of the horrors of the twentieth century, the millions who were killed and are still dying, the shambles that men made of the Earth, you seem optimistic. I get the feeling that implicit in what you're saying is that it took a nuclear catastrophe to liberate women. Is it worth it? Was that the only way?

BSA: No. It didn't have to happen that way.

18 GENDERLESS SEXUALITY: A MALE-FEMALE PSYCHOLOGICAL EXPLORATION OF THE FUTURE OF SEXUAL RELATIONSHIPS

by Lila Karp
and Renos Mandis

A Forward Moving Society

WHILE THE JUKE BOX in the campus diner blared out one of the moment's musical successes, "Love Is an Umbrella from the Rain," Janet, a young graduate student and friend of ours, spoke about what in the past would have been labelled her "marital problems." "It's just too weird," she said. "I'm married to Dan who would have an emotional collapse if he knew I was trying to have an affair with George, and George won't make it with me because I'm married and he doesn't want to feel responsible for the break-up of my marriage. What I'd really like to do is stop time for a while and pack my marriage into a trunk while I have an affair with George, and do whatever else I feel like doing, when I feel like doing it. There's so much feeling between my husband and me that I don't know if I want to split up with him. But he's not what I need right now. What I really should do is take a place of my own and get my head and my feelings together, but much as I hate to admit it, I'm scared stiff of being alone." She stopped talking for a few moments, long enough to hear the refrain of "Love Is an Umbrella from the Rain." "I love Dan," she said. "But he sure ain't no umbrella."

Janet is a young feminist and a product of the "youth culture." Before her marriage she tried communes, group sex, bi-sexuality, nudity, and drugs. Throughout her twenties she has been a Hippie, Yippie and every other "eeeee" that has come along.

In the following pages we shall try to gain insight into what is most likely going to happen to the Janets, Dans and Georges of the year 2000. By "most likely" we do not mean what "should" happen. Moral and ethical considerations can be instrumental within a "forward moving" society only if they are grounded upon an existing social reality, which they can directly influence and even forcibly "shake up." If they completely discard "what is," the possibility of their actualization becomes extremely remote, and they end up like so many fads, with no real grasp upon the future.

From the point of view of the future, "what is" is the "forward moving" section of our population: the Janets, the Dans, the Georges, etc. They represent the present trends within our society.

We will explore these trends, not only in their external forms, but from the point of view of their deeper implications. Believing, as we do, that our social, psychological, and sexual behavior are umbilically interconnected, we will look at the changing trends in these areas and try to perceive their impact upon the future. Only when we have grasped the real meaning of these present trends can we afford to take a guess at what might come out of them—with a little bit of luck. By with a little bit of luck we mean that no world cataclysm—such as an atomic war—takes place in the next twenty-five years, and that no dramatic series of political events occurs that would radically shift the course of history and set us back a thousand years.

Of course, when we discuss the future of sexuality, and we decide to take as our starting point the present trends in our society, we do not have in mind the rising price of food, the panic on Wall Street, or Doctor Kissinger's shufflings to keep the world "in balance." We do have in mind the powerful resurgence, these past years in the Western world, of the Feminist Movement. We have already witnessed a not particularly feminist president proclaiming a day in August as National Women's Day, and a Congress in Bucharest, of mostly sexist governments, accepting the principles of women's equality. Such events might be empty in terms of practical results. Nevertheless, they confirm what some knew but most tried to negate: that the Women's Liberation Movement is not just another passing fad but is here to stay. That it is not an isolated, marginal movement, but an indispensable element of historical evolution. That it is intrinsically connected with all other aspects of society and a ecessary partner in solving "world headaches," whether they be population explosion, labor unemployment, the making of a president, etc. Moreover, we view feminism not only as a partner in this process of historical evolution, but as THE *trend;* the major sociocultural factor presently taking place; a powerful catalyst that absorbs the economico-politico-ideological realities of the present and spells out its own culture and lifestyle.

Before we continue, it is important to clarify one thing. We will be focusing, in the following pages, on present and future avant-garde trends as the most important components of the cultural and sexual revolution, and as the spearhead of our forward moving society. Nevertheless, we are fully aware that these trends represent a very small portion of the population of this earth. This avant-garde minority, still centered today in a few sophisticated spots in the Western world, is important because it tells us more than the "conservative majority" does about things to come. We realize that by the year 2000 the adherents of a "new sexuality" will still be a minority, and that the majority of the world's population will not have caught up with them. We realize that Bucharest or no Bucharest, some strongly traditionalist nations are bracing themselves against any "modern" penetration; that Brezhnev's Russia is working surreptiously, but steadily, to strengthen the patriarchal family, and that China, with its mixture of feminism and Puritanism, is a still big question.

If one doesn't keep these considerations in mind, the following pages might often appear Utopian.

Women in Motion

The phenomenon of the Women's Liberation Movement is a phenomenon of "catching up" with history. It is the logical reaction to an absurd historical situation. It is this logical characteristic that gives the

Movement the power and impetus to spread across social classes and ideological positions, and makes its message hard to discard, even by those women afraid of its consequences. The absurd situation against which it reacts is the fact that although women have become a sizable and important part of the productive forces of society, they are still considered and treated as a "second sex." Although they are not a minority their status is still minor.

Early feminist demands, from the Suffragettes of the early part of this century up to the Sixties, focused mainly on practical and economic considerations. The new Women's Liberation Movement has made a dramatic switch. Taking its inspiration from Simone de Beauvoir's *The Second Sex,* it immediately went beyond the practico-material aspects of exploitation into a total reevaluation of what constitutes this "second sex." It made as its goal a thorough and methodical investigation of the psychological practices that kept this male supremacist society on its feet, the various roles that women have been forced into—mother, wife, lover, prostitute, etc.—and the biological and sociological myths supportive of such sex role stereotyping. Most important of all, the Women's Liberation Movement has revealed that the entire male supremacist system rests upon the mystification that results from the twisting of a sheer physical and functional differentiation into the notion of sexual gender.

The dictionary describes gender as: A grammatical classification of objects corresponding to the two sexes (masculine-feminine); property of belonging to such class. It is this classification by gender that has been used to determine what masculinity "is" versus what femininity "is." In such classification the feminine gender is defined primarily as a sexual being with particular sexual functions to fulfill. The Women's Liberation Movement refuses to accept this concept of womanhood.

From a psychological point of view, the new woman does not accept the relinquishing or denial of her own real and potential power in the social, psychological and sexual spheres. It was just this relinquishing of her power, and the projection of it onto the male sex, that women were forced to become experts at, or to suffer the inevitable economic, social and psychological consequences. The struggle, pain, and joy of sensing the responsibility for one's own life was totally denied to women of the past, and it is just this denial of responsibility and free choice that women will no longer accept.

Another psychological focus of the new woman is knowing herself.

The modern Feminist Movement started as a consciousness-raising process. The priority is not so much to change men as to change women; to understand not only the patterns of social-sexual exploitation and the myths that serve them, but how these patterns and myths have affected one's own behavior, manipulated one's own psyche, and invalidated the original possibilities of one's life.

By "women in motion" we mean the new women who go through such feminist consciousness raising, feeling the support emanating from the knowledge that "one is not alone," that "one is not crazy," that an entire movement is out there in the world to back one up. First there are few and then there are many. At first the many follow the movement only to a certain degree. The more they think about it, the more it becomes powerful and respectable, the more things they find right about it. The new woman is definitely the trend. She is in a state of motion, with part of herself ahead of herself while part of herself lingers behind. Her credo is not to be a "sucker" any more. She wants the maximum satisfaction of her psychological needs as well as her sexual ones. She'd rather go out into the world to work for her own security than pay for it with a loss of self. Her own sexual satisfaction is more important to her than someone else's sexual or psychological needs. She will try to understand her own sexuality independently of any "male cults." As we said, this new woman is in motion. She still has a long way to go. She started on her path alone. Are men about to follow?

Men in Trouble

Men's initial reaction to the Women's Movement has been hostile and sometimes violent. Today, men realize that feminism is here to stay, and their attitude has become more complex, wavering between repressed hostility and interested curiosity.

The often emotional quality of men's hostility towards feminism indicates that men feel threatened by it, and that such a threat is more than sheer fear of loss of material privileges. Men are not yet really concerned about women taking their jobs. They are concerned for their masculinity. They realize, more or less consciously, that the foundations of our Genderist (masculine-feminine) society are shakey and that it might collapse.

Man is a prisoner of his gender, even if his gender is the privileged one. Objectively, masculinity is a luxury. Subjectively, it is a must. For a man to be told that he is not a "real" man is as threatening as it is for a prefeminist or "feminine" woman to be told that she is not a "real woman." He has invested as much of his life in being a "man" as she in being a "woman." He feels that he has no choice. Only a "real man" will "make it" outside in the competitive world, and that means that if he does not "make it" outside, he is not a "real man," and therefore he will not "make it" at home or in bed. And vice versa, if his sexual masculinity is in trouble, it might seriously jeopardize his struggle for survival and his drive for success. Thus, his social, psychological, and sexual experiences are intertwined and dependent upon his masculinity.

It is a traumatic experience today for a prefeminist or "feminine" woman to free herself from her psychological conditioning. Nevertheless, she has an imperative motivation to help her make this "switch," and a clear and better alternative as her goal. For a male supremacist to cease to be a male supremacist is like jumping without a parachute into the unknown. Man has so deeply interiorized his identification with the "masculine gender," that he senses any possible loss of his masculinity as a loss of being.

Men are threatened by feminists. But they are also "attracted" by them. The reason for such ambiguity is important to understand here, because it puts the finger on a sensitive element of the male psyche that might provide a dynamic impetus for change. These reasons are to be found in the nature of masculinity itself.

What is masculinity? It is the "ideal" quality of the gender masculine. This gender is itself nothing else but a system of "qualities" that supposedly "make a man." Although the concept of masculine gender refers to a group of people who have male physical characteristics, it does not depend on it. A man can be feminine, a woman masculine. The masculine gender (as much as the feminine) is therefore an "ideal" concept. It has no substance. It is "in the head."

As an "ideal" quality of an "ideal" concept masculinity is also "in the head." It is not something that a man can say "he has." As a French poet put it, "Nothing is ever definite in man, neither his strength nor his weakness." Masculinity is not something that one can put one's finger upon within oneself, and say that it's there. If anything, it is experienced as a "lack," as something that "you have to have," which means that you are not quite sure that "you do have it"; something that you have to "prove" all the time and "act out" continuously. Don Juan cannot stop. He is in perpetual motion.

This "proving" or constant acting out requires a partner. For a man to know that he "has" masculinity he has to have an external manifestation of it, an outside "guarantee." In our sexist civilization the sexual role of women has been to be the provider of such a "guarantee."

The heterosexual man is "bound" to a woman in the pursuit of his masculinity. For such a pursuit to have any chance of success he has to be able to trust her judgement and to be sure that she is not "lying" to him for the sake of getting his approval. The weak, the afraid and submissive woman cannot give man a valid assurance of his own strength as long as he has reasons to suspect that her judgement is either motivated by need or fear, or that it is a fantasy distortion based on her own sense of powerlessness.

The so-called "boredom" that today, in our feminist times, man often experiences with his prefeminist or "feminine-submissive-sex-object" type partner, his need of freedom, escaping, etc. is not really boredom in the sense of "not having a good time" together. It is exasperation resulting from the "failure of the game." Such a man somehow feels that the only woman who can really satisfy his masculinity is a woman who is not dependent on him and therefore does not "need" his approval; a woman whose self-dependence is a guarantee of her own objectivity. Ironically, today's women who answer to these requirements are, by historical necessity, feminists or verging onto feminism, and the last thing they are concerned with is proving a man's masculinity.

So man is caught in a dilemma. On the one hand, he is "bored" by his "feminine" companion, who is not able any more to fulfill the needs of his masculine conditioned psyche; on the other hand, the women whose approval he really needs are actually engaged in destroying this concept of masculinity that has been his lifebelt up to now. In the past, men were often involved with so-called strong women who were willing to "play the game," and whose strength was a kind of "ersatz" guarantee of their objectivity. Today, women are obliged either to choose the feminist consciousness-raising process and follow its consequences or to psychologically "repress" the feminist consciousness, and fall inwardly, if not outwardly, into a more compulsive justification and perpetuation of masculine-feminine myths; myths which ultimately make them still less trustworthy—more boring—to the very males they are trying to please. The chauvinist man has a love-hate relationship with feminist women. He "wants" them, realizes that they reject him, not only as an individual but as a "redundant species," and he hates them for this. The acuteness of this unsolvable psychic puzzle is, we believe, going to provide the psychological impetus for man's reevaluation of the entire "masculine bandwagon" and give him the courage to jump off it.

To "jump off" is a painful and anxiety-ridden experience. No man will go through it for the sheer sake of feminist ideology. He will go through it only if and when he realizes that it is in his best interest, that he has no choice, and that in this forward moving society all the other ways are blocked to him. Such realization is already slowly, marginally, but surely taking place. It can start with a simple awareness that "something is changing" in the world, that his old sexist tricks have become redundant, that masculinity doesn't "pay off" anymore, that his interpersonal relationships are a failure, his sexuality confused, etc.

Nevertheless, it is only when he understands how deeply "in trouble" he is, that the full implications of his new existential situation, and the real nature of his ambiguous psychological love-hate relationships with feminists will be revealed to him. Only then will he fully realize that he has no choice "but to jump," and that by doing so he might be reaching towards a new and more fulfilling sexuality.

The Feminist Movement has already set "some" men in motion. It is still a slow motion. Men are still grudging about the privileges they feel they are losing, and not quite sure about what they are heading towards. Nevertheless, through a painful consciousness raising process, a still small, but definitely growing section of the male population is heading steadily to meet the challenges of the future.

Options for Women in Motion

To the extent that a woman is struggling to break out of her conditioned mind and lifestyle, she is a "woman in trouble." Today's young woman will of course have less "trouble" in experimenting with various lifestyles than older women. She has more lifestyle mobility tha these women because she has not become so entrenched in a way of life as to find it psychologically impossible to make a change. Her lifestyle, over a few years, may include living in a commune, living alone, living with a man or living with a woman. What the young woman does share in common with older women is the problem of holding onto, and constantly reinforcing her changing ideas about her role in society, while at the same time, confronting, in her everyday life, those who are threatened by her new nonappeasing, self-assertive behavior.

A married woman, who has been "set in motion" by the Movement, often finds herself in the extremely frustrating position of having to change her own self-image and psyche, while at the same time, living with a man who is not ready to change—a man upon whom she is extremely dependent as a result of many years of living together. The frustration of trying to break out of her daily role as "the wife," while the man she lives with persists in relating to her with stereotyped behavior, is often too much to bear. If she opts for remaining in the marriage situation and tries to make changes within it to free herself from stereotyped roles, she often finds herself engaged in constant battles over issues that were nonexistent before. The solution she sometimes chooses is the frightening and painful one of divorce. After years of living with a man, she finds herself alone for the first time. Like Nora, in "The Doll's House," she has gone from her father's "protective" house to her husband's "protective" house. The shock, pain and loneliness of being on her own is sometimes experienced as worse than the marriage she felt she had to leave.

If a woman is divorced, but has children, she is usually the one who must continue to raise and care for them. This often makes it impossible for her, particularly if the children are very young, to lead the "far freer" life she hoped for when she decided to get divorced. Today, young married women who have not yet had children also realize that, under the present organization of our society, they cannot both work successfully at careers and raise children. They sense that no matter how "helpful" their husbands are around the house, the children will primarily be their responsibility, and that, for at least several years, they will have to devote themselves exclusively to child rearing. Their solution seems simple: not to have children. This choice is also a painful one in that somewhere, in every woman's psyche, the inbred notion still lingers that she will be unfulfilled if she doesn't bear children. She is torn between what she has been conditioned to believe and what she rationally knows is best for her.

The young, single woman is in a different kind of "trouble." She may be living or spending time with a young man who is split between his past masculine conditioning and his desire for change. He may be likely to understand the changes the young woman is going through, willing to make efforts at changing himself, and less likely to indulge in stereotypical relating. Nevertheless, early conditioning is powerful, and the young woman may find that she is still often called upon to play the roles of housewife-mother and sexual object. She may join a consciousness-raising group and begin to spend more and more time with her sympathetic women friends. This can, and often does, lead her sexual partner into a feeling of "abandonment," and of being left out. The rage that accompanies these feelings in no way helps their relationship. The young woman may find herself reviewing her options. She can give up feminism and keep her man, accept the hard work and constant friction that goes with trying to change both herself and her lover at the same time, or give up her relationship altogether.

Although their options are increasing, the fact is that most young women, psychologically speaking, are still dependent on men and marriage as a means of survival. Walk into any restaurant, movie, theater, etc. and the obvious fact hits: couples are still "in." Whether one has a knowledge of karate or not, it is still a psychological ordeal for many women to take a stroll through a park alone for fear of being raped or just "hassled," to eat alone in a restaurant, go to a movie alone, or raise a child alone and earn enough money to support herself. Women still feel the need of male escorts and husbands. But as the "woman in motion" moves more and more towards self-dependence, and as she becomes sensitized to her real needs, she will no longer accept the company of "just any" male for the sake of an escort, nor will she be able to make herself believe that she is "in love" for the sake of getting a husband. As a result, more and more young women are beginning to make the conscious choice of remaining single, living alone, and socializing only when they choose to, and with whom they choose.

Last but not least, the changing woman is "in trouble" sexually. By "trouble," we mean here, the agonizing sexual split that many of today's women feel. Dreams and fantasies just do not change at the same rate of speed as our ideas. Women struggling towards independence still have many sexual fantasies that are directly connected to their social and psychological conditioning.

Today's woman tries to free herself from degrading sexual practices she has been accustomed to, such as the "lie in bed" for instance, where, by groaning and moaning, she pretends at pleasure she doesn't always feel, just for the sake of keeping up the man's image of his potency and sexual abilities. Today, she refuses to live on such an alienated, humiliating, and lonely sexual plane. But even if she ceases this and other such dominance-submission sexual practices, she may find that old sexual fantasies still cling. "My man beats me but I love him just the same," is not exactly the statement you'd hear from the changing woman, but it is hard to free oneself from internalized punishment and rape fantasies. The socialization of women, which teaches them to accept psychological rape by men as their only means of survival, has been translated into sexual fantasies. These fantasies, involving aggression by the man and submission by the woman, are often a source of sexual stimulation—a means of getting sexually "turned on." This sexual masochism is arrived at by sensing that safety and security are only obtainable by the acceptance of a set of social, and related sexual fantasies, in which women can only survive or get their "kicks" through victimization and objectification. Sexuality of this nature can have little to do with sensuality, and today's woman is aware of this fact, even if her past sexual fantasies still linger on. She can choose to suffer the torment of this psychic split while trying, through understanding, to rid herself of "victim" fantasies, or she can try homosexuality.

Homosexuality may also become the choice of women who find themselves in any of the social conflicts we have mentioned in this section. Often it doesn't start out as a conscious choice, but rather as "something that happens" as women find themselves spending more and more time relating to other women, rather than fighting the blatant male chauvinist, or the split man whose ideas are on one level while his psyche is on another.

The Homosexual Solution

Separatism, the habit of being only with one's own race or sex, is gaining momentum with various minority groups and within the ranks of feminist women. Homosexuality, both male and female, is spreading more and more. Its politicization makes it an important factor in influencing the cultural and sexual revolution, and some people view it as a transitional historical link with a future bisexual society. Homosexuality has already achieved some of its political and cultural goals.

For us, what is more relevant about the spread of homosexuality is that it is a biting statement against the failure of heterosexual relationships in our sexist society. Modern homosexuality represents that element within the cultural revolution that most vividly puts its fingers on the total fiasco of our sexist society in regard to male-female relationships: psychological misery, sexual dissatisfaction, nervous and spiritual breakdowns that are characteristic of so much of our bourgeois family life and make it seem like hell, mental instability, suicide, divorce, etc. etc. The gloomy picture of the reality of the coexistence of the sexes almost gives credence to those hard core homosexuals who view heterosexuality as a sexual and psychological perversion. (We recall one day, when we were holding hands and walking around the city, someone spat out at us with contempt, saying: "Disgusting heterosexual freaks!")

The important aspect of homosexuality, within the context of modern social experimentation, is the fact that it attempts to experience and prove the human possibilities of the sexual and psychological coexistence and relationship of two human beings who have not been subjected to a different socialization process and forced into opposite and incompatible sexual roles; in other words, the entire process that has placed an invisible, but no less effective, iron curtain between the two sexes, and divided humanity into two opposite "races" or genders—masculine and feminine.

For the homosexual, the sexual attraction towards one's own sex and the refusal of the opposite sex is partly based on the dread and fear of being sexually confined to one's gender by definitive sexual roles, or exposed to sexist objectification. From this point of view, homosexuality indicates the possibility of a future harmonious sexuality between *any* two persons, even if the one is a man and the other a woman, who have not been forced into two different genders. It is, after all, with such hope and belief in the sexual expansion generated by such "degenderization" of the sexes, that we write this chapter.

Nevertheless, homosexuality has indicated the problem, not resolved it. The fact of two people belonging to the same sex does not automatically eliminate the needs and patterns of psychological exploitation inbred in our sexist society. Sado-masochism still finds its way into homosexual relationships and new sexual roles are subtly redefined.

Homosexuality is handicapped by the fact that it often fails to break through the classical destructive patterns of interpersonal relationships.

Other Sexual and A-sexual Solutions

Our cultural revolution started as an explosion of freedom; as an attempt to liberate the individual from the social, psychological and sexual strains of an oppressive society. It looks as if at least some of it is going astray.

A large section of today's youth is heavily involved with mystical and spiritual experiences which generally end in abdication of one's individual freedom, the engulfment of one's consciousness in a "cosmic" consciousness, and finally, the desexualization and transmutation of sexual drives into a communal emotional experience. It's not exactly what Wilhelm Reich had in mind when he wrote of sexual liberation.

One of the reasons for this phenomenon is that today's young are in a sense not young enough. They had time to see their parents at work. They witnessed the misery of parental relationships, and this has often been a traumatic experience. By the time they got to rebel it was often too late. Today, only those children born into a parental situation where at least an "intellectual" switch has been made in the classical husband-wife-father-mother-child relationship have any chance of achieving relative psychic peace. The most deeply imbedded psychic factor in our society is the fear of loneliness. This fear has usually been the backbone of their parents' love affair. Fear of loneliness and need of love have been experienced and psychologically assimilated as two sides of the same coin.

The teenagers' fear of loneliness and need of love does not disappear with their parental rebellion. They do not want to love less. They want to love better than their parents. Their sexuality is torn between their fear of loneliness, their need of love, their original sexual drives, and the fact that they recognize, in their early sexual experiences, similarities with parental sado-masochist tendencies. Sometimes the choice of homosexuality is an unconscious attempt to "have" love, without becoming like one's parents. Their fear of becoming like their parents can turn into fear of heterosexual sex.

Today's youth often replaces the family by a larger spiritual community. Such community offers the possibility of an intense emotional outlet, in which sex, as a dreaded one-to-one experience, is transformed into a communion-type emotional and trans-sexual association. Love becomes the all-powerful, all-emotional experience, which encompasses and eliminates all needs for father, mother, husband or wife, and neutralizes sexual drives.

This new trend towards mystical emotionalism is today spreading beyond the youth culture and into bourgeois society under various forms. It is too complex a phenomenon to fully explore here. What is important for us is to state our belief that: a) this modern over-emphasis on spiritual communion and "love" is a temporary trend that restrains and distorts our present struggle towards changes in sexual relationships; b) there is bound to be—soon—a reaction against it because it does not offer appreciable and enduring psychological results.

This lack of appreciable and enduring results is already obvious. The young seem to pass from spiritual excitement to disappointment, from one spiritual adventure to another. Spiritual love does not seem to be "delivering" what it promises.

Against a social background of growing homosexuality and spiritual a-sexuality, a number of writers are taking up arms to "save" heterosexuality. They originate what could be called a "Futuristic Sexual Literature." The general characteristic of this literature is that it places the main responsibility for the sorry state of heterosexuality upon the hypocritical institutions and lifestyles with which heterosexuality has been associated. It therefore aims at the abolition of monogamy as it exists today. It proposes new forms of sexual associations, new rules for sexuality, new systems of cohabitation, etc. This futuristic literature has had wide publicity during the past year or so, and it is bound to grow. It represents the most recent trend in sexual philosophy. Evolving as a by-product of feminism, it accepts much of the feminist critique of the established sexuality and some of its psychological insight.

The Futuristic Sexual Literature is important and bound to have a strong impact upon the future. The abolition of coercive morality and antiquated institutions will have a positive liberating effect, not only on our social but also on our sexual and psychological life. Nevertheless, we feel that such literature does not go far enough. Its new lifestyle proposals can provide only limited results.

A sexual equilibrium cannot be achieved by replacing monogamy with an institutionalized or noninstitutionalized form of polygamy, or even by abolishing marriage and the nuclear family. A sexual equilibrium can only be achieved by breaking through the notion of the "couple" altogether, by liberating the individual from the psychologically conditioned fear of loneliness and "need" of a partner for the edification of what is called interpersonal relationship.

Many authors of this sexual futuristic trend still seem confused and torn between their desire to liberate sexuality and their attachment to a still mystified notion of love.

In this sense, we believe that the Futuristic Sexual Literature underestimates the future.

Of Sex and Love

When Christ spoke of Love he meant "agape," or the "caring for" humanity. When two people "fall in love," they mean "eros," or what was known in the past as "passion"—"the need" of someone else. This passion-need is what we today call love.

Today, the concept of love is used as a romantic sanctification of an otherwise very crude human relationship. Love in itself implies a "contract," even if it is not experienced in marriage. I love you today means I will love you tomorrow. I am in love does not mean I love, or care for, or am about to do something that is good for someone else. It means, I cannot do without someone else. Even if I do something to prove how much I love the other, I make sure that this something will bind this other more strongly to me. I would rather not do something that is good for my partner if I am afraid that this might make him or her more free from me. Love is not only need, it is also a chain. Love is surely not friendship. The more a relationship depends on need and fear of loneliness the more it relies on love, and the more it relies on love the more alienated sex will be. If love is meant to make sex more beautiful, it certainly doesn't make it.

On the other hand, a completely "non-loving" sexual act is experienced as an appropriation of one's personal body by another—usually a woman's by a man's—and a crude and unfulfilling experience. Prostitution is a sad example of it, and such body appropriation is not limited to houses of prostitution but is taking place in some of the most respected bedrooms. The reason why sex is often unfulfilling, both with or without love, is that both experiences are often the same—a sado-masochistic expression of hate and frustration.

We believe that sex is primarily a physico-emotional event. It is the skin of one's body wanting to achieve intense pleasure by intimate relationship with the skin of another person's body. The intensity of such pleasure, and the physical release it supplies, brings forth strong emotional feelings. These emotional feelings are physical in the sense that they are experienced as pleasure, but at the same time, they go beyond physical pleasure, and this by the fact that behind the two bodies there are two human beings. The quality of the emotional feelings will fluctuate according to the psychic "intentions" of these two human beings as to each other, or as to the act that they are performing together.

This transphysicality and emotionality of sex is what makes it more than sheer sensual pleasure. It intensifies it, beautifies it, and humanizes it. But it can also be the cause for its degradation, degeneration, and even desensualization. The dependence of the sexual act on the "intentions" of the two minds behind the two bodies makes it fragile to the psychological existential relation between the two human beings. If the intention in their relationship is to destroy each other, the sexual act will act out rape, fear, or paralysis, and only a brainwashing of the mind can turn such an act into an experience of pleasure. Love, in such a sexual act, is an attempt to cover up the crude reality of the situation by glorifying it.

It is only when two partners are psychologically independent of each other that their "intentions" will not be against each other but towards the common physical act. Only two psychologically self-sufficient human beings can experience the intense enjoyment in such physical intimacy.

What we today call interpersonal relationship makes such an experience highly unlikely. We believe that, although a sexual relationship is, and will remain, a psychological relation, it will more and more free itself from the pathological-psychological-interdependent-couple syndrome called Love.

The Individual Citizen—Monohabitation

The over-emphasis and exploitative degradation of love in our Western societies is a result of the intensification, during the past hundred years, of the psychological interdependency between men and women in Western bourgeois societies, and the trend of the nuclear family to become more and more restricted and defined by "The Couple."

The history of human socialization starts with tribes or clans—probably of matriarchal inspiration—passes through the period of the large monogamic and polygamic patriarchal family—still existing in many parts of the world—and ends up in Western societies with the modern small unit nuclear family. The nuclear family is identified mainly as husband-wife, to whom the status of mother and father is only provisorily added, and this for a relatively short period of time. Because of its smallness, because of the fact that the outside competitive world is increasingly felt to be an unrelaxing and hostile milieu of survival, this "reduced" nuclear family is more and more dependent on itself for the emotional release of psychological frustrations. The two partners in the "couple" situation, whether in marriage or outside it, feel more psychologically "bound" to each other today, even though the "wife" may have reached economic self-dependence. The two partners are indeed each other's "half." The use of a wider society as a milieu of intense psychological experience, including emotion, pleasure, and interest, is more and more lost, except in the specific domain of productive, competitive activity connected with the struggle for life and the need for personal assertion.

It is ironic that in the traditionalist, patriarchal, male chauvinist countries, although the economic dependency of the wife is total, and the institutional laws and ethical values oppressive to her, the couple is less "bound" to each other by psychological needs. The couple's psychological activity spreads out to the whole of the grand-family—uncles, cousins, etc.—and far beyond, into the social milieu. Friendships become important and highly emotional—both in pleasure and in pain—and one identifies with the whole village or city as a place "where one belongs" as an individual citizen. Of course, these societies are almost totally male supremacist; a virtually apartheid sort of world with a double standard of citizenship for males and females. One is the "upper world" with its public places, cafés, clubs, political gatherings, male entertainment, etc. The other, a more recluse world, confined mainly to the house. Nevertheless, the strong emotional attachments and friendships that develop outside the couple relationship result in a less tense marital situation which does not pretend to be anything else than what it is: a contractual arrangement that does not have to involve "falling in love." It is in the social milieu that the individual experiences his or her self more intensely. This intense social life, these attachments, likings, friendships, and affections lead us to believe that, if such sociability is possible in an unjust sexist and apartheid world, it might not only be possible, but also desirable in a non-sexist, genderless society. In such a society it might provide the basis for both a freer and better integrated sexuality.

We are now experiencing the collapse of this sexist, apartheid society. We are also experiencing—although this is a slow, confused, and still marginal reality—the effects upon our psyche of such an event. We turn more and more away from the "couple" unit and towards larger groups in the hope that in such groups we shall be accepted as free, participating individuals rather than as impotized, dependent "halves." Such a trend is taking different forms. Some people turn towards communes. These communes are either a place for relieving one's fear of loneliness—a sort of "bigger family"—and because of this they repeat the family power structure and don't work out too well, or they are agglomerates of free individuals, and in that case they are more like embryonic cities.

It seems to us that the trend that will finally prevail is a new "coming back to the city." By "coming back to the city" we do not mean that one has necessarily left it. It is more of a symbolic way to express a desire to live as an individual among other individuals. We realize that the cities, as they are today, are over-crowded and over-polluted, and that people are still leaving them. "Coming back to the city," means a new trend that is still marginal but bound to expand; a reaction to the still existing movement towards suburbia. The movement towards suburbia should be understood not only as an escape from over-crowding and pollution, but also as an attempt to put the couple "out of reach" of the new sexual upheavals and other cultural turmoils that might threaten it.

Today, "coming back to the city" means either rooming with someone or living alone. Rooming with someone is still often a "cover-up" for the fear of loneliness, and often it creates psychological complications that are disguised as practical issues. Living by oneself or Monohabitation is going to be, by 2000, the reality for quite a large section of the population in the most sophisticated cities of the Western world. This factor might even prove to be a dynamic reenergizing of city planning philosophies and techniques.

Monohabitation does not mean isolation or loneliness. Quite the opposite. With a video-telephonic system that will probably exist before the year 2000, it will mean more contacts with more people. It will mean a freer and more total commitment to the city, the neighborhood community, the group one is actively involved with, or simply with friends one likes most.

There are so many old widows and widowers today who have always cohabitated and dreaded the idea of loneliness. Suddenly, left by themselves, they are forced into Monohabitation. For the first time in their lives they start to get involved with the world around them. They like it.

Year 2000: Towards a Genderless Sexuality

We have tried to understand the present in as much as it is full of the future. We've seen feminism as a starting point of an evolutionary trend. We've seen the psychological problems it creates. We saw the different solutions that individuals give to such problems. We saw that the present involvement with emotionalism, love, and communal experience is a progressive—in relation to the past—but also a regressive—in relation to the future—factor. We've suggested that there will be a reaction against them, and predicted the advent of the "individual citizen" living in a "Monohabitat" society—a phenomenon that has already started to take shape. It remains now to draw the necessary conclusions about the nature of sexuality in the year 2000.

We wish to remind the reader here of what we said in the beginning. First, that even if one's analysis of the present is correct, any predictions about the future can only be "logical" and "probable." The future has often been known to play "tricks" and revert the "logical sequence" of historical development. Second, that when we talk about the year 2000 we are talking about the avant-garde section of the population in industrial Western societies, and that we are fully aware that the majority of the population of this earth will probably not have kept up with it.

We see as the main psychic factor that will determine the nature of sexuality for these avant-garde people of the future, the fact that they will have been born within a social milieu that has, at least intellectually, absorbed and dealt with the central issue of feminism—the analysis of the concept of gender as a construct of a male supremacist civilization.

The concept of gender—as the concept of race—is what has used meaningless physical differences to create a myth that has been "put on top" of these differences to reinforce the exploitation of one part of humanity by the other. If at an earlier time of our civilization the exploitation of all the short people by all the tall people, or vice versa, could have been wished and practical, we might have ended up today with two "categorical" genders: The Talls and The Shorts. A categorical gender lacks reality's "gradualism." If you are between four-feet and five-feet-six you are a Short. If you are between five-feet-six-and-a-half and seven-feet you are a Tall. Race is a "categorical" reality, and so is gender. Gender is a "categorical" conceptual definition, pretending to be a physical one. Genderism is what feminism is fighting against. Genderism has been analyzed and dissected. We know it well today either through personal experience, or by learning about it. But we have been born and raised within it. Our psyche and sexuality have been permanently affected. We believe that children who are born now will be less affected by it and that their sexual perception will be less "categorical" and more "real," meaning more "sensual," and that they will be able to better know and experience what they really like.

A genderless sexuality goes beyond heterosexuality, homosexuality, and bisexuality, in the sense that these can still be sexist while a genderless sexuality cannot. On the other hand, a genderless sexuality does not mean an a-sexual or a unisex sexuality. It does not imply esthetic standardization. On the contrary, it means that individuals will be more able to appreciate differences or similarities. Whether they are attracted by "opposites" or by "similars" they will know that such attraction is authentic, meaning physico-emotional, and not conditioned by genderic considerations.

What form will interpersonal relationships take, and how will sexuality be experienced in such a genderless society—a society of psychologically relatively self-dependent individuals? Are we heading towards one night stands and a sexuality completely devoid of psychological investment? We don't think so. Up to now such practices have been associated with sexist, sado-masochistic, seduction techniques. One night stands might take place only if one night friendships are possible. We believe that the pattern of interpersonal relationship and sexuality will closely follow the pattern of the individual's sociability. Friendship and "liking" will replace love and the "monopoly of the couple," and sexuality will find a new and fresh dimension within it.

The type of friendship we have in mind is one of individuals who come together for social enjoyment, and not only for competitive needs. One does not "fall" into such friendships or "divorce" from them. One is often not sure of when a friendship really starts and when it finishes. Such friendships can imply emotion, devotion, and a certain degree of loyalty. Sexuality within such friendships—between friends who sexually "dig" each other and for as long as they do so—has far reaching implications which are difficult to ascertain yet. It will probably: a) achieve the elimination of sado-masochistic sexual impulses which have been brainwashed into our society; b) create a new emotional dimension and a new psychology of sex; c) lead to a resurgence of a more sensualized sexuality.

Malinowski tells us that there have been some people, who because of a more intimate relationship with nature and a better integrated society, have lived through a sort of Golden Age of sexuality. Maybe we are heading towards such an era again. Of course, we are not Primitivists. We do not believe that history can go backwards. It is rather, through further sophistication, that we believe our society will decondition itself, and bring itself into an era of unstrained and genderless sexuality.

19 *YOUR TIME,*
YOUR STATION

by David Saperstein

THE SCREEN FILLS with a murky sunrise in a neat suburb; zooms in on a modest ranch house through the kitchen window. A woman, approximately age forty, is mixing frozen orange juice, getting out a box of "special" breakfast cereal and popping some frozen waffles into the toaster. Upstairs a man about forty-five is shaving with a new "double track" razor and canned aerosol foam shaving cream. A son and a daughter in their early teens and wearing jeans and tee shirts, bound downstairs to the kitchen for breakfast. Their hair is the same length.

The narrator tells us that we are about to witness a typical day in the life of a typical American family of the 1970's . . . As we sit here in the year 2000, the wall screen of the home "media" room proceeds to show how it was for Americans in those days, just a quarter century ago. The story explores how we lived—as though we were still colonial farmers, and as a result, had a rather dreary and wearing life.

Everyone got up about the same time. Everyone ate breakfast, traveled to work, entered offices or plants, had coffee, had lunch, traveled home, ate dinner—ate about the same kind of food—sat down and watched commercial TV and went to bed—All at about the same time.

The result of all of this, explains the narrator, was giant surges in electrical demand at specific hours, causing brownouts and blackouts, enormous traffic jams that polluted the air, overheated our cars, and caused anxiety in the drivers. In the cities it put an abnormal load on the public transportation systems and packed people sardine-like into buses and trains. We occupied giant office buildings and plants for about ten hours and then abandoned them for the remaining fourteen hours. Monuments to waste of space, construction materials and the vitality of cities.

The story continues to tell us about the prepackaged, preserved, air-filled foods we bought and ate, about the large gas-eating air-polluting, metal-consuming cars we drove, about the home gadgetry that freed housewives to tears of boredom. About the walls of silence that grew between couples and their children as did the rate of divorce, alcoholism and drug addiction. About the bland, insulting and unfulfilling television fare that was offered each evening, and how we watched the tube by habit, and in the meantime almost lost our ability to read and talk and write.

You are viewing an educational videotape program at home about life in the "seventies." Your children turn to you and ask, "Was it really like that?"

The program continues as the narrator talks about the way everyone worked during the week, and went off on the weekends to jam highways and recreational areas.

It was a time when we were depressed as a people, or rather confused about our national and personal goals. The American Dream was not working, and we were distressed by that thought. Some say we almost lost our Constitutional form of government—and consequently our freedom.

America in the 70's was surely a time of transition in the economic sense, too. Worry about inflation, shortages, interest rates, stock markets, unemployment. It was a time of transition.

Slowly those voices that insisted on saying "Italian" or "Black" or "Jew" or "Southerner" or "Socialist" or "Woman" for the reasons of separation and prejudice, died away. Slowly, as a people, we turned to the business of a new American Dream. We began reevaluating our goals and priorities. It had to do with redefining words like "happiness," "work," "equality," "sexuality," "morals," "consumerism."

Slowly, we began to ask some questions: Does a painter work? Yes, if he paints houses. But what if he paints pictures? Yes, if he sells them. But what if he does them for his own pleasure and the pleasure of others . . . to communicate feelings and ideas? Is he working?

Does a woman who wants to create advertising copy have to subvert that desire, and talent, because she is a woman and bears children? Does her sex make her a cleaning and cooking machine?

What should our goals be? A ranch house in the suburbs? A Cadillac car? A leopard coat? A country club membership? Thick steaks on the gas operated barbecue? Ten two-hundred-dollar suits in the closet? Children in the "best" colleges? Was that the promise of America?

Those questions asked in the forties or fifties would have been answered "Yes." In the 60's . . . "I guess so; I don't know; perhaps." In the 70's . . . "I don't think so; not for me, it doesn't work anymore." Now, in the year 2000 we can all have a good laugh at that life we once lived.

So the narrator closes the program and your wall screen fades to black. The conversation light automatically comes up to the comfortable, pre-set level. You are in your "media" room in the year 2000. 2000 will be a time of variety. This variety will manifest itself in every aspect of our lives. So it will be in our media, too.

You will have a place, a media room, and in it will be all of the technology that is available today, scattered and disconnected throughout your home as it is now, concentrated into one area. The center of it will be a screen—perhaps a whole wall, perhaps two of four walls. All video will appear on this screen, as it now does on your TV set. All audio will come through speakers recessed in the walls. Stereophonic or quadrophonic or octophonic, as it now comes through your telephone receiver or hi-fi or cassette player or AM/FM radio.

Sight and sound will combine in a variety of ways. The technology exists today. Some of it is still expensive and not yet mass produced. But it will be available to all by 2000.

In your "room" you will be able to listen to music, play along on the instrument of your choice and TV-record your performance at the same time. There will be programming that you can purchase or rent or swap. Just as you choose books and magazines today, so you will choose programs in 2000. More about the "room:" the picture phone is there. You will be able to converse and see each other, around the world. Think how pleasant to see a painting a friend just finished or a new baby or the family at Thanksgiving. Part of the "room" will be devoted to your own "productions." Home videotapes taken with your own color camera and color recorder. With sound, of course, and the ability to edit.

At any time, you will be able to receive the latest news on a worldwide, nationwide, statewide, and even local-block basis—via radio (continuous radio broadcasting is very much with us today as is closed-circuit TV news). You will be able to set a signal on your recorder that can be keyed to the news stations. This signal will turn on your recorder and tape items of special interest to you. It will be very much like the telephone recording units today that answer your phone and tape a message from the caller. It can play back at your convenience. There will be a similar remote control device that can be set to turn on at a given time and record a video program, too.

Your "newspaper" will be "printed" in your house via a facsimile machine attached to one of your closed circuit TV channels. We may well get as far as a simple holograph unit that will project three dimensional images on a special "stage" in the room.

All programming, news and events will come to us via video cassette, closed circuit cable television or worldwide satellite systems that beam down signals via laser beams. The limited channels that we all supposedly own today will diminish in commercial importance, and each person will truly own the airwaves.

Thus, in the media room-2000, you will be capable of as much variety in program selection as you want. But what of these programs? Will we be buying video cassettes of "The Beverly Hillbillies?" If that is the preference, then yes, you will be able to buy that program, or any other program. You will have the choice.

As our desire for variety, innovation, knowledge, specialized information and entertainment grows, so will the programming produced to satisfy those desires. The production and distribution of programming will be as diverse as the music industry is today. A sample of that variety can be found on Public Broadcasting today, most specifically in the potpourri found on NET—perhaps the forerunner of the programs for specific interests that will be available in 2000.

Certainly the imagination, innovation, quality and success of "Sesame Street," The Watergate Hearings, Professional Tennis, "Firing Line," "The Advocates," and the several fine educational series on health, all point out the possibility for innovation.

Repeating the same broadcast several times on different days, and in different languages will give you freedom to choose a program at your convenience.

Just imagine. It's three A.M. and you can't sleep. In the mail is the

"Cassette of the Month" selection, a new fiction film from China. You open the package and slap the cassette into your playback unit. Two hours of uninterrupted viewing follows. Do the same one night with "Gone With The Wind," or all the "James Bond" films; or have a Fellini festival party with some friends over a weekend.

If you're beginning to like the sound of this, stay well and live long. It is coming and it will happen by the turn of the century.

Now suppose you want to take a vacation in India. Borrow a cassette on India. The travel agent will probably have these available free for you to view at your convenience. The whole world, when and where you want it, so that you may understand and choose, and know what you are going to get. The cassettes won't replace travel, but they will give us more of a choice, so that we may make an intelligent decision.

Speaking of intelligent decisions, what about politics and voting? All this chatter about "equal time" and the cost of running a campaign is constantly with us of late. The candidates could state their programs and platforms on videotape and make them available to us. We would view them a number of times and really listen to the substance of these politicians and their views. If candidates chose they could tape debates and make them available. We may even be recording our vote through closed circuit TV. And that ought to increase the percentage of voters!

Now let me interrupt cassette programming and talk a little about closed circuit television. I believe this too will be a part of media in the future. Your receiver and taping unit will be linked by cable or secure laser beam to a multitude of channels. Literally thousands of channels can be made available on one beam. These can bring you your newspaper in the morning, supermarket specials direct from the supermarket ware-house, banking transactions, highly specialized programs dealing with your particular hobby or vocation, local political information, emergency information, stock market reports; the possibilities are endless.

Entertainment will come through closed circuit too. You will pay a fee for these programs as you view them, but the fee will be less than you now pay for a first-run film, and as many people as you want to invite can view it with you. Later you can decide to rent it and view it again, or buy a video cassette and have the show in your library.

Remember, it's your time, your station. So you'll be able to tune in anything that suits your interests or mood. How about a video version of *The Joy of Sex, Circa 2000* or a few erotic short stories of the kind that used to be called pornography back in the seventies? You can even make your own with your color videotape camera and recorder.

How about watching the Jets beat the Colts, 16-7, in that fateful January 12, 1969 Superbowl? You can get it in 2000.

You will be able to view what you want to view when you want to view it. The media will be at the very core of our lives for a long time. We crave information and we absorb and retain audio/visual messages as with no other media.

Back to education. Remember the controversy a few years back about sex education in the schools? There are many people who find it hard to tell their children, and educate themselves, about sex, reproduction, love, hygiene, morality and other so-called "difficult" subjects. Your media room, with the aid of tastefully produced programs, pre-screened by you, will be a private place to deal with those subjects.

The entire method of formal education, for both children and adults, will change by the turn of the century. Electronic media will play a key role in that change. Some schools will become studio centers that will disseminate courses via closed circuit television. This will differ from the pre-packaged cassettes I discussed earlier, because much of this education will be "live" and *two way*. That is to say, you or your child will be able to receive instructions from the "school," and send questions and answers back to the school. A worldwide system is possible. Many Universities and school systems exchange audio/visual courses today. Extended to 2000, live education will be a worldwide reality.

Much of our formal education in the past was designed to prepare us for a world in industrial revolution. We went to school on specific days and at specific times, just as our parents went to work. By 2000 that will have changed, and education will be as unregimented as our lives at that time. A new breed of teacher will develop. Part actor, part educator, knowledgeable in audio/visual techniques and programming concepts, innovative and interesting. We will make use of the best teachers for reaching a large number of students. I can even see the day when certain teachers will be "superstars" in their own right, and will command huge audiences.

Business, industry and government will also use the twenty-first-century media in all aspects of their operations.

Internal closed-circuit networks will be set up by the major worldwide organizations for the exchange of information. The new electronic media will be used to sell products, discuss problems, interview job applicants, change strategies, send memos and corporate communications. Many companies are using such techniques today, and each day new innovations are being explored.

Business will also sponsor much of the programming that you will buy or rent. The home cassette and closed circuit market is a new advertising outlet. With it, business will be able to reach not only mass audiences, but also the key, specialized audiences that are cropping up already in our fractionalized society.

On the subject of business and work—not having to commute to the office everyday, or take a grueling business trip to four cities in three days will be within your power. Your media room can become your office. You can work at home and communicate with fellow workers via closed circuit or picturephone. You can make sales presentations to customers in the comfort of their houses, and show them your product in action. All the time spent commuting and traveling can be better spent on productive work. And this will open many new job opportunities for women.

Suppose you want to have a meeting with an important client. She is in Rome and you are in Tulsa. You both agree that it would be nice to meet on the beach in Rio. Instead of traveling to Rio you project a motion picture, with sound, of the beach. She does the same on her screen, you aim your camera at yourself with the beach behind you on your screen, she does the same . . . you superimpose each other onto the other's screen and you have your meeting. Why not sip some rum punch while you talk? Interesting fantasy?

If we project business use of the electronic media, then it follows that consumer use will be as exciting. Your media room can be a shopping center. Although you may still want to touch a fabric, or talk face-to-face with an expert, or test drive a transportation device, the bulk of your day-to-day shopping can be accomplished through the media.

Centrally located supermarket warehouses will broadcast continuously. They will present specials for the day, new products, etc. This will come to you over a closed-circuit TV channel. You can choose your purchases by code, and either phone them in, or send them back to the "store" via another TV channel. By using a special number your purchases will automatically be debited to your account and credited to the store's account and your order delivered.

Perhaps you want to shop for a dress in Paris. By using a dataphone attachment to your picturephone you will be able to dial the store in Paris, and receive pictures of the merchandise. You will talk to the salesperson and make your choice. Or maybe you'll yearn for furniture in Stockholm. Once again you dial them, but this time you send them a picture of the room you wish to furnish. They assemble your room and project it back to you. You then discuss changes, accessories, color and finally wind up with the room you want. The order is then placed and confirmed including shipping instructions.

Almost all of the media will make use of computers. So will we. Every media room will have a computer terminal that is connected to a main central computer. With the terminal you will be able to call on the data stored in the main computer, or be patched into any specialized computer program that you may require. Much of our educational data will come to us this way, and certainly a great deal of research material.

We may, by 2000, own small computers of our own in which we store personal data and data required for our work. In fact, picture a computer program that holds the sum total of a person's life being a most valuable asset to future generations, especially your own family. This is what you can leave behind . . . your records, knowledge and experience . . . securely locked in a little black box on disk or tape or captured within memory bubbles.

If you are wondering why I have only occasionally talked about women thus far, please understand that, in fact, I have been talking about women, and men, all the time. I believe by 2000 we will have passed that self-conscious state where sexual separation dominates every subject.

Young men and women are increasingly sophisticated about media and about life. They buy soap because of the way it cleans, not because a commercial tells them they will get a husband or wife by using it. They buy a certain car for the way it functions, not because an ad promised them status. And they have very basic attitudes toward humanity, gained largely through the media. They have watched a war on TV; they have watched their government on TV; they see their music flourish on TV; they have watched the power of their voices topple a President on TV; they understand the media, and they cherish and respect its value to the society.

Women are certain to be as much a part of media 2000 as men. There will be a tremendous need for people to create, write and produce for the coming media explosion. . . . In large measure, the treatment of women in the entertainment media has just begun to change. This is due in part to the women's movement, in part to the "growing up" of our country, and in part to the entry of women into responsible and creative positions in the media.

If you doubt this, then reflect a bit on the way women were portrayed on TV a few years ago. Dumb . . . in menial jobs . . . doing cooking shows . . . subservient to their husbands; or constantly and cutely tricking their even dumber husbands. How many women were doctors, lawyers, politicians, newscasters, reporters, detectives, athletes, astronauts?

Now think of today. True, the TV networks still pump some outdated characterizations at us, but this is swiftly changing. Women are seen and heard today, as real people: doctors, cops, lawyers, politicians. All of the news shows have women reporters . . . not reporting on "women things" . . . just reporting. Women's sports are fast gaining equal time with "men's" sports.

Women today are writers, producers, reporters, directors, photographers, painters, dancers, composers, technicians, editors . . . in fact, I cannot think of a single craft, talent or profession in the communications business that does not now involve and employ women. More important, women's involvment grows each day.

Because I do not believe in 2000 we will still be separating the sexes as some who control media do today, I find it illogical to extract women's roles in the media in 2000 from men's roles. The media will be even closer to the core of our life in 2000 than it is today. Communicators will be equivalent to the high priests of ancient times. They will have similar power and responsibility. I can think of no more exciting or rewarding field than communications in 2000, and, as it is now, so it *will* be wide open to women.

As we were learning to live with the electronic media, it may have been true that "the medium was the message." In 2000, we will have come far from the time when we were overwhelmed and mesmerized by the medium, and to quote my partner, Joe McDonough, "the *message* will be the message . . ." This means that because of our various interests and life styles in 2000, we will need and demand an infinitely larger scope to our programming.

The control of today's programming is in the hands of very few people, namely the three networks, a handful of motion picture distributors, the hodgepodge of censorship and a fluctuating government control. In no way will these few outlets and narrow program matter satisfy us.

Today the distribution, and therefore content of programming is tightly controlled. I believe that the production and distribution of programming in 2000 will be exploded out to all of us. Again, I take my cues from the music business. It is fractionated and keyed to specialized markets and needs. I believe that with our media rooms, cameras and recorders, we will, in effect, all be producers. We will demand and get much more. In 2000 we will have the tools. If today, the means of distribution are rooted in mass audience appeal, then tomorrow they will be attuned to specific local needs. We can see the first signs of change right now:

- Every population center has several "local" TV stations.
- There is more and more local programming.
- There is an upsurge in local theater and local live entertainment.
- Advertising is spending more and more money in local marketing rather than large amounts on national campaigns.
- Films are being shot on location all over the world . . . not just on back lots in California.
- Television series in prime-time have a fast turnover rate.
- Civic affairs draw large TV audiences . . . people are interested in their government, and the government is beginning to understand that fact —and respond to it.
- More and more specialized programming is available through independent syndication.
- Colleges and universities, even high schools are teaching film and videotape production to thousands of students.
- Business and industry is making use of the electronic media more and more each day.
- We are receiving an enormous percentage of our information and entertainment at home, over TV and radio.

I believe that the electronic media will be the overwhelming means of communication in 2000. However, we will still have the printed word and beyond that, the arts. And they will all interlock and reinforce each other.

The year 2000 will be a time of options and variety; with so many frontiers being conquered each day; it becomes apparent that one great frontier we haven't begun to touch is our own inner potential. It will be a time of exploring and expanding those potentials and the media will be a great tool in that exploration.

If we transport ourselves for the stimulation electronics gives our senses, then why not bring the stimulation to ourselves? If business requires that we see people or things, then why travel to them . . . why not bring them to us?

What we say in a letter, may we not say better on tape? Must a traveling saleswoman physically transport her body and wares from customer to customer instead of teletransporting them and remaining in one place? The media is a visible part of the electronic revolution. The technology exists in some form today, and in 2000 will be a reality for all of us. At the core of it will be quality, creativity, and usefulness of the programming we need. In effect, we all now live in a global village and we have more and more in common each day.

In George Orwell's *1984* we see a world controlled by the electronic media. We see the extreme abuse of it. This *is* possible if we are not careful and if we leave the control of the media in the hands of a few. Signposts are pointing to a decentralization of programming control for the benefit of all of us. We will require programmers who are not afraid to experiment and explore new ideas, because that is what we will all be doing in 2000 . . . outwardly in our physical world, and inwardly in the infinite recesses of our minds. We know that in order to survive we must communicate and we must be honest. We all saw our small fragile blue planet on TV from outer space. We saw it through the media. We watched a terrible war and all its horrors. We saw it through the media. A security guard at the Watergate and two Washington Post reporters began a chain of revelations that brought us to the brink of Constitutional crisis. We understood it through the media.

With women playing key roles in the production of what enters the communication media and with women's lives changed by the total choice of education, services and entertainment they receive from the electronic media, we will, someday soon, have an historic opportunity to realize the full potential of human beings.

So there it is . . . the door to your media room–2000. Fill it with what you want, with what you need to know. Laugh and cry at your convenience. Learn at your leisure, and create for your pleasure. Stay in touch with the rest of the world. 2000 will be your time . . . and your station.

20 X: A FABULOUS CHILD'S STORY

by Lois Gould

ONCE UPON A TIME, a baby named X was born. This baby was named X so that nobody could tell whether it was a boy or a girl. Its parents could tell, of course, but they couldn't tell anybody else. They couldn't even tell Baby X, at first.

You see, it was all part of a very important Secret Scientific Xperiment, known officially as Project Baby X. The smartest scientists had set up this Xperiment at a cost of Xactly 23 billion dollars and 72 cents, which might seem like a lot for just one baby, even a very important Xperimental baby. But when you remember the prices of things like strained carrots and stuffed bunnies, and popcorn for the movies and booster shots for camp, let alone 28 shiny quarters from the tooth fairy, you begin to see how it adds up.

Also, long before Baby X was born, all those scientists had to be paid to work out the details of the Xperiment, and to write the *Official Instruction Manual* for Baby X's parents and, most important of all, to find the right set of parents to bring up Baby X. These parents had to be selected very carefully. Thousands of volunteers had to take thousands of tests and answer thousands of tricky questions. Almost everybody failed because, it turned out, almost everybody really wanted either a baby boy or a baby girl, and not Baby X at all. Also, almost everybody was afraid that a Baby X would be a lot more trouble than a boy or a girl. (They were probably right, the scientists admitted, but Baby X needed parents who wouldn't *mind* the Xtra trouble.)

There were families with grandparents named Milton and Agatha, who didn't see why the baby couldn't be named Milton or Agatha instead of X, even if it *was* an X. There were families with aunts who insisted on knitting tiny dresses and uncles who insisted on sending tiny baseball mitts. Worst of all, there were families that already had other children who couldn't be trusted to keep the secret. Certainly not if they knew the secret was worth 23 billion dollars and 72 cents—and all you had to do was take one little peek at Baby X in the bathtub to know if it was a boy or a girl.

But, finally, the scientists found the Joneses, who really wanted to raise an X more than any other kind of baby—no matter how much trouble it would be. Ms. and Mr. Jones had to promise they would take equal turns caring for X, and feeding it, and singing it lullabies. And they had to promise never to hire any baby-sitters. The government scientists knew perfectly well that a baby-sitter would probably peek at X in the bathtub, too.

The day the Joneses brought their baby home, lots of friends and relatives came over to see it. None of them knew about the secret Xperiment, though. So the first thing they asked was what kind of a baby X was. When the Joneses smiled and said, "It's an X!" nobody knew what to say. They couldn't say, "Look at her cute little dimples!" And they couldn't say, "Look at his husky little biceps!" And they couldn't even say just plain "kitchy-coo." In fact, they all thought the Joneses were playing some kind of rude joke.

But, of course, the Joneses were not joking. "It's an X" was absolutely all they would say. And that made the friends and relatives very angry. The relatives all felt embarrassed about having an X in the family. "People will think there's something wrong with it!" some of them whispered. "There *is* something wrong with it!" others whispered back.

"Nonsense!" the Joneses told them all cheerfully. "What could possibly be wrong with this perfectly adorable X?"

Nobody could answer that, except Baby X, who had just finished its bottle. Baby X's answer was a loud, satisfied burp.

Clearly, nothing at all was wrong. Nevertheless, none of the relatives felt comfortable about buying a present for a Baby X. The cousins who sent the baby a tiny football helmet would not come and visit any more. And the neighbors who sent a pink-flowered romper suit pulled their shades down when the Joneses passed their house.

The *Official Instruction Manual* had warned the new parents that this would happen, so they didn't fret about it. Besides, they were too busy with Baby X and the hundreds of different Xercises for treating it properly.

Ms. and Mr. Jones had to be Xtra careful about how they played with little X. They knew that if they kept bouncing it up in the air and saying how *strong and active* it was, they'd be treating it more like a boy than an X. But if all they did was cuddle it and kiss it and tell it how *sweet* and *dainty* it was, they'd be treating it more like a girl than an X.

On page 1,654 of the *Official Instruction Manual*, the scientists prescribed: "plenty of bouncing and plenty of cuddling, *both*. X ought to be strong and sweet and active. Forget about *dainty* altogether."

Meanwhile, the Joneses were worrying about other problems. Toys, for instance. And clothes. On his first shopping trip, Mr. Jones told the store clerk, "I need some clothes and toys for my new baby." The clerk smiled and said, "Well, now, is it a boy or a girl?" "It's an X," Mr. Jones said, smiling back. But the clerk got all red in the face and said huffily, "In *that* case, I'm afraid I can't help you, sir." So Mr. Jones wandered helplessly up and down the aisles trying to find what X needed. But everything in the store was piled up in sections marked "Boys" or "Girls." There were "Boys' Pajamas" and "Girls' Underwear" and "Boys' Fire Engines" and "Girls' Housekeeping Sets." Mr. Jones went home without buying anything for X. That night he and Ms. Jones consulted page 2,326 of the *Official Instruction Manual*. "Buy plenty of everything!" it said firmly.

So they bought plenty of sturdy blue pajamas in the Boys' Department and cheerful flowered underwear in the Girls' Department. And they bought all kinds of toys. A boy doll that made pee-pee and cried, "Pa-pa." And a girl doll that talked in three languages and said, "I am the Pres-i-dent of Gen-er-al Mo-tors." They also bought a storybook about a brave princess who rescued a handsome prince from his ivory tower, and another one about a sister and brother who grew up to be a baseball star and a ballet star, and you had to guess which was which.

The head scientists of Project Baby X checked all their purchases and told them to keep up the good work. They also reminded the Joneses to see page 4,629 of the *Manual*, where it said, "Never make Baby X feel *embarrassed* or *ashamed* about what it wants to play with. And if X gets dirty climbing rocks, never say 'Nice little Xes don't get dirty climbing rocks.' "

Likewise, it said, "If X falls down and cries, never say 'Brave little

Xes don't cry.' Because, of course, nice little Xes *do* get dirty, and brave little Xes *do* cry. No matter how dirty X gets, or how hard it cries, don't worry. It's all part of the Xperiment."

Whenever the Joneses pushed Baby X's stroller in the park, smiling strangers would come over and coo: "Is that a boy or a girl?" The Joneses would smile back and say, "It's an X." The strangers would stop smiling then, and often snarl something nasty—as if the Joneses had snarled at *them.*

By the time X grew big enough to play with other children, the Joneses' troubles had grown bigger, too. Once a little girl grabbed X's shovel in the sandbox, and zonked X on the head with it. "Now, now, Tracy," the little girl's mother began to scold, "little girls mustn't hit little—" and she turned to ask X, "Are you a little boy or a little girl, dear?"

Mr. Jones, who was sitting near the sandbox, held his breath and crossed his fingers.

X smiled politely at the lady, even though X's head had never been zonked so hard in its life. "I'm a little X," X replied.

"You're a *what?*" the lady exclaimed angrily. "You're a little b-r-a-t, you mean!"

"But little girls mustn't hit little Xes, either!" said X, retrieving the shovel with another polite smile. "What good does hitting do, anyway?"

X's father, who was still holding his breath, finally let it out, uncrossed his fingers, and grinned back at X.

And at their next secret Project Baby X meeting, the scientists grinned, too. Baby X was doing fine.

But then it was time for X to start school. The Joneses were really worried about this, because school was even more full of rules for boys and girls, and there were no rules for Xes. The teacher would tell boys to form one line, and girls to form another line. There would be boys' games and girls' games, and boys' secrets and girls' secrets. The school library would have a list of recommended books for girls, and a different list of recommended books for boys. There would even be a bathroom marked BOYS and another one marked GIRLS. Pretty soon boys and girls would hardly talk to each other. What would happen to poor little X?

The Joneses spent weeks consulting their *Instruction Manual* (there were 249½ pages of advice under "First Day of School"), and attending urgent special conferences with the smart scientists of Project Baby X.

The scientists had to make sure that X's mother had taught X how to throw and catch a ball properly, and that X's father had been sure to teach X what to serve at a doll's tea party. X had to know how to shoot marbles and how to jump rope and, most of all, what to say when the Other Children asked whether X was a Boy or a Girl.

Finally, X was ready. The Joneses helped X button on a nice new pair of red-and-white checked overalls, and sharpened six pencils for X's nice new pencilbox, and marked X's name clearly on all the books in its nice new bookbag. X brushed its teeth and combed its hair, which just about covered its ears, and remembered to put a napkin in its lunchbox.

The Joneses had asked X's teacher if the class could line up alpha-betically, instead of forming separate lines for boys and girls. And they had asked if X could use the principal's bathroom, because it wasn't marked anything except BATHROOM. X's teacher promised to take care of all those problems. But nobody could help X with the biggest problem of all—Other Children.

Nobody in X's class had ever known an X before. What would they think? How would X make friends?

You couldn't tell what X was by studying its clothes—overalls don't even button right-to-left, like girls' clothes, or left-to-right, like boys' clothes. And you couldn't guess whether X had a girl's short haircut or a boy's long haircut. And it was very hard to tell by the games X liked to play. Either X played ball very well for a girl, or else X played house very well for a boy.

Some of the children tried to find out by asking X tricky questions, like "Who's your favorite sports star?" That was easy. X had two favorite sports stars: a girl jockey named Robyn Smith and a boy archery champion named Robin Hood. Then they asked, "What's your favorite TV program?" And that was even easier. X's favorite TV program was "Lassie," which stars a girl dog played by a boy dog.

When X said that its favorite toy was a doll, everyone decided that X must be a girl. But then X said that the doll was really a robot, and that X had computerized it, and that it was programmed to bake fudge brownies and then clean up the kitchen. After X told them that, the other children gave up guessing what X was. All they knew was they'd sure like to see X's doll.

After school, X wanted to play with the other children. "How about shooting some baskets in the gym?" X asked the girls. But all they did was make faces and giggle behind X's back.

"How about weaving some baskets in the arts and crafts room?" X asked the boys. But they all made faces and giggled behind X's back, too.

That night, Ms. and Mr. Jones asked X how things had gone at school. X told them sadly that the lessons were okay, but otherwise school was a terrible place for an X. It seemed as if Other Children would never want an X for a friend.

Once more, the Joneses reached for their *Instruction Manual.* Under "Other Children," they found the following message: "What did you Xpect? *Other Children* have to obey all the silly boy-girl rules, because their parents taught them to. Lucky X—you don't have to stick to the rules at all! All you have to do is be yourself. P.S. We're not saying it'll be easy."

X liked being itself. But X cried a lot that night, partly because it felt afraid. So X's father held X tight, and cuddled it, and couldn't help crying a little, too. And X's mother cheered them both up by reading an Xciting story about an enchanted prince called Sleeping Handsome, who woke up when Princess Charming kissed him.

The next morning, they all felt much better, and little X went back to school with a brave smile and a clean pair of red-and-white checked overalls.

There was a seven-letter-word spelling bee in class that day. And a seven-lap boys' relay race in the gym. And a seven-layer-cake baking contest in the girls' kitchen corner. X won the spelling bee. X also won the relay race. And X almost won the baking contest, except it forgot to light the oven. Which only proves that nobody's perfect.

One of the Other Children noticed something else, too. He said: "Winning or losing doesn't seem to count to X. X seems to have fun being good at boys' skills *and* girls' skills."

"Come to think of it," said another one of the Other Children, "maybe X is having twice as much fun as we are!"

So after school that day, the girl who beat X at the baking contest gave X a big slice of her prizewinning cake. And the boy X beat in the relay race asked X to race him home.

From then on, some really funny things began to happen. Susie, who sat next to X in class, suddenly refused to wear pink dresses to school any more. She insisted on wearing red-and-white checked overalls—just like X's. Overalls, she told her parents, were much better for climbing monkey bars.

Then Jim, the class football nut, started wheeling his little sister's doll carriage around the football field. He'd put on his entire football uniform, except for the helmet. Then he'd put the helmet *in* the carriage, lovingly tucked under an old set of shoulder pads. Then he'd start jogging around the field, pushing the carriage and singing "Rockabye Baby" to his football helmet. He told his family that X did the same thing, so it must be okay. After all, X was now the team's star quarterback.

Susie's parents were horrified by her behavior, and Jim's parents were worried sick about his. But the worst came when the twins, Joe and Peggy, decided to share everything with each other. Peggy used Joe's hockey skates, and his microscope, and took half his newspaper route. Joe used Peggy's needlepoint kit, and her cookbooks, and took two of her three baby-sitting jobs. Peggy started running the lawn mower, and Joe started running the vacuum cleaner.

Their parents weren't one bit pleased with Peggy's wonderful biology experiments, or with Joe's terrific needlepoint pillows. They didn't care that Peggy mowed the lawn better, and that Joe vacuumed the carpet better. In fact, they were furious. It's all that little X's fault, they agreed. Just because X doesn't know what it is, or what it's supposed to be, it wants to get everybody *else* mixed up, too!

Peggy and Joe were forbidden to play with X any more. So was Susie, and then Jim, and then *all* the Other Children. But it was too late; the Other Children stayed mixed up and happy and free, and refused to go back to the way they'd been before X.

Finally, Joe and Peggy's parents decided to call an emergency meeting of the school's Parents' Association, to discuss "The X Problem." They sent a report to the principal stating that X was a "disruptive influence." They demanded immediate action. The Joneses, they said, should be *forced* to tell whether X was a boy or a girl. And then X should be *forced* to behave like whichever it was. If the Joneses refused to tell, the Parents' Association said, then X must take an Xamination. The school psychiatrist must Xamine it physically and mentally, and issue a full report. If X's test showed it was a boy, it would have to obey all the boys' rules. If it proved to be a girl, X would have to obey all the girls' rules.

And if X turned out to be some kind of mixed-up misfit, then X should be Xpelled from the school. Immediately!

The principal was very upset. Disruptive influence? Mixed-up misfit? But X was an Xcellent student. All the teachers said it was a delight to have X in their classes. X was president of the student council. X had won first prize in the talent show, and second prize in the art show, and honorable mention in the science fair, and six athletic events on field day, including the potato race.

Nevertheless, insisted the Parents' Association, X is a Problem Child. X is the Biggest Problem Child we have ever seen!

So the principal reluctantly notified X's parents that numerous complaints about X's behavior had come to the school's attention. And that after the psychiatrist's Xamination, the school would decide what to do about X.

The Joneses reported this at once to the scientists, who referred them to page 85,759 of the *Instruction Manual.* "Sooner or later," it said, "X will have to be Xamined by a psychiatrist. This may be the only way any of us will know for sure whether X is mixed up—or whether everyone else is."

The night before X was to be Xamined, the Joneses tried not to let X see how worried they were. "What if—?" Mr. Jones would say. And Ms. Jones would reply, "No use worrying." Then a few minutes later, Ms. Jones would say, "What if—?" and Mr. Jones would reply, "No use worrying."

X just smiled at them both, and hugged them hard and didn't say much of anything. X was thinking. What if—? And then X thought: No use worrying.

At Xactly 9 o'clock the next day, X reported to the school psychiatrist's office. The principal, along with a committee from the Parents' Association, X's teacher, X's classmates, and Ms. and Mr. Jones, waited in the hall outside. Nobody knew the details of the tests X was to be given, but everybody knew they'd be *very* hard, and that they'd reveal Xactly what everyone wanted to know about X, but were afraid to ask.

It was terribly quiet in the hall. Almost spooky. Once in a while, they would hear a strange noise inside the room. There were buzzes. And a beep or two. And several bells. An occasional light would flash under the door. The Joneses thought it was a white light, but the principal thought it was blue. Two or three children swore it was either yellow or green. And the Parents' Committee missed it completely.

Through it all, you could hear the psychiatrist's low voice, asking hundreds of questions, and X's higher voice, answering hundreds of answers.

The whole thing took so long that everyone knew it must be the most complete Xamination anyone had ever had to take. Poor X, the Joneses thought. Serves X right the Parents' Committee thought. I wouldn't like to be in X's overalls right now, the children thought.

At last, the door opened. Everyone crowded around to hear the results. X didn't look any different; in fact, X was smiling. But the psychiatrist looked terrible. He looked as if he was crying! "What happened?" everyone began shouting. Had X done something disgraceful? "I wouldn't be a bit surprised!" muttered Peggy and Joe's parents. "Did X flunk the *whole* test?" cried Susie's parents. "Or just the most important part?" yelled Jim's parents.

"Oh, dear," sighed Mr. Jones.

"Oh, dear," sighed Ms. Jones.

"Sssh," ssshed the principal. "The psychiatrist is trying to speak."

Wiping his eyes and clearing his throat, the psychiatrist began, in a hoarse whisper. "In my opinion," he whispered—you could tell he must be very upset—"in my opinion, young X here—"

"Yes? Yes?" shouted a parent impatiently.

"Sssh!" ssshed the principal.

"Young *Sssh* here, I mean young X," said the doctor, frowning, "is just about—"

"Just about *what?* Let's have it!" shouted another parent.

"... just about the *least* mixed-up child I've ever Xamined!" said the psychiatrist.

"Yay for X!" yelled one of the children. And then the others began yelling, too. Clapping and cheering and jumping up and down.

"SSSH!" SSShed the principal, but nobody did.

The Parents' Committee was angry and bewildered. How *could* X have passed the whole Xamination? Didn't X have an *identity* problem? Wasn't X mixed up at *all?* Wasn't X *any* kind of a misfit? How could it *not* be, when it didn't even *know* what is was? And why was the psychiatrist crying?

Actually, he had stopped crying and was smiling politely through his tears. "Don't you see?" he said. "I'm crying because it's wonderful! X has absolutely no identity problem! X isn't one bit mixed up! As for being a misfit—ridiculous! X knows perfectly well what it is! Don't you, X?" The doctor winked. X winked back.

"But what *is* X?" shrieked Peggy and Joe's parents. *"We* still want to know what it is!"

"Ah, yes," said the doctor, winking again. "Well, don't worry. You'll all know one of these days. And you won't need me to tell you."

"What? What does he mean?" some of the parents grumbled suspiciously.

Susie and Peggy and Joe all answered at once. "He means that by the time X's sex matters, it won't be a secret any more!"

With that, the doctor began to push through the crowd toward X's parents. "How do you do," he said, somewhat stiffly. And then he reached out to hug them both. "If I ever have an X of my own," he whispered, "I sure hope you'll lend me your instruction manual."

Needless to say, the Joneses were very happy. The Project Baby X scientists were rather pleased, too. So were Susie, Jim, Peggy, Joe, and all the Other Children. The Parents' Association wasn't, but they had promised to accept the psychiatrist's report, and not make any more trouble. They even invited Ms. and Mr. Jones to become honorary members, which they did.

Later that day, all X's friends put on their red-and-white checked overalls and went over to see X. They found X in the back yard, playing with a very tiny baby that none of them had ever seen before. The baby was wearing very tiny red-and-white checked overalls.

"How do you like our new baby?" X asked the Other Children proudly.

"It's got cute dimples," said Jim.

"It's got husky biceps, too," said Susie.

"What kind of baby is it?" asked Joe and Peggy.

X frowned at them. "Can't you tell?" Then X broke into a big, mischievous grin. *"It's a Y!"*

21 TRANSHUMANS—2000

by F.M. Esfandiary

HERE WE ARE AT LAST—year 2000.

The beginning of a new century—the beginning of a whole new millennium.

All over the planet and across the solarsphere transhumans are celebrating. Unicom has teleconnected everyone in a Super Festival.

Astroville L-91 put on the most spectac display of all. They laser-relayed fantastic stellar and Crab-Nebular Kaleidoscope. Many of us had never seen such colors before. You could hear the cheering across this planet and on all the astrovilles.

Last week at exactly new millennium we tried our first 24-hour day. We turned on daylite over the whole planet. The solar sats deployed beautifully. No nite—no sleep. We wanted EVERYONE to be up celebrating at the same time. Super video screens were suspended everywhere and we linkedup with fellow transhumans. For a full 24 hours everybody across the solarsphere was on Universal Time. What a galactic bang.

Mega color illuminations decorate nite and day skies. Some of these playful images flash messages on and off in unilang—

> Happy Universe Day
> Year One Millennium Three
> All Go On 21st Century
> We Will Storm The Universe
> Trans Are Up . . . Trans Are Up . . . Trans Are Up . . . and so on.

Listen carefully and you realize that the celebrations really have little to do with calendar and chronology. A new Up spirit has been spreading across the solarsphere the last few years and it lasered on this occasion to explode.

People are celebrating not so much the liftoff to a new century or to a new millennium—but the upflow to whole new spectra in evolution.

In the last two three decades farout things have been happening all around us. There is growing awareness that we are bursting out of primitive childhood. Emerging in the universe creators of our own trajectories.

A galactic confidence is spreading that we can now cancel any problem realize any dream attain any Time/Space.

Fatalism pessimism resignation and other downs which slowpaced the world for several thousand years are on fadeout.

Not that we are suddenly free of problems. Not at all. We have many problems. But they are problems at a higher orbit of history—a higher evolution.

Very few of the old survival hurdles stand. Our tieups are mainly post-survival.

Poverty famine war overpopulation pollution—these were feudal and industrial breakdowns. They phased out when the industrial age itself began to fall apart around twenty thirty years ago.

We are now close to global cybernation which already monitors resources—manages community needs—runs production. Our new seventh-generation supercomputers are programmed to run everything in mobilias communities biospheres and the solarsphere.

In most farfront communities people work two or three days a week—eight months a year. Much of this work is unnecessary and the demand is spreading for more leisure.

Very few nations remain. Following mid century decolonization came a steady buildup of regional blocs and common markets. In the last few years nations have given way to continental and subcontinental formations. We now have a United Europe—United Africa—United South America—United States of North America—United West Asia etc. . . . These and other united continents are interlinked via unicom and world organizations.

No one is now grounded to specific communities. We are transplanetary. Mach 9 hypersonics zip a thousand people at a time to any spot on the planet within fifty minutes. Several times a month astroshuttles ferry people and stuff back and forth between Planet 3 and astrovilles.

Life expectancy which rose all through the 20th century is now over 100 years. Tens of millions of vigorous trans are well beyond 110 years old. Many will live indefinitely.

Overviewing the past we realize that the two greatest events in all human history—perhaps all our evolution—are the Space Extension and the Bio Lib.

Our extension into Space catapulted us beyond this micro planet —into the vast universe. We have been spreading out farther and farther—the more we spread out the more we grow. No limits to our growth. We are free at last in the universe.

The Bio Lib is helping us extend ourselves across Time. We are creating new bio designs to help us live forever.

Both these cosmic events tookoff around the second half of the 20th Century. They have been feeding each other and gaining momentum since the 50's and 60's.

We are now absorbing their impact. Blazing ahead in new unmonitored directions—full of wayout marvels. Evolution has picked up speed.

What triggered these thoughts is an old application form I found today dating back from the 60's. The questions on the form make me laff and realize again the liteyear speed with which things are overturning.

Name of Applicant?
Male or Female?
Married or Single?   Children?
Education?
Profession?
Residence?   Nationality?

Today these questions are no-where. We are—

Transsexual   Multiprofessional
Multiinvolved   Transmobilia
Uniparents   Transplanetary
Teleeducated   Extraplanetary

In the 60's these answers would have made no sense. Today the questions make no sense.

What brought on these farout changes? Looking back now I can see many of the worldforces of the last forty fifty years which catalyzed the overturns—

—Linkup of peoples and cultures via unicom.

—Spread of social and humanistic sciences.

—Post-industrial technologies and resources.

—Space-extension.

—Liberation movements—Youth and Women's Libs of the 60's Sexual and Nudist Libs of the 70's Gender Lib of the 80's the great Bio Lib of the 90's.

—Bio breakthroughs—from new methods of contraception to sex cell banks—genetic counseling and engineering—embryo transplants—out of the womb reproduction—cloning etc . . .

All through the second half of the 20th Century these forces heatedup to breakdown family patriarchy marriage parenthood puritanism sexism exclusivity . . .

These systems are now in rapid decompress.

Family marriage parenthood belonged to the oldworld of exclusivity. They are now as archaic as tribe clan fatherland.

Instead a new range of processes have been upcoming in pace with the rapidflow of our times.

People now wing singly or translive in mobile communes. In fact we don't even say commune anymore. Mobilia is more mobile and Up.

Mobilias actually started in the 60's and 70's. Strangers would converge usually in the summertime to share a resort mobilia for a few weeks or months—then deconverge. I think some of the first mobilias were in California on Long Island and in southern France. But then they spread all over the planet.

Today mobilias are everywhere. Want to be unalone? Land at a mobilia spend a few hours days or weeks—then liftoff.

More and more people are super mobile. That's another reason we are called trans. We no longer belong to specific groups communities or regions. We are transplanetary—we wing and flow across the planet. Some chic trans are even extraplanetary—they love to satellite-hop.

Movement is up. Rootedness down.

As someone once input—transhumans are not carrots to need roots. Today anyone who pads at a mobilia a community or a job longer than a few weeks or months is considered frozendown.

What happened to reproduction? Didn't people throughout history pride themselves on having many children? I think it was around mid-century that reproduction began to decelerate. Worldforces dismantled family marriage and other traditions. People had fewer and fewer babies. Three then two then one then zero. By mid 70's tens of millions of adults had never reproduced. Making babies was considered antifuture. Antisocial they called it.

By mid 80's several communities around the planet required genetic counseling before child output. Some communities also began licensing parenthood.

The idea was that since parenthood is irreversible if parents have recessive genes or are emotionally offcourse the damages to the child may be severe and permanent. It was felt that since a child does not *choose* its parents the community had the responsibility to make reasonably sure that prospective parents were genetically psychologically and socially fit to produce new life.

Today even these once enlightened measures of the 80's are wayback. To us private reproduction itself is neanderthal.

We are amazed that women in the past subjected themselves to pregnancy walking around for months like a cow with a child in them. There was no other way to reproduce so women and men were programmed to romanticize childbearing.

In the old days two people would linkup and decide to have a child. Just like that. Have a child or two or five or ten. As though new life were cabbage you grew in the field. It was all crude and haphazard. People never paused to ask—can our community or the world accommodate new life? Should we not first attend to all the poor and unhappy children in the world before reproducing new ones? Have we sought genetic counseling as safeguard against producing genetically defective children? Are we psychologically and economically able to provide for all the many subtle needs of a new life?

People were like sheep. They reproduced because their parents had reproduced. Because the community expected them to reproduce. Because their narcissism impelled them to reproduce.

Today the very idea of an individual or a couple unilaterally having a child is primitive. A new life is an important event which cannot be left to the whims of individuals. It is an event in which everyone must be involved.

How do we now join to create wholesome healthy new lives? We all deposit our sex cells at one of the World Child Centers. Genetecists biologists social scientists and others with the help of telecomputers study the cells. They also study the psycho and physio backgrounds of donors and their ancestries. The info is then telefiled at Centers all over the planet and on astrovilles.

Universal monitors regularly put out demographic info which helps us decide when to create new life. We select our best sex cells to fertilize. We strive not only for qualities of transhumanity and intelligence but also bio diversity.

Until recently we implanted the fertilized eggs in female bodies. But very few trans now want to subject themselves to carrying a baby. Anyway we now have outbody wombs far superior to the old inbody wombs. The new wombs are super safe and totally monitored. We leave very little to chance. No more slam-bang breeding.

Infant mortality and genetic defects very high at one time hardly occur today. Every newborn is healthy strong attractive intelligent. Every newborn takesoff into life with good genes and healthy constitutions. Little wonder that trans are much healthier and happier than humans ever were.

Another gain is that nobody knows whose sex cells have been fertilized. Who cares anyway? The donors may even be dead in suspension or transing across the solarsphere.

By not knowing the bioparents we are phasing out exclusive parenthood. No one can now say—this is *My* child. *My* parent. We consider private parenthood destructive chauvinism and monopolism.

We are all parents to all children. Every newborn belongs to all transhumanity.

Each child spends its first few years in monitored mobilias around people who like children and are good with them. Later at around ten or twelve the child is released into the universal process free to choose mobilias anywhere.

Children do not belong to specific parents. They are not frozen into a one-to-one relationship with a mother a father or a parent-substitute.

They grow up around a constant flow of multiparents. They feel wanted and loved by many many people. They therefore do not grow up possessing and needing to be possessed. They are not trapped in anyone's bio or psycho orbit. They flow with fellow trans.

Phasing out the mother-child one-to-one relationship is helping decouple all later linkups. A person is no longer black-holed in an exclusive coupling. You are no longer conditioned to hold on to another for dear life. Nor do you ever need to breakup with anyone. Since linkups are no longer exclusive painful breakups are very rare. Why ever breakup with anyone?

Jealousy rivalry competitiveness possessiveness loneliness rejection—these were prevalent downs in the oldworld of one-to-one relationships. Now they are on fadeout particularly among the young. We do not prove our aliveness through suffering—but through Up feelings.

In the past people approached sex as though it were a tarantula. To us sex is *Fun*. Nothing more.

We enjoy it more than ever before. Fuss over it less than ever before.

Sex is no longer central to linkups. Whether people fuse sexually or not is no longer an issue.

A more farout advance is our ability to convert gender. We not only routinely plan the gender of every newborn—we also reprogrammed gender after birth.

I think it was around thirty or forty years ago the two sexes began to connect. Their appearances hairstyles clothes roles merged indistinguishable. Unisex many called it then. Unnatural others called it.

Around the same time people sought sex conversion through surgery. Transsexuals increased from a few thousand in the 70's to tens of thousands in the 80's.

Today among the lib mob gender is irrelevant. In fact the chic are offended if you refer to them as women or men. They are transsexual. Free of gender chauvinism.

Gender libbers think it is antitrans to be only and permanently a woman or a man. What a galactic bore they say. Why not a woman for a while then a man then a woman again and so on?

Some consider all this unnatural. The hell with nature others say.

Those who change their genders often are called loose or crazy radicals. The lib trans consider them righton.

In recent years gender lib has been spreading. Bodies are not for reproduction people are saying. They are for communication and fun.

Here in the year 2000 we are transing beyond the primal concept of woman and man.

Changes explode at rocketspeed now. Not enough to deprogram gender. The entire anatomy must be liberated.

There is buildup of excitement about the most farout liberation of all—the Bio Lib.

Through lasergery prosthetics transplants we make many biotransfos. Telemed routinely replaces brokendown fleshware with durable nonflesh implants. We also implant micro-TV to restore sight to the blind. Micro-antenna for the deaf and so on . . .

Transhumans are no longer biostatic. We are emerging biofluid. Our bodies have interchangeable parts.

We are defleshing and deanimalizing many areas of our anatomies.

Why suffer or die simply because the heart or the kidney has broken down?

Why be doomed to a terminal body? Why fester a lifetime in a programmed mind and personality?

Why should such a beautiful phenomenon as a transhuman die simply because this perishable animal body has conked out?

We are designing modular bodies which can grow and flow forever and ever.

We are creating a new entity in evolution.

We are already more evolved more refined more comfortable more joyful than life has ever been on this planet. Because we are now less and less vulnerable to external and internal threats to our existences we are also more at peace with ourselves and the world.

This is why the millennial celebrations are so super nebular these days. This is why all across the planet and the solarsphere you hear people cheering from the bottom of their pacemakers.

I think we all sense that we are on the verge of some marvellous new worlds. That the greatest breakthroughs are still ahead. That we are on our way to new wavelengths in evolution. On our way beyond animal beyond human beyond transhuman—to a post-human dimension—free of suffering free of death free forever FREE FOREVER IN THE UNIVERSE.

ABOUT THE CONTRIBUTORS

BELLA S. ABZUG, a member of Congress since 1971, is a lively, articulate and nationally-known leader of the women's rights movement. She and Mim Kelber have been friends since they attended high school and college together in New York. Ms. Abzug became a lawyer, and Ms. Kelber a newspaper editor and professional writer. Their paths joined again when, in response to the resumption of nuclear testing, they helped to organize Women Strike for Peace and spent the next decade in the peace movement. Ms. Abzug, who had long ago decided that women had to acquire political power, won a seat in Congress on her first try and went on to become a founder of the National Women's Political Caucus. Ms. Kelber joined her congressional staff as a writer and legislative aide and is also active in the Caucus. Bella Abzug is an irrepressible optimist and believes that people, if they are organized, can solve any problem. Mim Kelber is the resident pessimist who hopes that Bella is right. Each has a husband and two daughters and each considers herself a personally conventional, politically radical feminist.

CAROLINE BIRD is an author, a social critic and a feminist. She was a member of the editorial staffs at Fortune and Newsweek, and has written over two hundred articles on economic and sociological subjects. Her 1968 landmark book, *Born Female: The High Cost of Keeping Women Down*, documented discrimination in female employment; and her 1973 book, *Everything a Woman Needs to Know to Get Paid What She's Worth*, delineated what women can do about it. In 1972–73 Caroline Bird was Froman Distinguished Professor at Russell Sage College.

RONA CHERRY is currently working on two books: one on life cycles and one on old age—not ordinary subjects for a twenty-six year old. But Rona Cherry is an independent journalist with an established specialization in medical-science reporting. She gradually moved into this field as she progressed from reporter on daily papers in Guadalajara, Mexico, Virginia and Ohio to The Wall Street Journal and to associate editor at Newsweek. Her medical reporting has appeared in The New York Times' Sunday Magazine, The Christian Science Monitor, Reader's Digest as well as several publications abroad. One of her main preoccupations is keeping out of doctors' offices.

SHEILA COLLINS is Director of Publications for a national ecumenical church agency and an organizer of guerrilla activities among women within religious institutions. She speaks and writes on three interlocked subjects: social ethics, the women's movement and religion. *A Different Heaven & Earth: A Feminist Perspective on Religion* is her manifesto on these subjects. In her spare time Sheila Collins teaches at the New York Theological Seminary, works with a women's poetry collective and the Women's Political Caucus, paints in batique, talks to her seventy-five plants and shares housework, stimulating conversation and the care of two daughters with her clergyman-lawyer husband.

F. M. ESFANDIARY is teleeducated multiprofessional transplanetary. His last three tracts —*Optimism One, Up-Wingers, Transguide*. His articles on the future have appeared in The New York Times, The New York Sunday Times Magazine, The Village Voice, The Futurist. He has held seminars on Up-Wing philosophy at the New School for Social Research, U.C.L.A., the Smithsonian Institution and elsewhere. Esfandiary was formerly with the United Nations. His philosophy—Optimism Universalism Immortality.

ROBERT AND ANNA FRANCOEUR write together, live together and bring together a serendipitous collection of talent and experience. Anna Kotlarchyk Francoeur, born and raised in Manhattan's Ukranian settlement, has taught history, started a family—two daughters——and shifted to a career as a general accountant for a large corporation and co-author with her husband. Dr. Robert Francoeur, a former priest who is married with Vatican permission, holds graduate degrees in both biology and theology. Now a Professor of Human Sexuality and Embryology, he also teaches bioethics and medical genetics. He is the author of seven books on evolution and human sexuality including—with Anna as co-author—the recently published *Hot and Cool Sex: Cultures in Conflict.* Anna Francoeur, according to Robert H. Rimmer, author of *The Harrad Experiment,* "has a cool capable Middle European peasant style that was unfortunately lost by millions of women in the powder-and-lace urban environment of the eighteenth and nineteenth centuries." The same author describes Robert as "the dreamer, the utopianist, the cross-culturist, the man who can bridge knowledge in different disciplines and reveal striking parallels."

LUCINDA FRANKS is an experienced young reporter who worked for UPI. She dodged bullets in Belfast while covering Irish politics, covered the Miss World Beauty Contest and reported the tragic events of the Munich Olympics from inside the Israeli compound. Her story on the life of Diana Houghton, who went from rich girl to radical and died when her own bomb went off in the "house on 11th Street," won a 1971 Pulitzer prize. Lucinda Franks' book, *Waiting Out a War: The Exile of Pvt. John Picciano* was published in 1974. She is now with the New York Times doing investigative reporting. Having been excluded from neighborhood baseball games as a kid (weak hitter), she reports that writing "Women in Motion" for this book has given her renewed hope.

LOIS GOULD, a native and incurable New Yorker, one-time reporter and magazine columnist, quit her last job in 1968 as executive editor for a leading women's magazine to turn her full attention to writing fiction. Her novel *Such Good Friends* became a best seller and a movie. Her two succeeding novels, *Necessary Objects* and *Final Analysis,* have received much critical acclaim. Lois Gould also writes short articles and fiction in such magazines as Ms., New York, McCalls and Redbook. She lives with her professor-psychiatrist-author husband and her two independent sons who "pretty much run the household."

RENOS MANDIS AND LILA KARP live together in Soho, sharing their hope for a genderless society. Lila Karp, author of the novel *The Queen Is in the Garbage* teaches a course in The Sociology of Women's Literature at the State University of New York at New Paltz, and The New School for Social Research. She has also taught at Bryn Mawr College and The University of The New World in Switzerland. At both of these schools she taught Creative Writing for Women, and at The University of the New World she organized and ran workshops on various aspects of Contemporary Feminism. Renos Mandis is Greek. He studied philosophy at the University of Geneva, and drama in London. Since then his interests have been shared between philosophy and the theater, in which he works as both actor and director. Most recently he has directed an experimental version of Sartre's "No Exit" at the LaMama Theater in New York City, and an adaptation of Sophocles' "Oedipus Rex" at The State University of New York at New Paltz. He also taught Existential Phenomenology and a course on Simone de Beauvoir at The University of The New World in Switzerland.

LETTY COTTIN POGREBIN is a writer, lecturer and feminist activist with special interest in two areas of women's lives—work and child-rearing. An editor of Ms. Magazine, she worked on the "Free to Be . . . You and Me" projects for the Ms. Foundation which became a record album (with Marlo Thomas and Friends), a TV Special and a book. Letty Pogrebin contributes a monthly column to Ladies' Home Journal. Her annual list of non-sexist toys in Ms. is used by educators, child care experts and women's groups. A book reviewer herself, she is also the author of *How to Make it in a Man's World* and the forthcoming *Getting Yours: How to Make the System Work for the Working Woman.* She is a member of the Chancellor's Commission on Sexism and Sex Discrimination in New York City Public Schools. With her twin daughters, a son and a husband, Letty Pogrebin shares "a little tennis, fishing, beach walking—and the inability to ever get enough sleep."

CAROL RINZLER is a writer, an editor, a reviewer and an observer of the facts, fancies and foibles of everyday living. Her eye for what is "fashionable" has been turned to good effect for New York Magazine, Life, Ladies' Home Journal, MS., and more. Carol's serious side has been revealed in her 1969 book, *Frankly McCarthy* and in The New York Times and Publishers' Weekly book reviews. Her book *Nobody Said You Had to East Off the Floor* is a minimalist's guide to housework. Carol Rinzler lives, in her own words, "with two extraordinarily talented and beautiful children, and an extremely vicious cat."

CAROLE ROSENTHAL, Chicago-born and Virginia-raised, is a Penn State graduate. She holds an advanced degree from New York University and is completing her doctoral work at The Graduate Faculty of the New School. She has been a reporter, done psychological counseling and dug for artifacts in the ruins of Guatemala and Mexico. She is now an Assistant Professor of English at a Brooklyn College. And from her desk overlooking the construction of New York's newest subway, Carole Rosenthal writes successful short fiction.

DAVID SAPERSTEIN is a writer, film maker, lyricist, futurist and ardent fly fisherman. In his role as owner of Skyline Films, his work takes him around the world and into every form of audio-visual communication. David Saperstein's films have found their place as television shows and commercials, educational material and documentaries for schools, businesses and closed-circuit broadcasts. He hates stuffy people, neckties, and enjoys being with his wife and two children.

DORIS L. SASSOWER, feminist attorney, speaker and writer, worked for women's equality long before it was popular. A past president of the New York Women's Bar Association, she has been active in matrimonial law reform and was instrumental in the passage of the Gleason Bill, a law designed to remedy one of the most glaring inequities for women in our divorce law. She chairs the Subcommittee on Matrimonial Law Reform of the Association of the Bar of the City of New York, co-chairs the National Conference of Lawyers and Social Workers, is Special Consultant to the Professional Women's Caucus, of which she is a founder. Ms. Sassower is a member of the Board of the International Institute of Women's Studies, the Institute on Women's Wrongs, the Executive Woman, and a member of the Association of Feminist Consultants and a fellow of the American Academy of Matrimonial Lawyers. As practicing lawyer, writer, speaker, bar leader, women's rights organizer, wife and mother of three, she has earned the description "Renaissance Woman."

NORA SAYRE, daughter of the writer Joel Sayre, was educated at Radcliffe and has spent much of her life in New York City. From 1965 to 1970 she was the New York correspondent for the *New Statesman,* for which she wrote on a wide variety of political, urban and cultural subjects. She is currently film critic for The New York Times. Her articles, essays and reviews have also appeared in *Esquire, The Progressive, The London Magazine.* Nora Sayre's observations of the passing parade of literary, political and social trends of the times are recorded in her book, *Sixties Going on Seventies.*

GLORIA STEINEM is a journalist and a leading spokeswoman for the women's movement in America. A Phi Beta Kappa graduate of Smith College, she has written and lectured widely on the politics of women's position in society. Ms. Steinem is on the advisory board of the National Organization for Women and helped convene the National Women's Political Caucus. She is co-founder and editor of *Ms.* magazine.

ALVIN TOFFLER is a former Associate Editor of *Fortune,* a former Visiting Professor at Cornell University, a former Visiting Scholar at the Russell Sage Foundation. His books include *The Culture Consumers* and *The Schoolhouse in the City,* as well as the bestselling *Future Shock.* His articles have appeared in scholarly journals, as well as such varied pulications as *Reader's Digest, Playboy, The New York Times,* the *London Observer,* and others.

JANE TRAHEY heads her own advertising agency and has helped inject a note of reality into women-directed advertising with such famous headlines as "It's Not Fake Anything—It's Real Dynel." She was voted Advertising Woman of the Year and also received the Harper's Award as one of the Hundred Most Accomplished Women. Ms. Trahey's talents range far beyond the advertising business, however. Her book, *Life with Mother Superior,* was made into two movies starring Rosalind Russell. She is also a playright and the author of four cookbooks: *The Taste of Texas, The Compleat Martini Cookbook, The Gin & Butter Diet* and *The Son of Martini Cookbook.* And breaking one more precedent, Jane Trahey is a founder and Board Member of the First Woman's Bank of New York.

MAGGIE TRIPP, Philadelphia-born and bred, has long been an outspoken advocate of freedom of choice for women. Her own career has ranged from business woman to serious art student and gallery owner to innovator of courses on women's role in society. She was an early Sixties' activist in the Continuing Education program at the University of Pennsylvania. She created two courses at the New School for Social Research: *The Changing Consciousness and Conscience of Women—Liberation How?* and *The Present and Future World of Women.* Her articles have appeared in *Aurora* and other feminist publications. She helped initiate a Women's Center for the YWCA together with the first course on *Women's Consciousness.* Maggie Tripp's husband, whose business is the creation of new products, claims that she is his best invention: a contemporary woman who loves contemporary houses and contemporary art but who lives in the future.

INEZ TURNER, DOROTHY EUGENIA ROBINSON, DEBORAH SINGLETARY AND MARGO JEFFERSON are friends who formed a collective to write for this book based upon a deep respect for the difficulty of finite statements on the future of black women. Inez Turner teaches Basic Education and is developing her skills as a fiction writer. She is active in the Black Feminist Movement. Dorothy Robinson, a graduate of the City College of New York, is a television associate producer and a free lance film writer. Deborah Singletary is a Black Feminist writer and a student at Hunter College. Margo Jefferson was graduated from Brandeis University and received her Master's degree from Columbia University. She is an Associate Editor at *Newsweek.*